THE FRENCH REVOLUTION

THE
FRENCH REVOLUTION
1788-1792

by

GAETANO SALVEMINI

*Professor of History in the University of Florence and
Emeritus Professor of Harvard University*

Translated from the Italian

by

I. M. RAWSON

New York
HENRY HOLT & COMPANY

FIRST PUBLISHED 1954

PRINTED IN GREAT BRITAIN

CONTENTS

CONTENTS

TRANSLATOR'S NOTE

THIS book was first published in Italy in 1905. Since then it has run through many new editions, and has come to be regarded as a classic in its field. It was received in France with warm appreciation: the great historian of the Revolution, Albert Mathiez, wrote in 1907, 'Voilà un excellent manuel, le meilleur sans contredit qui existe sur l'histoire de la Révolution ... M. Salvemini ne s'est pas seulement inspiré des travaux les plus autorisés, il en a repensé les conclusions et son œuvre a une valeur originale ... Je n'en finirais pas si je voulais signaler toutes les pages pénétrantes qui m'ont arreté dans ce livre.' And in 1926, Alphonse Aulard greeted the appearance of a revised edition with the comment: 'C'est à la fois un récit et une philosophie. J'ai lu son livre avec soin. Je l'ai lu avec profit, je l'ai lu avec plaisir. Ce sont des pages robustes et instructives, où il y a un talent original, et où nos points de vue sur la Révolution sont intelligemment critiqués et renouvelés.' The book is, moreover, the only general study of the Revolution by a non-French writer to be cited — together with the works of Carlyle, Kropotkin, Gooch, Gershow, etc. — by Louis Villat in *La Révolution et L'Empire* (Paris, Presses Universitaires de France, 1947).

It may seem strange that a work so well known on the continent should not have been made available to English readers long ago. The explanation lies in part in the fact that the author, an exile for over twenty years from his own country and actively engaged in the struggle against Fascism, as well as in writing a number of works on modern politics, had no time to give his study of the great Revolution a further revision in the light of recent historical research, and was unwilling to allow it to appear in English before this had been done. The present version has been made from a text carefully revised by the author. It differs in a number of ways from the latest Italian edition (1949) and contains many minor emendations as well as new material. I should like to take this opportunity of expressing my gratitude to Professor Salvemini for all the help and advice he has given me during the course of my work.

I. M. RAWSON

PREFACE

THE word 'revolution' may mean either the forcible overthrow of an established social or political order (when an unconstitutional change is effected by the Government itself it is called a *coup d'état*) or any great change brought about in a pre-existing situation, even slowly and without violence. It is used in the former sense with reference to the two Paris revolutions of 1830 and 1848, or the Russian revolution of 1917. It is used with the latter significance when we say that Columbus brought about a revolution in mediaeval geography, Copernicus in astronomy and Galileo in scientific method: and that an industrial revolution began in England during the second half of the eighteenth century.

The word can be used in both senses for the upheaval that took place in France towards the end of the eighteenth century. In so far as it consisted in the violent destruction of the feudal and monarchical régime, the French Revolution may be said to have come to an end on September 21st, 1792, when the monarchy was formally abolished. But as the creation of a new social and political order it continued until the *coup d'état* of Brumaire, indeed, up to the time of the Consulate for Life, when nineteenth-century France appeared finally constituted.

This book is concerned with the French Revolution as understood in the first sense. Its aim is to explain why and in what way the feudal monarchy was destroyed.

In this endeavour it has been necessary to present the four revolutionary years in relation to a complex system of cause and effect the origins of which must be traced to former times, often centuries before the Revolution itself. A considerable part of the book, therefore, is devoted to social conditions, ideas and events chronologically remote from, but logically bound up with, the revolutionary period. The author's aim has been, not to bring new facts to light, but simply to put before his readers, in a rapid synthesis, the conclusions he has reached in the course of extensive study of the subject.

The history of these years is covered by a single term, the

'French Revolution', which conjures up in our minds a general picture of its events. But the use of proper names has so accustomed us to seeing, in our mind's eye, the real entities behind them that we often come to regard collective and abstract nouns as personifications. And just as we think of disease as something extraneous to ourselves, and say that the malady has killed the patient (who in fact has simply died showing certain morbid symptoms) so we are apt to treat the Revolution as having an existence apart from the men of the time, and say that it destroyed the feudal rights, proclaimed the Rights of Man, dethroned Louis XVI and so on. But the *Revolution* did nothing of the kind. It is merely an abstract term by means of which, to save time, we refer to the way in which all these events of the revolutionary period were brought about.

The practice has its advantages, provided that one is always ready mentally to replace the abstract by the concrete term. We can say that the Revolution did away with feudal dues, so long as we remember that after the fall of the Bastille it was the peasants who refused to pay them, the Constituent Assembly that failed to enforce them, the Legislative that formally abolished almost all of them and the Convention that completed their legal suppression. There is no harm in asserting that the Revolution was dominated by two ideas, those of equality and popular sovereignty, if we bear in mind that the metaphor simply implies that all the democratic agitators of the time and the majority of deputies in the revolutionary assemblies had an unshakable faith in these two philosophical dogmas. And we may very well say that 'Paris was the heart of the Revolution', on the understanding that this is only taken as a concise and effective way of stating that the most zealous revolutionaries were to be found in the capital, and that their actions had a powerful influence upon those in the rest of France.

The trouble begins when we come to regard the Revolution as an historical force in itself. For instance, it is a fact that both the Constituent and Legislative Assemblies and the Convention were largely composed of lawyers, and that very few of the industrialists, tradesmen, bankers and other men of affairs who really formed the *bourgeoisie* were elected to it. Such citizens as these have their own business to attend to, and find little time for politics; lawyers, on the other hand, besides being facile speakers — a great asset in public life — find in politics an excellent way of making a name for themselves and of increasing the scope and gains of their calling. For this reason the electors of the revolutionary period usually had a choice of various candidates belonging to the legal profession, but were rarely free to choose between a lawyer and, for instance, an engineer.

This circumstance, though not unusual in modern representative assemblies, was of considerable importance during the French Revolution: for it meant that the policy of these bodies, in emanating, not from the *bourgeoisie* proper but from its legal experts, was not always in conformity with the interests of the economically dominant class: being, in fact, an outcome of moral and intellectual habits of mind different from and even at times opposed to theirs. This explains certain ultra-democratic measures of the Constituent and Legislative Assemblies that would never have been passed by a chamber of bankers and industrialists.

Yet so eminent an historian, for instance, as J. L. Jaurès is not satisfied with such a simple explanation. He writes: 'If the Revolution sent only a handful of merchants and tradesmen to the Constituent and Legislative Assemblies and to the Convention, this was because it instinctively felt reluctant to give its great work the stamp of too narrow a class; and because, prompted not only by the economic growth of the *bourgeoisie* but by the whole trend of contemporary thought, it wanted the law to give full expression to the nation's real wishes and to all the complex interplay of human relations. For this reason the Legislative — better-fitted for its task, without doubt, than an assembly of industrialists and manufacturers, accustomed to the hierarchy of commercial life — proclaimed universal suffrage after August 10th.' The Revolution thus appears in person, and, endowed with instincts and reasoning power, votes in place of the electors, to whom no one would have thought of attributing such political sagacity.[1]

When the Revolution is represented as though directing men's actions from above we are apt to award it responsibility for events

[1] The author is aware that his warning as to the use of abstract terms may seem unnecessary to English readers, who are accustomed to a more direct style of writing. It may, however, be not entirely out of place in view of the influence in England of such outstanding continental writers as Michelet or Jaurès. Nor should it be forgotten that Carlyle himself often treats the Revolution as though it were a being of flesh and blood.

which should, in fact, be assigned to some real person or group of persons. The Revolution that glorified Lafayette in July 1789, but forced him to flee the country in 1792; that proclaimed the Rights of Man, yet persecuted the non-juring priests; that perpetrated the September massacre, and then made its courageous stand at Valmy, seems to us a monstrous, incomprehensible force. And since this mythological Revolution gave political power to the middle classes and at the same time committed innumerable crimes, historians of liberal sympathies make every effort to minimize its misdeeds, or, taking their courage in both hands, maintain that with all its excesses it must be acclaimed for the results it achieved; while those who deplore the fall of the *ancien régime* are shocked at the evil they have to record, and in their regret for the beneficent institutions of the past, assert that it would have been a blessing for mankind had the Revolution never taken place.

When, on the other hand, we stop thinking in terms of Revolution, and turn to the revolutionaries themselves, seeking to understand their characters and the motives by which they were guided, we find among them men of every sort — able and incompetent, disinterested and self-seeking, resolute and cowardly, the criminals of September and the stalwarts of Valmy: all of whom contributed, largely unawares, to a great political and juridical transformation which was, in fact, the necessary outcome of previous social and economic development in France, but which, violent in form owing to the blind resistance of the privileged classes, ended in a republic, owing to the crass stupidity of the King and his advisers.

THE FRENCH REVOLUTION

CHAPTER I

SOCIAL CONDITIONS IN FRANCE IN THE EIGHTEENTH CENTURY

I

IN feudal France, during the tenth and eleventh centuries, all political and administrative power, and nearly all the land, was held by the nobility and clergy. The King was only one of the feudal lords, and had little effective authority outside his own domains. The population consisted almost entirely either of peasants, who were serfs of the glebe, or of artisans who, when they, too, were not actually serfs like the workers on the land, were still subject to the lay and ecclesiastical lords.

During the eleventh century there was a gradual decline in the economic and political predominance of the nobility and clergy. The population was growing in the towns; division of labour began to develop, and a new social class — the *bourgeoisie* — composed largely of merchants and craftsmen, was becoming steadily more prosperous. They filled all the lucrative and honourable liberal professions, organized themselves into guilds, and gained control of the municipalities. Their rapid economic and social progress enabled them to exert an ever-increasing political influence.

In the country districts the serfs banded themselves together and by means of strikes and risings, or through purchasing their freedom, waged a ceaseless war of attrition against the feudal rights, little by little gaining ownership of the land.

As six centuries passed and the commons prospered, the kings slowly consolidated their own position. They made alliance with the new middle-class, conferred the seal of legality on their trade-guilds, and, with their support, gradually subjugated the lay and

B

ecclesiastical nobility, putting an end to independent feudal rule and creating political and administrative unity.

By the eighteenth century the old feudal order in France had already disintegrated, and amid the ruins of the past the broad outlines of a new *bourgeois* society were beginning to appear.

The area of France amounted to some fifty million *hectares*; of these a large part had already passed into the hands of the commons. In the north, on the eve of the Revolution, the peasantry possessed 32 per cent of the land, the city *bourgeoisie* 16 per cent or 17 per cent, the nobility 22 per cent and the clergy 19 per cent or 20 per cent. The rest belonged to the Crown or to charitable institutions, or was communal property. In the western provinces the proportion was less favourable to the commons, who owned only a fifth of the land; but in the centre, the south-east and the south, they held as much as half, or even more. Altogether, it may be said that the clergy, who constituted the 'First Estate' of the realm, still owned a fifth of the landed property of France; the nobles, or 'Second Estate', also a fifth; while the property of the Crown, the communes and of charitable institutions accounted for another fifth of the country. Of the property in private hands, half belonged to the 'Third Estate': this was, in fact, the most productive in the kingdom, whereas the forests, marshes, untilled and badly-cultivated areas were almost all included in the patrimony of the feudal classes.

The commons numbered 25 millions; there were 130,000 clerics (of whom 70,000 belonged to the 'secular' clergy, or priesthood, and 60,000 to the 'regular' clergy, or monastic orders); while the *noblesse*, or 'Second Estate', amounted probably to some eighty thousand families. Nearly a million labourers were still subject, in some Crown and Church lands, to feudal servitude, which, however, in many districts had been considerably lightened. More than twenty million small peasant proprietors, tenant-farmers, *métayers* (share-croppers), agricultural labourers and peasant artisans, had already gained personal freedom. The rest of the population was concentrated in Paris, Lyons, Bordeaux, Marseilles, Le Havre, Nantes, Rouen, Amiens, Tours and other big urban centres.

In the cities, the feudal orders were confronted by the commercial *bourgeoisie*: ship-owners and ship-builders, owners of mines, foundries, tanneries and glass furnaces, or of china, earthenware and paper factories; manufacturers of silk, wool and cotton, shareholders in banking companies, members of importing and exporting firms; proprietors of vast domains in the colonies cultivated by slave labour and of refineries in the mother-country; and contractors, financiers, physicians, engineers and lawyers.

Manufactured goods were still chiefly produced by small firms employing few workers, or by independent craftsmen supplied with raw materials by the merchant-capitalist. The most important factories, like the iron foundries at Montbard, cost scarcely three hundred thousand *livres* to set up; less than the value of the ground they stood on. But already, especially in the glass, wool and cotton industries, in those of spinning, dyeing, and the manufacture of hats, the big capitalist distributing raw materials among many hundreds of workers, and supplying wide and distant markets, was beginning to appear: at Sedan, twenty-five cloth manufacturers were employing 10,500 workers. In the metallurgical and paper trades, and some textile industries, the first factories requiring heavy capital expenditure and equipped with machinery driven by steam or water-power, were already to be seen, with a working population concentrated around them. Réveillon, a paper manufacturer in Paris, had 400 workers; a factory at Roanne making china ornaments employed a similar number, and the muslin factory at Puy-en-Velay 1200. They were forerunners of the great industrial capitalism that was to transform economic and social life in the nineteenth century.

Trade between France and her colonies in America, which in 1716, carried by 300 vessels, had brought in 25 million *livres* a year, had risen by 1786 to 239 million *livres*, with 1219 vessels engaged on it. That with the Barbary Coast, which in 1740 had amounted to 1 million *livres* a year (apart from the corn trade) had grown to more than six millions in 1788. In 1789, the total value of imports and exports amounted to more than 1100 million *livres*: in comparison with 1715 the movement of trade had increased fourfold.

'All experts', wrote the economist Messance in 1766, 'are agreed that the country has made surprising progress in the last forty years. More goods are being manufactured now than in the past, and not only have our traditional products improved, but many new ones, unknown to our fathers, have been introduced.'

Agriculture, too, was trying new methods. Many bogs were drained and much untilled land broken up. Between 1779 and 1789, 1900 *hectares* were newly put under the plough in Languedoc. It was estimated in 1780 that during the previous twenty years 305,000 *hectares* had been added to the land under cultivation in France. Potatoes were being increasingly grown, and plantations of mulberry trees for the silk industry were spreading. The system of leasing large properties to farmers with considerable capital resources was in many districts replacing the small-scale agriculture that had impoverished the countryside. Land-values were rising everywhere.

Apart from the income derived from their own estates, from trade, commerce, and the liberal professions, the *bourgeoisie* held nearly all the shares in the Public Debt, the interest on which amounted in 1784 to 207,000,000 *livres* a year. Moreover, the local administrative bodies, clergy and nobility were all in debt to the *bourgeoisie* to an extent that, though it is difficult to determine, was certainly very considerable.

While the Third Estate was thus improving its position, the nobility still clung to the social values of mediaeval times, when landed property and the profession of arms denoted rank and power, and wealth from other sources implied inferior status. The nobles, save for some rare exceptions during the last years of the old régime, would have thought it beneath them to engage in the commons' activities. Thus, aristocratic families, exposed like all others to vicissitudes of fortune, had no means of repairing financial loss, and the nobility, as a class, became more and more impoverished. Although the right of primogeniture, which entitled the eldest son in a noble family to inherit two-thirds of the family property, staved off the ruin of a part of the nobility, it merely hastened that of the rest: for if the younger brothers of one generation shared a third of the paternal inheritance, those of the next divided the third of a third, and after three or four generations, as Chateaubriand observed, the patrimony of their descendants consisted of no more than a rabbit, a pigeon or a hound.

Those nobles not yet ruined lived at court. Many of them knew neither what their incomes were nor where their estates lay:

a great lord would have thought it beneath his dignity to discuss such matters as fertilizers or the housing of his peasants. It was the business of the bailiffs and attorneys to keep his accounts, and his to spend the money. 'My lord Archbishop,' said Louis XVI to Monseigneur Dillon, 'it is said that you have a great many debts.' 'Sire,' replied the prelate ironically, 'I will inquire of my *intendant*, and shall have the honour of rendering an account of them to Your Majesty.'

Naturally, they were riddled with debt. The Duc de Lauzun, at twenty-six years of age, had squandered the whole capital of his 100,000 crowns' income and was in debt to the sum of two million; the Prince de Conti, with 600,000 *livres* a year, had a horde of creditors at his heels; the Comte de Clermont, Abbot of Saint-Germain des Prés, went bankrupt twice in succession; the millions of the Comte d'Artois and the Cardinal de Rohan went to pay the interest on their debts; the Duc de Choiseul had property worth 14 millions and debts amounting to 10 millions; while the Duc d'Orléans had creditors claiming 74 millions. When the revolutionaries confiscated the property of the *emigré* nobles they found that the richest were all mortgaged. If a fifth of the landed property of France was held by the nobles before the Revolution, this was largely due to the fact that the richer commoners, by gradually entering the ranks of the aristocracy either through the purchase of posts carrying ennoblement, or by obtaining ennoblement directly from the King, were at least in part filling the gaps produced by the disintegration of the authentic feudal families.

Step by step with economic decline went political decline. Not only the high dignitaries of the Church, for whom in the past ecclesiastical office had meant political and military power, but also the descendants of those feudal lords who, in the Middle Ages, had exercised sovereign rights throughout their own lands, were in the eighteenth century almost wholly excluded both from politics and the administration. The kingdom was governed by the royal officials. At the centre was the King's Council, which drew up laws, levied taxes, and was the supreme authority in all branches of public administration. Next came the Comptroller-General, who saw to the enforcement of the laws and royal ordinances, and directed all the internal administration of the country, from finance to the police, and from public works to poor relief. In the provinces, the *intendants*, under the orders of the Comptroller-General, and — in less important areas — *sub-délégués* under those of the *intendants*, supervised communal administration and governed former lay and ecclesiastical fiefs. Through these officials the Comptroller's orders were transmitted to the remotest corners of the country. Administrative centralization was not, as many believe, created by the revolutionaries: it was the result of long and patient labour by the kings and their officials, and was already highly developed before the Revolution. The revolutionaries perfected the system and made it work efficiently.

As time passed and the King's authority gradually became extended to the whole of France, an ever-growing army of employees was required by the administration, which every day was becoming more complicated. The King could no longer administer his affairs himself, as he had done in the twelfth century. What had originally been under his personal supervision was now the collective responsibility of the bureaucrats. The officials who, according to juridical theory, were instruments of the royal will, became in reality the true depositaries of power: they dealt according to their own lights with most of the work of administration, interpreting and applying the laws that emanated from the King. They suggested such measures to him as were in their opinion necessary, and in effect were themselves the ruling class. As Frederick of Prussia said, in referring to the French ministers, they were 'subaltern kings'.

These 'subaltern kings' rarely belonged either to the feudal nobility or to the clergy. The kings were careful to exclude both classes from the administration. The royal officials were generally *bourgeois* — for the most part lawyers — without family traditions or personal connections, who could be dismissed from office at the King's will and who carried out his orders unquestioningly. In the seventeenth century and still more in the eighteenth, the custom of ennobling high state officials became common; but this 'nobility of the robe' remained distinct from the 'nobility of the sword', which as a rule was still excluded from the more important administrative posts. When Louis XIV died, there was an attempt, under the Regency of the Duke of Orleans, to restore

authority to the feudal lords; but the 'nobles of the sword' soon
tired of governing, and left it once more to the bureaucrats, con-
tenting themselves with such offices as were merely lucrative sine-
cures. In the reign of Louis XVI only three ministers were of un-
questionably feudal origin. The nobility of five others dated only
from the fifteenth or fourteenth centuries; the rest came from the
nobility of the robe, and most of these had acquired their rank
no earlier than the seventeenth or eighteenth centuries. Among
the *intendants* very few indeed belonged to the old noble families:
the majority had been ennobled no more than four generations
back.

II

The prerogatives enjoyed in eighteenth-century France by the
feudal nobles and clergy were but sorry survivals of their early
wealth and sovereignty: the last visible remains of a great continent submerged by the waters.

One of these prerogatives consisted in immunity from taxation.

In the Middle Ages this privilege had been justified by the fact
that, while the commons served the King by paying the expenses
of public administration, and the clergy by praying to God for
his prosperity, the nobles lent him free military aid. But in the
eighteenth century few, even among the clergy themselves,
believed that prayers were an adequate substitute for taxes. As for
the nobility, since the feudal levies were no longer called upon for
service, such nobles as served in the standing army received
regular pay, like all other servants of the state.

Furthermore, in mediaeval times, when the royal imposts were
comparatively few, exemption from taxation had represented no
great benefit for the privileged class nor an excessive burden upon
the rest. But by the eighteenth century the days were long past
when Sully, minister of Henri IV, had been wont to say, 'It is
easy enough to talk of a hundred thousand crowns, the difficulty
is to find them.' The rising number of employees required by the
central administration, the maintenance of a large army, foreign
wars and general social progress, all threw a growing burden of
work and expenditure upon public administration, and forced
the central Government to augment its revenue by increasing old
imposts and creating new ones. Ordinary revenue, which in the

23

time of Louis XI amounted annually to 4,700,000 *livres*, had risen to 70,000,000 under Richelieu, to 85,000,000 in 1661, to 119,000,000 in 1683, to 166,000,000 in 1715, to 283,000,000 in 1757, and to 476,000,000 in 1789.

It is true that the increase in taxation was accompanied by an increase in wealth. But tax privileges prevented the imposts from being levied on the wealth which should have borne them.

Of the 476,000,000 *livres* of ordinary revenue in 1789, about three-fifths represented indirect taxation (on wine, liquors, salt, tobacco, the circulation of manufactured goods, etc.); which, as was natural, weighed most heavily upon the poorest classes. In addition, many of the privileged class succeeded in obtaining further exemption for themselves, either by breaking the law or through direct concessions from the Government.

Among the direct imposts, the *taille* or property-tax was levied in some provinces only on landed property (the *taille réelle*), and in others on personal wealth whatever its origin. Whereas in 1439 it had produced 1,800,000 *livres* a year, it was bringing in 91,000,000 towards the end of the old régime. The *capitation*, a progressive tax on personal income instituted in 1695, brought in 42,000,000 *livres*. The *vingtième*, also levied on income, and derived from successive transformations of a tax of one-tenth (*décime*) introduced in 1710, brought in 76,500,000 *livres*.

The privileged orders were almost entirely freed from payment of the *taille*. They were not supposed to be exempt from the *capitation* and *vingtième*; but the clergy had succeeded in commuting their obligations by payments (*dons gratuits*) to the Exchequer; and the nobles, by obtaining reductions and special favours, or by rendering false returns, contributed on a ludicrously low scale. The nobles and clergy paid only half of what should have been their share in *vingtièmes*; even the Princes of the Blood only contributed 188,000 instead of 2,400,000 *livres*. As to the *capitation*, it is calculated that in ten provinces the commons paid 11,636,000 *livres* and the nobility and clergy 1,450,500; in Champagne, out of a million and a half of *capitation*, the nobles paid scarcely 14,000 *livres*. Altogether, the privileged classes bore only an eighth part of the *capitation* to which they should have been liable. Twelve *arpents* of land owned by a noble paid nine *livres* of direct taxation: four *arpents* of land in plebeian hands paid fourteen.

The injustice of this system was increased by the fact that wealthy commoners too could acquire immunity if they bought one of the four thousand financial, administrative or judicial posts conferring nobility and total exemption from the *taille*. Another forty thousand offices, without conferring nobility, assured partial exemption from this tax.

Thus the growing burden of taxation fell not on the class best able to bear it but upon those in no position to defend themselves. At a time when the conditions that had once justified or restricted exemption were disappearing, the privileged orders were arousing more and more resentment by their extravagance. The Exchequer's needs put too hard a strain on the commons, whose capacity to pay was rapidly nearing exhaustion. Sooner or later the Government would be forced either to suppress many political and administrative offices for lack of funds, or to do away with feudal tax prerogatives and proclaim equality for all citizens in face of this obligation.

Just as immunity from taxation was incompatible with the new needs of public finance, so the ancient feudal division of France was at variance with the more recent administrative system. Three hundred and fifty dukes, princes, counts, and marquises drew four and half millions a year from the Exchequer in salaries, apart from their accessory rights, which amounted to double the ordinary ones: yet they had no duties to fulfil, since their former political, administrative and military functions had passed into the hands of the *intendants* and other state officials. France was therefore maintaining and paying two different administrative organizations: the new one did the work, while the old enjoyed a decorative and parasitical existence.

Furthermore, the new administrative system had arisen little by little, without definite plan, as the old fiefs gradually became absorbed into the Crown domains. In consequence, there were *intendances* comprising two million inhabitants and others with only two hundred thousand. The judicial division of the country did not coincide with the administrative, nor the latter with ecclesiastical spheres of authority. Taxation varied from one province to another and often within the same province. Not only was France divided by customs barriers from other countries, but every one of her provinces levied its own duties on goods crossing its borders. This helped to keep the different regions estranged from one another; and, in conjunction with the 1500 tolls on roads, bridges and rivers— payable to the royal Exchequer, the feudal lords, the churches, abbeys, cities and guilds— slowed down transport and entailed heavy expenditure in collection: all of which naturally raised the cost of the goods. There was no uniform system of weights and measures. Nor, despite repeated efforts by the kings to unify civil and penal law, was there legislative homogeneity: the various cities and regions jealously preserved their mediaeval legal privileges, and there were 360 conflicting codes of local customary law. Everywhere the old authorities were at odds with the new. The various courts and tribunals— administrative, feudal, ecclesiastical, military, financial, city and corporative— all clashed with one another. Justice, at the best slow-moving and costly, was hard to seek in such a maze of contradictory laws; and, with its endless complications of procedure, was only too easily side-tracked altogether, in the course of revocations, appeals and counter-appeals. In Brittany alone, before 1789, there were about 2500 feudal courts, with 3500 judges.

This tangled growth of local independent authorities, dating from far back into the Middle Ages, hindered any development of a simple and uniform system of law and custom, such as is indispensable, in the modern world, to the free circulation of ideas and wealth. As trade and industry progressed, this cumbrous administrative legacy from times long past became more and more exasperating to the commons.

III

Other discredited survivals were ecclesiastical tithes and feudal dues.

The *dîme* (tithe) levied upon the crops by the clergy brought them about 120 million *livres* a year. Its origin lay, like all their other privileges, in the Middle Ages, when the clergy saw to the building and repair of roads and bridges, helped to maintain public order, administered justice in the ecclesiastical courts, and were responsible for education and for care of the poor and sick: carrying out, in other words, many functions of benefit to the community which the civil authorities were incapable of exercising. In the eighteenth century, however, the lay bureaucracy had taken over most of this social and administrative work. The *dîme*, therefore, which mostly went to swell the revenues of the rich and indolent higher clergy, seemed to those who paid it a totally unjustifiable burden. All attempted to evade or to reduce this obligation; and although it had, in many places, dropped to a twelfth, a twentieth or even a fortieth part of the produce of the land, it was a source of greater bitterness than in former times, when it had in reality weighed more heavily upon the rural population.

Similar resentment was aroused by the countless feudal rights exercised by landowners for their own benefit. The first category of these were relics of feudal sovereignty: imposts, such as the hearth-tax, road and bridge tolls, dues levied on the transit of flocks and herds through feudal property, and taxes on the sale of certain goods; juridical rights, such as the power to nominate judge and attorney in rural law-suits and feudal litigation; and monopolies, such as exclusive rights of hunting and fishing, and of owning flour-mills, pigeon-cotes, bakehouses and slaughter-houses. The other category— charges levied on produce, dues exacted in cash or in kind, the use of forced labour (*corvées*), payments demanded in respect of the inheritance or sale of property or in lieu of labour, rights of pre-emption and redemption, etc. — were derived from the feudal lord's former rights of ownership over the land and serfs of the glebe, and represented compensation secured by the nobles and clergy in the original agreements giving the peasants use of the land and personal freedom.

In mediaeval times these seigniorial rights had found justification in the fact that the feudal lords lived on their estates, maintained public order and helped to defend the country from external attack. Such socially-useful services received their natural recompense in the levying of taxation, possession of monopolies and exercise of juridical rights. In the same way, the feudal dues had at one time represented a great step forward on the road both of social and agricultural progress, for through them the peasants had freed themselves from servitude and gained ownership of the land they cultivated.

But in the eighteenth century the lay and ecclesiastical nobles no longer carried out their local political and administrative functions; where the feudal lord's authority had once been supreme the State officials now ruled. Recollection of the old agrarian compacts between lords and vassals had faded: the land had passed through many hands, feudal rights had been sold by one owner to another, and the peasant proprietors no longer remembered that their holdings had once belonged to some noble or abbey, and that the land-dues they paid were only survivals of the original feudal property-rights. In their eyes, this complicated system of annual payments and petty restrictions was an intolerable burden that hampered them at every stage of production, decimating their agricultural profits and proving a source of endless disputes, litigation and ill-feeling. Moreover, it acted as a brake upon agriculture, which, under the pressure of increasing consumption, was struggling to expand and find freedom of action. In the eighteenth century the feudal rights, like ecclesiastical tithes, were but a shadow of what they once had been, owing to anti-feudal encroachments by the State officials, and because the peasants were ever on the look-out for opportunities to reduce or commute their obligations, or to let them fall into disuse. But, like tithes, these rights were detested largely because their justification was no longer apparent: 'They gave more trouble to those who paid them than gain to those who benefited.'

It should also be noted that some feudal rights had, in fact, become more burdensome than in the past. For instance, in mediaeval times the chase was free to all; indeed, since the forests were infested with wild beasts, hunting was one of the feudal lord's duties. In some places the peasants used to bring him special gifts, such as baskets of oats or wheat, if he hunted longer than was, according to local custom, incumbent on him. But with agricultural development the forests became reduced in size, and game grew scarce. The nobles then claimed as an exclusive right what had formerly been an obligation; whereupon the game once more increased and prospered, roaming undisturbed and in broad daylight over cultivated ground, damaging vegetables and fruit trees and in some places ruining up to a third of the crops. Yet woe betide the peasant who killed even a hare or a partridge: the game-laws were inexorable, protecting the beasts of the field as though they were human and persecuting men as though they were beasts. 'There go the nobility', grumbled the peasants at sight of the wild creatures they might not touch; making no distinction between game and feudal lords, in their hatred towards all privileged beings.

But even apart from their privileges, the landed wealth still remaining to the nobility and clergy was in itself galling to the commons. Twenty million *hectares* of land were owned by scarcely 300,000 persons in a population of 26 million. The property of the clergy alone was valued at 3 milliards, and brought in about 100 million *livres* a year. Moreover, these estates could not, under canon law, change hands; while the law of primogeniture impeded the breaking-up of the nobles' property. So vast an amount of land concentrated in the hands of so few was not only a challenge to the rest but was a barrier to the development of wealth, and to the spirit of enterprise that imbued the new French *bourgeoisie*. With increasing prosperity, the need for commercial expansion became acute. It was little wonder that city capitalists, small farmers and peasantry all cast covetous eyes on land held by the nobles and the Church.

IV

Thus in eighteenth-century French society, the needs of the modern *bourgeoisie* were totally at variance with the customs inherited from feudal times. This clash of interests gave rise to the great crisis in which the last bulwarks of mediaevalism finally went down, and a new social order emerged.

Yet it may well be asked whether so sanguinary an upheaval as that of the great Revolution was necessary, to crown the long struggle of both commons and State officials against feudalism with ultimate success. Was it inevitable that the monarchy itself should be overthrown by the last stage of a policy which it had for so many centuries openly supported? Could not Louis XVI, like his predecessors, have enlisted the help of the *bourgeoisie* — now the largest, richest and most cultivated section of the community — and so made an end of feudalism whilst avoiding the horrors of revolution?

If we suppose that Louis XV and Louis XVI, instead of being the men they were, had been endowed with the genius of Henri IV or of Richelieu, and had pursued a line of conduct differing from that which, in reality, they chose — a line easy for us to point out, in the light of after events — we may possibly conclude that the French Revolution of the eighteenth century was unnecessary. But history is not made by suppositions. To deduce the probable course of events had some historical factor been different may, to a certain extent, help us to clarify the causes of the real facts by contrasting them with hypothetical ones; but it is no substitute for knowledge of the real facts.

The truth is that, like the kings and their officials in their political victories over the feudal classes, the men of the *tiers état*, in extending their economic influence, were always prompted by their immediate personal interests, and never tried to put forward a comprehensive plan for rooting-out feudalism altogether. They wanted to enrich themselves and gain control, little by little, of the land, as opportunity offered. But they never gave a thought to the social and political effects which their continual encroachments were bound in the end to bring about. In the same way, the kings and their officials had gradually ousted the feudal lords and their agents as expediency demanded, only suppressing their former powers in those areas where they most obviously clashed with the royal authority. This unconscious empiricism on both sides in the centuries-old struggle for power explains the survival of so many mediaeval practices well into the eighteenth century.

The *tiers état* were bound to continue their work until feudalism was wholly destroyed, since the ancient privileges of both nobles and clergy conflicted everywhere with the needs of the new *bourgeois* society. But the kings and State officials were under no such compulsion. Their conflict with the feudal lords arose, not from the latter's oppression of the commons, but from their resistance to the central authority. So long as it was necessary to wrest political power from the feudal lords the kings were naturally allies of the commons; but once this aim had been achieved, they had no further cause for combating the privileged orders. Such feudal rights, therefore, as did not conflict with the royal prerogative were regarded by the kings as time-honoured possessions, to be respected and safeguarded in the same way as — indeed in preference to — every other form of property. Fundamentally, the monarch was only first among the great lords of the realm.

Nor should it be forgotten that in France the influence of the kings in public administration had become, in recent centuries, far less effective than that of the all-powerful officials. And although the latter, on the one hand, did their best to exclude the old feudal classes from political or administrative power, on the other they themselves had every wish to rise above the commons. The more highly-placed among them were ennobled by the King and thus gained many privileges appertaining to the first two orders of the realm; and this new nobility of the 'robe', as opposed to that of the 'sword' and the Church, was nevertheless clearly removed from the lower sphere of the *tiers état*. Having themselves become a privileged class, immune from taxation, and with the distinctions accompanying noble rank, the higher officials ended by defending the remains of feudalism from attack by the commons; employing, for this purpose, the very powers that in former times they had acquired with the commons' help for use against the feudal classes.

This lack of consistency between what might be called the neo-feudal policy of the kings and the State bureaucracy, and the anti-feudal tendencies of the commons, became increasingly apparent as both nobility and clergy grew politically weaker and more servile towards the King. During the last years of his reign, Louis XIV had effected a new alliance between the lay and ecclesiastical feudal lords and the monarchy. The aristocrats, by then deprived of power owing largely to the policy of Richelieu and Mazarin, were — if not dragging out a useless existence in the provinces — entering the army to seek their fortune, or living at court, which had become the centre of national life and fount of all authority. Here they gathered round the King, rendering him homage and leading a decorative but altogether parasitical existence. Louis XIV, who wished to destroy all political influence on the part of the nobles, encouraged them to become courtiers, uprooted them from their old *châteaux*, severed all contact between them and their former subjects, and kept them wholly in his power. In return, he declared their feudal rights imprescriptible, recognized their monopoly of the chase, and revoked the Edict of Nantes, dispersing the Protestant *bourgeoisie* to please the Jesuits, after forcing the clergy to accept the articles of the Gallican Church. He entertained lavishly and created lucrative posts for his *protégés*, showing an interest in their family affairs, helping them in their financial troubles, and showering favours and pensions upon them.

There was no end to the favours and pensions, because according to the theory propounded by legal experts of the *tiers état* to justify confiscation of feudal property, the King was owner of France and the French, and no distinction could be made between his privy purse and the public revenue. Nor was it possible to keep the courtiers' needs within bounds, owing to their unbridled extravagance — encouraged by the royal example — and to the growing disorder on their estates. In consequence, court offices, as unnecessary as they were costly, increased in number year by year: palace officials, governors of the royal households, masters of the chase, chamberlains, grooms, gentlemen-in-waiting, gentlemen of the bed-chamber, almoners, chaplains, maids of honour, ladies-in-waiting and ladies of the bed-chamber. They were attached to the King and Queen, their sons and daughters, and to every branch of the royal family. The daughter of Louis XVI, when one month old, had eighty persons in her service: well might Marie-Antoinette resolve to give her a good upbringing and not encourage her in 'sentiments of pride'. An army of about fifteen thousand gilded idlers existed at court who, with their salaries, pensions and gratuities, consumed, during the last years of the old régime, forty million *livres* a year; in other words, a twelfth of the public revenue.

The nobles in the army, too, had to be compensated for their former power with the glory of military conquest and its accompanying gains. Thus there were the great international wars, not dictated by any real need on the country's part: the so-called 'wars of magnificence', which imposed an enormous additional strain on the Exchequer.

To keep pace with so much expenditure, taxation rose, as we have already seen, from 85 million *livres* in 1661 to 166 million in 1715. But the usual sources of revenue proved inadequate. Louis XIV had to seek others, and thus had recourse to borrowing, to pledging revenue in advance, to lotteries, the issue of paper money, the sale of State property, the sale of formerly elective municipal posts, the institution of artificial monopolies and a number of other immoral and ruinous expedients. When he died in 1715 France was already reduced, according to

Fénelon, to the state of 'a desolate and starving poor-house'; with a public debt — unheard of in those days — of 3 milliards.

Although Louis XIV had, during the second half of his life, sacrificed his country's prosperity to the greed of the privileged classes, he had excluded them from the King's Council and from administrative, diplomatic and ecclesiastical office. During the eighteenth century, however, episcopal sees, canonries, conventual posts, and about two thousand benefices, which under Louis XIV had been invaded by clergy belonging to the lower orders, were all seized for members of noble families. Military posts were multiplied for the nobles' benefit, while the exclusion of those of common birth became more and more the rule. When, in 1769, Choiseul established twenty-three as the minimum age for obtaining a colonelcy in the army, the Court was shocked, having been accustomed to seeing boys of sixteen — if the sons of dukes, counts or favourites — nominated to colonel's rank. On the eve of the Revolution the French army consisted of 35,000 officers (of whom 1171 were generals) and 135,000 men. The officers were maintained at a cost of 46 millions a year, although only 3500 were on the active list; the maintenance of the rank and file amounted to 44 millions in all.

Taxation trebled in seventy years. In times of great stringency, when it was no longer possible to force it beyond all reasonable limits, recourse was had to so-called 'extraordinary' measures, although there was nothing unusual about them, since the crisis was continual: money was borrowed at exorbitant rates of interest, official posts were created for sale at a high price, municipal posts — already purchasable — were suppressed and others established that had to be bought afresh, and monopolies were abolished in order to be revived and re-sold. From time to time, when funds were entirely lacking and all other expedients had been exhausted, the Exchequer was made more or less openly bankrupt; after which the same process began all over again.

V

This spendthrift economy, growing worse from year to year, made its effects felt in every sphere of public and private life.

The fact that municipal posts were purchasable prevented any influence or control over local government by the citizens. Such offices became monopolized by a narrow oligarchy of rich men who had bought the right to administer cities and looked upon the people as born to servitude. Indirect taxation became almost the sole basis of communal economy. The *octrois* — duties upon articles of consumption entering the towns — weighed heavily upon the people's foodstuffs, but did not affect luxury products. Unscrupulous contractors, speculators and bankers flocked around the administrations, eating up communal wealth; while the municipalities were almost all insolvent or in a state of the utmost financial disorder. In 1778 the commune of Lyons, with a revenue of 2,118,142 *livres*, was paying interest on debts to the amount of 2,411,030 a year. About the same time the commune of Marseilles, with a revenue of a million and a half, was struggling to make ends meet, while the syndicate collecting the duty on wine alone made 181,725 *livres* in three years.

The horde of inspectors, controllers, inspector-controllers, visitors, assayers, surveyors, supervisors and so forth — which had been increased by Louis XIV and his successors to ludicrous proportions under the pretext of supervising industry and commerce, but in reality in order to profit by the sale of office — was an intolerable burden upon every sphere of economic life: in itself unproductive, it lived at the expense of production, and multiplied restrictions rather to justify its own existence than for any valid reason. These officials encumbered the streets and marketplaces, invaded shops and factories, levied fines to right and left, and held up all technical progress. So soon as invention or fashion triumphed over old restrictions, new regulations came in to strangle further progress and to raise fresh barriers against the movement of capital, always in search of easier investment and greater freedom.

The Government's financial policy had a ruinous effect upon the guilds of artisans. These associations certainly did not, as has been thought, constrict the nation's whole commercial and industrial life: because not only rural industries but also the growing capitalistic undertakings were free from corporative control. It was only in the cities and in various traditional trades that mediaeval regulations persisted. But where this was so, the guilds had, little by little, turned themselves into exclusive organizations assuring their members a monopoly in the local market. The Government had seconded this change by sanctioning new prohibitive measures demanded by the guilds themselves and by making them in return pay heavily for royal protection. Thus, many free trades were arbitrarily transformed into closed associations and forced to buy their charters and monopolistic privileges. This had a crippling effect on the country's economic structure; for these small monopolistic groups, jealous of one another, were an arbitrary brake upon free enterprise. Furthermore, while the Government was propping up old guilds and endeavouring to create new ones, it was at the same time violating their former privileges; it would sell charters of mastership to non-members, grant exclusive rights to practise a trade to whole cities, or to new quarters of a city already subject to the traditional system, and would at one stroke abolish all the charters of a trade in order to force the artisans to buy themselves new ones again. Thus, even within the same trades, monopolies clashed with free competition, and free competition made monopolistic privileges illusory. In free commerce, no less than in privileged trades, the Government's dishonest fiscal policy caused widespread confusion and resentment.

Capital, prevented or discouraged from finding an outlet in production, sought safer and more convenient investment in the public debt. The Government, always short of money, created life annuities, perpetual annuities, revertible annuities, premium loans and State lotteries, offering high rates of interest. But when payment fell due, difficulties were raised: and suspension, reduction of interest or refusal to pay ensued, to the detriment not only of the bond-holders but of the contractors and purveyors involved. These became debtors in their turn: so that all delay or failure by the Government to meet its obligations had disastrous repercussions throughout the business world.

The *bourgeoisie* suffered not only materially but in their *amour-propre*. In the eighteenth century, differences between them and the nobles in wealth, culture and tastes were tending more and more to disappear. 'The middle-class,' wrote Voltaire, 'has enriched itself through industry, and commercial profits have increased; there is less luxury amongst the nobility than formerly, and more in middle-class life, so that the contrast between them is not so marked.'

Differences in legal status between the classes, however, remained clearly defined. The nobility still, as in mediaeval times, regarded itself as superior in every way to the commons. It was the nobles who filled the more honourable and lucrative offices; they alone could become dignitaries of the Church or officers in the army, and none but they had *entrée* to the Court. They were exempt from taxation; they claimed that they could not be summoned for debt, or challenged to a duel by a commoner, even after personal assault; and in 1779 they obtained a decree which, in prohibiting duels altogether, made any *bourgeois* who challenged a noble liable to death by hanging. The middle-classes, forced to give way in every respect to the nobles and conscious of the latter's disdain, were continually exasperated by this disparity. During the eighteenth century the desire for 'equality before the law' had become almost an obsession with the *bourgeoisie*. In 1789 the burghers of La Rochelle even went so far as to complain of the law by virtue of which a noble, if condemned to death, was beheaded, while a commoner was sent to the gallows. Whenever an intelligent *bourgeois* came into contact with a noble, there was immediate friction, and hatred flared up. And indeed, in view of the injuries inflicted upon the middle-classes in every circumstance of their lives, the fury with which the French revolutionaries sought to root out the nobility from the nation's life is easily explicable.

If such were the moral and material condition of the middle-classes, it is not hard to imagine how bad must have been that of the urban working-classes. These, for the most part, were employed in privileged trades. Employers' associations laid down standards, wages and limitations of work, and fixed inordinately severe penalties for every offence. The workers were looked upon as inferior beings, without rights of any kind. A worker who left his master had to obtain the latter's consent and a certificate of good conduct, or no other would engage him. Officials of the masters' associations were entitled to arrest workers found in inns or other places who could not produce certificates. A worker could not leave his employer without giving due notice, in default of which he was liable — as, for instance, in the Paris watchmakers' guild — to a sentence of three years' hard labour.

The rest of the city proletariat clustered round centres that were immune from corporative restrictions. Those most highly-skilled and fortunate went to swell the class of small independent artisans or expert craftsmen. Others were absorbed by the growing heavy industries and dockyards, or formed the great reserve of unskilled workers who lived from hand to mouth or, if unemployed, by begging. Behind them swarmed the real beggars and vagabonds; men and women for whom no hope remained.

This crowd of workers, oppressed both by the ancient trade guilds and newly-developed capitalism — bled white by the implacable taxation levied by the Government and the local administrations — harboured many secret associations for resistance. At every crisis in industry or in the supply of foodstuffs, strikes and rebellion broke out.

The most dangerous city was Paris, with its more than half a million inhabitants. With the growth of a centralized administration, the capital had attracted to itself a crowd of fortune-seekers, both rich and poor. To satisfy the diverse needs of all these people new houses and factories were built, which absorbed a stream of workers and peasants from the provinces. The Government, disturbed yet gratified at such an increase in population — embarrassed at having so large a city to administer, but thankful for additional sources of revenue — wavered between distributing favours and privileges, and imposing absurd restrictions, in an effort to stem the flood. But the colossus went on growing, with or without the King's permission; rearing up within itself an army of rebels that was to become a most efficacious weapon for destroying the old France. On the eve of the Revolution employers in Paris were complaining that 'the workers were dictating to the Government and making leagues of resistance: what with insolent speeches and insulting letters, they seemed to think that anything was permissible'.

VI

The beasts of burden in this society were the peasants.

We do not know precisely how the 20 million *hectares* belonging to the commons were divided between the citizens and peasants of France; nor how many peasants were entirely independent or had land burdened with feudal charges; nor how many small free-holders also cultivated property belonging to the privileged classes and *bourgeoisie* as tenant-farmers or *métayers*, or worked, when free to do so, for other landowners, as day-labourers. How many peasants, furthermore, were entirely without land of their own and lived as tenants, *métayers* or labourers, and how much each rural family was able to add to its earnings by working at home-handicrafts, then very widespread, it is not possible to estimate, in the present state of our knowledge; especially as conditions varied considerably from region to region and between commune and commune. All sources agree, however, upon the wretched state of the French peasantry as a whole.

In eighteenth-century France the land was cultivated by most antiquated methods. Tools were poor; in some districts, only wooden ploughs were used, and very few fertilizers were available. The capital invested in agriculture was only a third of what it became a century later. Arthur Young, comparing French and English agriculture in 1789, found that whereas the produce of an acre in England was worth £36, in France it was scarcely worth £25. It may well be imagined how hard was the life wrung from a few *hectares* of land by a family of small peasant proprietors.

Worse still was the state of tenants and *métayers* (share-croppers) who did not own their land. The great landowners, and in particular the higher nobility and clergy, either entrusted their estates to bailiffs, or leased them *en bloc* to a general lease-holder; the latter would sub-let small lots to others, who sub-let in their turn. Thus the land not only supported its distant owner but a whole series of intermediaries, all of whom weighed upon the peasants. Rents were high and leases of short duration. The *métayage* system had deteriorated owing to special clauses which reduced the peasant's share to a third or even a quarter of the produce.

As to the agricultural workers, Taine calculates that a rural day-labourer could before the Revolution buy 959 *litres* of grain with his year's wages, while in the nineteenth century he could buy 1851, or almost double. Wages were about ten to nineteen *sous* a day, whereas a century later they were forty; fête-days and bad seasons reduced the labourer's earnings by a third; and house-rent alone absorbed about thirty *livres* a year. In addition he had to pay the *capitation* and salt *gabelle*, and work in the *corvée* for road-making. It was abject poverty.

Progress in agriculture during the last decades of the old régime, far from turning out to be of benefit to the rural population, brought even greater hardships upon them. Formerly the peasant had been entitled to take wood from the forests for fuel, or for building his house and making his own rough furniture; he could graze his flocks on uncultivated land, and glean after the harvest had been gathered in. In short, he enjoyed a thousand petty rights over others' property which, survivals, as they were, of mediaeval collective ownership, represented a source of additional income for the poor. In the second half of the eighteenth century many landowners — especially newly-ennobled *bourgeois*, anxious to exploit their land by more modern methods — cut down the forests to sell wood to the factories, or to extend the area of tillage; in many districts they turned pasture into arable land; and they endeavoured to exclude the peasants' flocks and herds from cultivated ground, and to prevent gleaning and other petty depredations on their property. In consequence, the poorest of the rural population found themselves forced to buy wood for fuel, to give up their flocks and to buy larger quantities of grain. Rents rose, and also the price of furniture. In many places, a desire to increase production led to the merging of small lease-holdings into large agricultural units, and this technical progress reduced many former tenant-cultivators and *métayers* to the condition of day-labourers. The nobles, clerics and more powerful *bourgeois*, attracted by rising land values, began everywhere to lay hands on common land. The plight of the peasants became ever more desperate as general wealth increased.

Naturally, so wretched a rural population was ill-equipped to withstand the crisis produced by an incursion of capitalism into the countryside. It was totally unfitted to bear the crushing burden of taxation. It has been estimated that out of 100 *livres* of net profit derived from cultivating the land — that is, after expenses of production, interest on capital, losses, etc., had been deducted — direct Government taxation (the *taille, capitation* and *vingtième*) absorbed fifty-three, ecclesiastical tithes fourteen and other dues fourteen *livres*. Only 19 per cent of the profit remained to the peasant; but out of this, indirect taxation — beginning with the salt *gabelle* — had to be paid. Then there was the *corvée*; and finally there were the communal taxes for the repair of local roads and bridges, for maintenance of the church and town hall, for the doctor, midwife and other communal employees and for the cost of legal proceedings undertaken by the commune. It seems incredible that the peasants survived at all, under such ruthless extortion.

They certainly led a life unfit for beasts. Their houses were hovels, without windows and with earthen floors. Their food rarely included meat or wine, and their bread was made of rye, barley, oats, maize or chestnuts; wheaten flour was reserved for fête-days or for the sick. Shoes were little worn. Many possessed neither furniture nor beds. Infantile mortality was extremely high and epidemic disease continual. A bad harvest was sufficient to bring them to the very brink of starvation and despair.

Taxation was not only very high but was levied in an exasperating manner. The direct taxes, for example, were collected by certain peasants of the parish, chosen by their companions in misfortune, and forced to accept the task. No more dreadful office can be imagined: the tax-payers protested their poverty, objected to the quota assigned them, and refused to pay; had they done otherwise they would have been mulcted of yet more the following year. The collectors were for ever in pursuit of defaulting tax-payers; if they failed to collect the required sum they had to pay it themselves, or were imprisoned either until they could produce the money or extract it from the original debtors. In some communities during the eighteenth century tax-collectors were to be found in every jail. One administrative area of Champagne had ninety-five under lock and key in 1785.

The use of the *corvée*, up to the time of Louis XIV, had been a feudal right appertaining only to the seigniorial lords and the communes, and the main roads were maintained out of the taxes. Under Louis XIV the Government began in some places to employ forced labour also for public works. This system of using the labour of the poor to lighten expenditure for the rich seemed so good an idea that in 1737 it was extended to all France; and gradually, as trade developed and new roads were made while the necessity of keeping the old in better repair was everywhere apparent, increasing recourse was had to the *corvée*. It was also used for transporting condemned criminals and sick persons, for building barracks and for military convoys. Contractors often obtained permission to make use of it.

The most hated tax was the salt *gabelle*. Every family had to buy so many pounds of salt for each of its members over seven years of age, and the necessary quantity had to be acquired all at once from public storehouses which opened twice a week. This salt might be applied only to kitchen use; for other purposes a special kind had to be bought. The *gabelle* officials were entitled to enter the homes of the poor at any moment of the day or night, to search them from top to bottom and to impose fines at will. Since the price of salt varied from province to province owing to various local privileges, reaching in some places sixty-two *livres* a hundredweight and in others only sixteen, smuggling was naturally rife. Twenty thousand *gabelous* were employed in searching houses, vehicles or pedestrians on the roads. On the eve of the Revolution there were in one year alone 3700 instances of the sequestration of contraband salt, and 2300 men, 1800 women and 6600 young persons in prison for the crime of smuggling.

The fiercest resentment aroused by this state of affairs was to be found, not among the day-labourers, who had no crops of their own, paid neither *taille* nor *vingtième* and had almost nothing to lose, but among the small proprietors, tenant-farmers and *métayers*: in other words, among those very sections of the community which as a rule are anything but revolutionary in their sentiments. When the peasant, sober, tenacious and fiercely attached to the soil, had succeeded by means of rigid economies in adding year by year to his hidden savings, and had bought or leased some land for himself— feeling that in so doing he had improved his social position— he found descending upon him the noble with his claims for feudal dues, the cleric with his demand for tithes, the game that he might not kill, and the tax-gatherers, *gabelle* officials and agents for the wine-tax: a whole horde of oppressors who threatened him with expropriation if he did not at once pay up, who woke him at night and ransacked his house, who demanded tolls at every step he took, and prevented him using his own goods how and where he pleased. Continually harassed, at harvest and vintage-time, on the threshing-floor, in the mill, and in the very act of selling his produce, he was always under threat of fines, arrest or judicial proceedings. No wonder he nursed an ineradicable bitterness in his heart.

Many, especially during the last years of the old régime, sold their accursed land to feudal lord or wealthy *bourgeois* and flocked city-wards in search of more remunerative work. Others emigrated or took to a life of vagabondage. The more stubborn lived by poaching: upon the confines of the forests there was a constant slaughter of keepers and their dogs. Or they turned to smuggling, and — men, women and children — stormed the customs-barriers and cleared a passage between one province and another. Many plunged into brigandage, which flourished throughout France; the peasants secretly helped these outcasts, giving them information and hiding them from reach of the law. Often whole villages, in desperation, rose in revolt against the revenue officials, attacked the town halls and looted the granaries. During the eighteenth century troops were continually on the move, imposing order and suppressing riots, often at the expense of human life.

But what was to happen were the whole countryside to rise at once? If a revolt of the urban population were to be added to rural insurrection, and one general impulse explode all these inflammable elements that were included under the single designation of the *tiers état*? How then were the privileged orders, the King and his bureaucrats to be saved from utter ruin? In other words, what forces could the conservative element in the feudal monarchy muster against a revolt of the whole Third Estate together?

VII

Very few among the privileged classes ever considered the possibility of a revolution. In free countries, where discontent has an outlet through the press, or by means of demonstrations, discussions, and stormy parliamentary debates, revolutionary parties come out into the open: the Government and ruling classes are kept continually on the *qui vive*; they become aware of every change in the balance of political forces and are quick to defend themselves. But in eighteenth-century France a political press was almost entirely lacking, and there was no legal way in which the country could make known its desires and grievances. Not only the King and his officials, but the ruling classes themselves were without any means of gaining an accurate idea of the dangers that threatened them.

The bureaucracy had some regard for the needs of the cities, where the populace, crowded around the monied and intelligent middle-class, could, to a certain extent, make itself felt, and represented a tangible danger. But to the peasants — scattered, ignorant and unable in any way to gain a hearing for themselves — no one gave a thought, except the tax-gatherers. The Government did not even know how many there were of them; when rural statistics were required, the priests were asked to report on the number of communicants at Easter and the population was estimated accordingly.

The King, at court, was entirely cut off from the life of the country, while the nobles who surrounded him knew no more of it than he did. Having nothing to do, they sought to pass their time as best they might: there were balls, theatrical performances and hunting-parties; they discussed philosophy, read fairy tales, acted charades, flew kites, or 'worked'. Having nothing to do, they even 'worked' to escape boredom: playing musical instruments, painting, learning some handicraft or unravelling brocade in order to pick out the gold and silver threads. There was great excitement when the dentist came to court to extract one of the Dauphin's teeth — fortunately only a milk tooth; but political alliances, battles lost or won, were no concern of theirs: or at most, were the occasion for an epigram or a song, after which diversion was sought elsewhere. Having lost all contact with the mass of the people they were totally ignorant of conditions prevailing either in the cities or the countryside, and imagined the peasants as they were portrayed in tapestries and painted porcelain, in plays and madrigals: gentle and charming beings, clothed in silk and satin, who made love in well-rhymed verse. Between nobles and working-class all humane and charitable relations had ceased; the peasant only knew his master through the brutal administrators, agents and contractors who exacted feudal dues. In the Clermont district, the Prince of Condé's game-keepers reared wolves at the castle to loose, when winter approached, for their master's sport; the wolves, immune from harm, killed the peasants' livestock, and sometimes carried off a child. What wonder if the peasants, at the first opportunity, were to set fire to the castle and murder their lord, with his hated retainers?

The lower ranks of the nobility and clergy, especially in country districts, remained in touch with the people. But those nobles who stayed at home did so only because they could not afford to go and ruin themselves at court. Privilege and prejudice raised a barrier between them and the peasantry. Even in church they had a special place reserved for them. They met the peasants only when they had to collect their scanty revenues or extort their remaining feudal dues. At such times, being poor themselves and crippled by debt— forced to live in a manner worthy of their rank on so miserable a source of income, and, in very truth, goaded by necessity— they were ruthless, grudging and impossible to please. The peasant, more stubborn still, disputed every stage of the proceedings, growing more embittered towards the familiar, impoverished noble than towards the distant great lord. The latter, at least, sometimes allowed some small crumb to fall from his table, if only out of carelessness.

For that matter, even when they possessed some moral ascendancy over the peasants, these provincial nobles were unlikely to use it in favour of the Government. Hard up as they were and envious of the great nobility at court who gained all the favours for themselves, the country lords blamed the Government for neglecting them and looked on the court as source of all their ills. At the approach of the Revolution they were so exasperated at the way in which their own class had failed them that they regarded themselves almost as democrats, wanted to abolish the court nobility, and refused to nominate the great lords as their representatives in the States-General.

Less conservative still was the attitude of the lower clergy. The stipend of 700 *livres* a year for the *curés* and of 350 for the *vicaires* barely sufficed to keep them from starving; yet out of this they had to contribute almost all the *dons gratuits* (benevolences) which the clergy offered the King from time to time in return for non-payment of property-tax: an obligation which the prelates always took care to shift on to the shoulders of the lowest ranks in the hierarchy.

In 1775 the *curés* and *vicaires* sent a petition to the King demonstrating the inadequacy of their stipends. In 1780 the parish priests of the Dauphiné, comparing their own poverty with the luxury in which the great ecclesiastics lived, asked that their subvention should be raised, out of the proceeds of tithe, from 500 to 1000 or at least 900 *livres*. The higher clergy continued to oppose their claims.

Every one of them of noble birth, the high ecclesiastics themselves absorbed more than half the tithes and revenue from land or feudal dues. One hundred and thirty-five bishops alone divided among themselves 14 millions in revenue; in other words, an average of more than a hundred thousand *livres* each. In the episcopal palaces and abbeys, and in the chapters where canons and canonesses dwelt in comfort, receptions were held and life was lived much as in high society. In the Abbey of Saint Germain des Prés the honours of the house were performed by a dancer, Mademoiselle Leduc. Many great dignitaries of the Church did not live in their dioceses. They kept stables and followed the chase; their kitchens were equipped with utensils of solid silver and they held confession in satin-lined confessionals. '*Liberté, facilité, M. l'Abbé*,' the Cardinal de Rohan used to say to his secretary; he was no stickler for morality, being of the opinion that 'it is impossible to sin in good company'.

The lower clergy grew exasperated at so insolent and scandalous a display of luxury, and canons, abbots, priors, bishops and archbishops were all detested by the humble parish priests. This dissension between the higher and lower ranks of the clergy was one of the most potent causes leading to the early victories of the Revolution.

VIII

In the second half of the eighteenth century, therefore, French society might be said to resemble an ancient city, grown up in past times without design or order, built of diverse materials and according to the methods of different ages; with old and out-of-date buildings huddled together amongst new and solid structures. Almost all the inhabitants — working-class, middle-classes and even a large part of the privileged orders — were ill at ease and discontented, amidst the discordant claims of old and new.

The state officials had become the instruments of a corrupt and reactionary system against which the nation needs must revolt, if it were not to relapse into feudal darkness. The privileged classes plundered the Exchequer, disrupted the administration and paralysed the country's economic life. They had reached the very brink of the abyss without perceiving it, and continued to wrangle with one another, when all were about to be engulfed.

The commons, forced to choose between their own ruin and the destruction of every vestige of feudalism, had hoped that the King might return to the traditional anti-feudal policy that had been the glory of his dynasty in times past. In the end, tired of waiting in vain, they overthrew what was left of feudalism together with the monarchy that intervened in its support, freed themselves by their own efforts from their last remaining fetters, and set the new seal of the Republic upon modern society.

CHAPTER II

THE INTELLECTUAL MOVEMENT

I

IN a small country, social inequality and the discontent arising from it are sufficient in themselves to produce a successful revolt, if the malcontents have material preponderance over satisfied members of the community. In large ones, on the other hand, opposition groups cannot achieve victory unless they are numerous and widely disseminated. But this very dispersion subjects them to local pressure and may lead to contradictory and ineffectual action if they do not follow some common policy. To achieve success, the leaders of single groups must share similar aspirations and be guided by an accepted programme to which all contribute, while each adapts his own actions to local conditions. Such a programme cannot be improvised and suddenly imposed upon a people from one moment to the next. It must be the outcome of experience and disappointments, of hopes and fears and illusions that have existed for a considerable time. A great revolution, in fact, is already mature in men's minds when it reveals itself in deeds; it is not simply an outbreak of unreasoning violence, but the result, above all, of intense thought and of an entirely new moral attitude.

For this reason the social conflicts of modern states are always accompanied by the widespread expression of political sentiments and theories, whilst those of the small mediaeval communes, in many respects so similar to our own, were virtually without such intellectual preparation. The French Revolution was preceded by a great spiritual crisis, the elements of which, accumulated from many varied sources, had been maturing during the course of several centuries.

Even at the height of the feudal period, when all public administration was reduced to a question of mutual obligation

47

between the lord and his vassals, Incmarus, Archbishop of Rheims (806-82), had stated that political society is based upon a contract between the subjects, who elect their sovereign, and the sovereign, who must govern them wisely. In the eleventh century, during the great struggle between emperors and popes, and in the twelfth, when the social and political revolution of the *bourgeois* communes was coming to a head, we find that the supporters of pontifical supremacy and those who promoted the anti-feudal and anti-Imperial movements denied any divine character to the sovereign, and regarded monarchical government as derived from the free will of the people, who chose a ruler to act in the common interest and for common defence: the King's subjects, therefore, had every right to rise against him if he did not fulfil his compact, and above all if his actions were not in conformity with the divine laws as transmitted to mankind by the Church. Such theories were opposed by those who upheld the Emperor's supremacy; they believed in the divine origin and hereditary character of sovereignty, and the duty of the subject to obey even a bad monarch. In the end, even the Ghibelline Marsilius of Padua, in his *Defensor pacis* (1324), accepted the theory of the contractual and elective origin of the civil authority: but according to him, in electing their sovereign, the people — not the Pope — were interpreters of the divine will, and endowed their chosen Emperor with divine right and unlimited sovereignty.

In all these mediaeval disputes, however, supreme authority in the social order — whether of Pope, Emperor, or People — was always held to be of divine origin. The duty of earthly governments was to guide men not so much on the way of terrestrial well-being as to future beatitude. Every writer supported his arguments with the authority of the Bible and the Holy Fathers.

In the twelfth century, European culture began to throw off its mediaeval dogmatic traditions, with the revival of Roman law. In this mighty structure, fruit of the wisdom and experience of the ancient world, the new *bourgeois* class found, ready to hand, a juridical system on purely rational lines, well-adapted to their own economic advancement. *Omnis jurisconsultus*, it was said in mediaeval times, *male de religione sentit*: which might be rendered as 'all lawyers are unsound on religious questions'. After the renascence of Roman law came that of Aristotelian philosophy; and despite every effort to reconcile the traditions of the Church with this further expression of classical rationalism, intellectual unrest steadily grew. In the fourteenth and fifteenth centuries a revival of classical learning in every field extended the secularization of culture begun by the jurists. Church teaching, forced on to the defensive, progressively lost ground.

Niccolò Machiavelli (1469-1527) was the first political thinker to treat statecraft as an exclusively worldly art, having as its only aim the conservation and strengthening of the public authority. After him, in the great religious and political disputes of the sixteenth and seventeenth centuries, to which the protestant Reformation and the constitution of absolute and national monarchies gave rise, the theories already adumbrated in mediaeval times on the natural and contractual origin of law, on popular sovereignty and the relationship between the Government and the individual, were systematically studied and developed.

The eighteenth century opened under the influence of two great English thinkers, for whom mediaeval scholasticism, even in the political field, was already over and done with. Hobbes (1588-1679), the theoretician of absolute monarchy, deduced his whole political system from mankind's need to escape from barbarism and natural violence: an aim achieved by means of a contract in which the authority of the individual is transferred to the sovereign, who is given full powers over the property, religious faith and education of his subjects, in order that he may preserve the peace. But Hobbes makes it incumbent upon the sovereign to obey 'natural laws'. The King must not be a capricious despot, but one 'enlightened' by Reason.

To Locke (1632-1704) — the theoretician of what, in the nineteenth century, was to be called liberalism — the function of the social contract was to preserve personal freedom and private property from external attack and disorder at home; he affirmed the necessity for religious tolerance and outlined a theory of education founded on persuasion and freedom. Locke maintained that the individual possessed rights independently of the sovereign's will, and that a sovereign must respect these rights if he wished to be a just ruler and not a tyrant. The people were entitled to dismiss state officials who failed to carry out the contract upon which their political constitution was based, and to exercise this right through a legislative authority elected by themselves and distinct from the judicial and executive powers.

England was the centre of this movement during the second half of the seventeenth century. France remained almost wholly excluded from it during the reign of Louis XIV. After the latter's death in 1715, Frenchmen too began to use their minds more or less freely. They gradually threw off their lethargy and plunged into the thick of the fight. French writers, trained in the Cartesian tradition of deductive rationalism, awarded the force of an ordered philosophical system and the value of absolute truths to observations and theories which English writers had presented in fragmentary and empirical form; while criticism of theological and absolutist beliefs, confined, in England, to the field of abstract study, was turned, in the fevered atmosphere of French society, into a formidable weapon of revolutionary change.

The first indications of these trends of thought were the early works of Voltaire (*Oedipe*, which came out in 1718, *Épitre à Uranie*, written in 1722, but published ten years later, and the *Henriade*, published in 1723); and the *Lettres persanes* of Montesquieu (1721). In 1724 a club devoted to political studies, known as the *Réunions de l'Entresol* and presided over by the Abbé de Saint-Pierre, was set up in the house of the Abbé Alary. Here the discussions were wholly dominated by admiration for English political life. The club was closed by order of the Government in 1731; but, during the ensuing twenty-five years, admiration for English freedom spread and became fashionable among cultivated persons.

At the same time the desolation of the last years of Louis XIV's reign had become a distant memory. In all branches of social life a progressive awakening was to be felt. Prosperity increased. Evils endured in silence while there had seemed no remedy for them became intolerable so soon as deliverance appeared a possibility.

On the other hand, such hopes as were engendered by the accession of Louis XV, at the age of five, rapidly faded. With advancing years the King revealed himself as self-indulgent and irresponsible. He left the government of his country to the greed and caprice of court officials and favourites, squandered the revenue extorted from his subjects in debauchery and on ill-fated wars, and dissipated the monarchy's prestige with criminal thoughtlessness.

It was under the pressure of all these factors — economic progress leading to increased dislike of the feudal régime, propaganda by Voltaire and other liberal publicists, together with the study of English habits and ideas, and growing distrust of the King — that the great crisis maturing in men's minds was precipitated. Voltaire rightly puts it as coming to a head about the year 1750, when, as he said, 'the nation turned to discussing grain'; in other words, economic, political and social problems.

The *Pensées philosophiques* of Diderot came out in 1746; Montesquieu's *Esprit des Lois* and *L'Homme-machine* by La Mettrie in 1748. In 1749 Diderot published the *Lettre sur les aveugles*, Buffon the first volume of *L'Histoire naturelle* and Rousseau his *Discours sur les Sciences et les Arts*. The publication of the *Encyclopédie* began in 1751. The *Code de la Nature* by Morelly, and Rousseau's *Discours sur l'origine et les fondements de l'inégalité* belong to 1755. In 1756 Voltaire's *Essai sur les mœurs* was issued; in 1758 a treatise by Helvétius entitled *De l'Esprit*; in 1761 Rousseau's *Nouvelle Héloïse* and *Contrat social*, and in 1762 his *Émile*. The year 1770 saw the publication of the *Système de la nature*, and 1772 that of the last volume of the *Encyclopédie*, out of which undertaking the publishers had made a profit of almost 300 per cent on their capital. During the same period *Le Tableau économique* (1758) by Quesnay, and two works by the Marquis de Mirabeau, *l'Ami des Hommes* (1757) and *La Théorie de l'impôt* (1760) were published. Meanwhile, Voltaire was carrying on his tireless liberal and anti-clerical propaganda by means of tragedies, epic poems, epigrams, letters, madrigals, fables in prose and in verse, didactic poems, translations, comedies, melodramas, histories, scientific treatises, essays on political economy and philosophy, literary criticism, controversial discussions on religion, law and politics, and campaigns against wrongful judicial sentences: in addition to which we have the twenty volumes of his letters, packed with wit and penetrating thought. In all these writings he heaped scorn upon the clergy and superstitious practices. Voltaire gave clear and lively expression to the most abstruse ideas, and was undoubtedly the true father of journalism and modern popular literature.

Besides the output of such leading writers, there was a flood of other books, pamphlets, essays, inquiries, periodicals, and proceedings of philosophical, scientific and economic societies. In 1777 the first daily paper, the *Journal de Paris*, began publication, and was immediately followed by a rival, the *Journal de politique et de littérature*. Sociology and political economy had become the most common studies; having invaded literature they displaced poetry to such an extent that during the second half of the century it almost died out.

This tremendous outburst of new religious, moral, political, economic and social doctrines gave men an entirely fresh view of life. By discrediting the beliefs of the old régime it undermined the social structure upon which they had been founded. 'Everyone talks of a necessary and imminent revolution,' wrote the Marquis d'Argenson in 1751, in his *Mémoires*. 'All classes are discontented. Inflammable material is accumulating on every hand. A riot might lead to a rising, and a rising to a general revolution in which there would be tribunes elected by the people, legislative assemblies and independent communes, and in which kings and ministers would be deprived of excessive power.'

The Assembly of the Clergy stated in 1757 that 'it must be recognized that in religion, morals and even politics the spirit of the times reveals a threat of revolution portending complete social destruction'. And in 1760 the Marquis d'Argenson wrote: 'Fifty years ago the public was wholly uninterested in the news. Today all read the *Gazette de Paris* even in the provinces. They talk a great deal of nonsense about political matters, but they take an interest in them. English liberty has conquered us.'[1]

Rousseau, in 1762, declared that 'the time of crises and the century of revolution' were approaching. In 1764 Voltaire wrote: 'Everywhere the seeds are being sown of an inevitable revolution which I shall not have the joy of witnessing. Happy are the young, for they will see great things!' In 1778, when he revisited Paris after an absence of twenty-eight years, he had a triumphal reception by the Academy, at Court, in high society and from all persons prominent at the time.

The Revolution was already mature in men's minds.

[1] The struggle of Wilkes and his supporters in defence of a free press and the right of free election was followed with deep interest in France. When Wilkes returned to England from his exile abroad, Diderot compared him with 'a nobler Coriolanus', bent not on the destruction but the salvation of his country.

All this literature overflows with optimism. Saint-Just (Robespierre's disciple, who was destined to die on the scaffold in the same hour as his master) had good reason for saying that the eighteenth century 'discovered happiness'. Christian doctrine had condemned man, through original sin, to affliction. The eighteenth-century *philosophes* — as the intellectuals were then called — returning, by way of the Renaissance, to the beliefs of classical antiquity, asserted that at the birth of humanity there had been no sin, but innocence: man was born not to suffer but to be happy. Happiness could be attained if Reason, enlightened by philosophy, destroyed prejudice and reformed the institutions inherited from a barbarous past. In this great work Reason would have a sure guide in 'natural law'; that is, in the moral precepts with which Nature imbues the heart of man at the very moment of his birth. It was only necessary — as the Stoics had taught — to seek out these principles and to find inspiration in them. The Christians, who had taken over the doctrine of 'natural law' from the Stoics, had put God in the place of Nature. But the *philosophes*, coming, as they did, after the time of Newton, who had made of the Deity a kind of constitutional king in the English pattern, either relegated God to the background or denied him outright. They went back to 'Nature'. The eighteenth century was the age of 'Reason' and 'Nature', of optimism and 'enlightenment'. It was known as *le siècle des lumières*.

Under free governments, the citizens gain practice in politics by administering their common affairs; they learn how institutions work and come to see both their good and bad sides. Thus they realize the risks attending innovations, and are unlikely to be carried away by political illusions. Freedom is a great instrument of social conservation; and the nearer a party feels itself to power, the more its ideas become tempered and adapted to the requirements of real life.

But in eighteenth-century France politics and administration under the monarchy were an occult science practised by the State officials. The public were not allowed to interfere in 'the King's affairs'. Writers and readers, confined to the limbo of abstract ideas, had no way of trying out their theories through daily practical experience; they did not realize how much resistance even just and beneficent reforms arouse when in conflict with interests and prejudices inherited from the past, and they could not distinguish between what should be got rid of, and what would be better preserved. They felt weighed down by the past, and condemned it *en bloc*; with their Utopian visions and unshakable, almost religious faith in the omnipotence of knowledge, they were dazzled by the novel splendour of free thought, and convinced that it was possible to build a perfect society by the power of reason alone.

At the approach of the Revolution free thought, humanitarianism and cosmopolitanism were the fashion in literature. Unlimited possibility for progress in the arts and sciences, in customs, institutions and the social order, was a dogma accepted by all. Europe, having reached the peak of an enlightened civilization, would advance step by step in moral, intellectual and social improvement, and would extend these benefits to the whole human race.[1] Never in history, as in that age of hope, has there been a greater respect for universal truth, a more ardent faith in the power of thought, or so passionate a desire to understand all and to attempt all.

The Government saw no threat to its authority in these philosophers who preached an enlightened despotism and apparently knew the secret of how to give mankind freedom and happiness without causing social upheavals. The privileged classes amused themselves by patronizing the new ideas. For a century they had been deprived of any practical experience of affairs, and they had no suspicion of the abyss that was yawning before them. At banquets, conversation would be on religion, political economy and science. The nobles prided themselves on being unbelievers; to a certain extent they respected the outward forms of religion, but they regarded it as 'superstition': good only for their lackeys, and the poor in spirit. The ecclesiastics, too, who moved in high society, were *philosophes*, and preached 'in the Greek manner'; that is to say, they never quoted the Bible, referred to Jesus Christ as 'the law-giver of the Christians' and only expounded moral and

---

[1] In the darkest days of the terror, Condorcet was to develop this theme in his *Esquisse d'un tableau historique des progrès de l'esprit humain*, written in hiding after he had been proscribed by the Convention, and only shortly before his arrest and death.

philosophical themes. The *philosophes* were an indispensable ornament of the *salons*: when Voltaire appeared at a reception, fashionable ladies turned pale and threw themselves into his arms, while at the sight of Rousseau they burst into tears. They wore dresses *à la Rousseau* — as near as they could go to a state of nature — and even took to breast-feeding their own infants, by way of obeying the master's precepts.

The masonic lodges, which had arisen in England at the end of the seventeenth century and towards 1730 were imported into France — where for about forty years they existed as societies for mutual aid and entertainment — became, after 1770, centres of free-thinking, anti-clerical and humanitarian propaganda. On the eve of the Revolution they numbered about seven hundred, with a central council, the Grand Orient. The Grand Master was the young Duc de Chartres, a prince of the blood and the future Louis Philippe. Many *grands seigneurs* and high prelates were members, and among those of the ladies' lodges were to be found friends of Queen Marie-Antoinette. The lodges did not preach revolution; according to the German, Grimm, they were 'academies, lyceums, clubs, rooms for dancing and banqueting'. But they enabled nobles, *bourgeois*, and different ranks of the civil administration and army to meet together on common ground, and helped to create that atmosphere of *laisser aller* which was to make resistance by the privileged orders to the revolutionaries at first so weak and unco-ordinated.

Another factor of importance at this time was the revolt of the American colonies against England (1775-81), which had an immense influence upon French political thought. A new society was rising beyond the seas, rebelling against traditions inherited from the past and claiming a right to govern itself according to the dictates of reason rather than the capricious will of despots. It was a triumph for eighteenth-century 'enlightenment'. When the French Government intervened on the insurgents' side, the popularity of American ideas in France became unbounded. Benjamin Franklin, who came to Paris in 1777 as American ambassador, had an enthusiastic reception. The capital was flooded with portraits and busts of him, a number of which were inscribed with Turgot's celebrated line '*Eripuit fulmen coelo sceptrumque tyrannis*': hailing him as inventor of the lightning-conductor and victor over the King of England. Many French officers who had fought with the insurgents — most famous among them being the Marquis de Lafayette — returned home desirous of utilizing in their own country the stirring experiences of America.

For the nobles, high prelates and ladies, philosophy and sociology were an innocent pastime: they played at revolution. 'Liberty', the Comte de Ségur wrote later, 'delighted us by its daring, and equality by its agreeableness. It is always pleasant to descend when one knows one can rise again at will. Unthinking as we were, we enjoyed the advantages of patrician life and the delights of a plebeian philosophy at one and the same time. And although our own privileges and the remains of our former power were being undermined beneath our feet, we were not alarmed, because as yet we did not feel the impact of the blows directed at us. We never dreamed that this wordy warfare might threaten the exalted life that was ours and that for so many centuries we had regarded as unassailable.'

But so soon as their real interests appeared affected by the first timid reforms, the 'democratic' ladies and their 'patriotic' cavaliers grew resentful, and their foolish resistance provoked a revolution in earnest. They had all condemned privilege in the abstract, and each was ready to sacrifice the privileges of his neighbour; but none dreamed of renouncing his own, which were naturally held to be sacred and inviolable rights.

No one ever met the intellectual *bourgeoisie*, outside the *salons*: the lawyers, doctors, civil servants, journalists and writers, who devoured the new literature and found reflected in it their own dreams, their own passions, their bitterness of heart. Certainly, the *philosophes* did not destroy the old social order, for it was disintegrating of itself. Nor did they bring about the Revolution, the roots of which lay deep in the preceding centuries. But in their writings the future revolutionaries found not only moral justification for sweeping away the past but the materials they needed in setting up a new society. It was through the works of the *philosophes* that they learned, rightly or wrongly, the causes of their troubles and a possibility of better things. In this way the middle-class intellectuals trained themselves for leadership over the army of peasants, workers and artisans: the ignorant crowd that, driven desperate by poverty and shut out by illiteracy from the intellectual movements, was ready to revolt at the first opportunity.

In the last few years of the eighteenth century, Edmund Burke attacked French 'enlightenment' in his famous *Reflections on the Revolution in France*. In Burke's view, perfect happiness is unattainable; no man born of woman can escape suffering. There is no such thing as 'natural law'. Laws are evolved empirically by man out of the experience of the centuries, in accordance with changing social conditions and the moral ideas associated with such changes. For the *philosophes*, tradition was of no account. But to Burke, tradition alone mattered. Burke's Englishman feared God, honoured the King, supported parliamentary government and respected the nobility and clergy. Reason had nothing to do with this. It was so because it always had been so. Institutions inherited from the past might need renewing: but beware of shaking them from their foundations. Any such attempt must be either mischievous or futile, and mischievous precisely in so far as it was not futile.

Burke was on sure ground in affirming that perfect happiness is an illusion, and that human rights are the historical creation not of a non-existent 'Nature' but of men themselves, who have elaborated them, to the best of their ability, according to the moral, intellectual and social stage they have reached. No wholesale break with the past is possible, for the past is always with us, even where we least expect it. The *philosophes* knew what they were about when, in the name of 'natural law', they assailed a social order that justified itself simply by its appeal to tradition and antiquity. They confronted this very tradition and antiquity with the 'law of Nature': a law as old as man himself, in existence before the most ancient of institutions, inalienable and eternal. 'An admirable, instinctive move', as Jaurès observes, 'by which privilege was dislodged from the fastness of time, in which it had tried to barricade itself; and the authority of the centuries was transferred to the new conception of freedom.'

During the nineteenth century, the doctrines of the *philosophes* were carried on into the various schools of Liberalism (in the Continental meaning of the word), of Democracy and Socialism. The aim was still the attainment of such justice and happiness as each

held to be possible, after subjecting tradition to criticism enlightened by reason. The revolt against reason, however, proclaimed by Burke, continued in the Romantic movements.
Among these, one school of thought — the clerical-conservative —
in upholding tradition, found Christian revelation, and in
Christian revelation a natural law of divine origin; thus returning
to the doctrine of natural law condemned by Burke. Another
discovered that tradition was largely national sentiment, and
proceeding along these lines ended up in nationalism and Bis-
marckian militarism. Others again, reacting not only against
Reason but against tradition, glorified instinct, intuition, inspiration, the unconscious, and the 'vital urge'; rejecting such restraints
as common sense and a sense of morality — last survivals of the
doctrine of a natural law — might impose. Thus they found,
finally, a vent in the criminal excesses of Fascism and Nazism.
Burke would have been hard put to it to recognize his own disciples
in these rebels against Reason.

III

The first bulwark to feel the assault of the *philosophes* was that
of the clergy.

In embarking upon the anti-clerical campaign the intellectuals
were able to take their stand on a long series of scientific victories,
each one of which had been a defeat for the religious tradition.
Moreover, the royal officials, although ostensibly in alliance with
the clergy, were often embroiled with them over their attempts
to encroach upon matters of State jurisdiction: and for this reason,
anti-clerical writings were not always suppressed, or were treated
with a leniency they would not have received had the State been
defending itself rather than the Church. The writers themselves
felt that they were duelling with a caste that was their natural
enemy, since not only all education but the censorship of the
press were in its hands. In other words, by attacking and discrediting the clergy they were combating tradition at its most
vulnerable point and fighting for their own freedom of thought
and expression; they were avenging their persecuted forebears,
and finding an outlet for the bitterness that each one had stored

up in his breast in the course of many personal differences with the ecclesiastical authorities.

Furthermore, in the early eighteenth century, the faithful themselves had been responsible for often ridiculous scenes of fanaticism and hysteria during the violent disputes that broke out between the *ultramontanes* (who supported the Pope's authority) and the Jansenists (who would not accept Papal infallibility as an article of faith). These polemics — over correct understanding of the dogma of predestination and grace, and the disciplinary relations between the Gallican Church, the Curia Romana and the French King — often went beyond the bounds of all reason. On the one hand, they engendered bitter hostility among believers towards the Bishops and Jesuits, who with Government support had oppressed the Jansenists; and on the other, afforded the sceptical ample occasion for scoffing not only at both parties but at the nature of Catholicism itself.

In ground so well prepared for the spread of anti-clericalism it is easy to understand the enormous influence of Voltaire.

Voltaire (1694-1778) believed in a God who dealt out 'rewards and punishments'; he accepted Providence and the immortality of the soul, and recognized the necessity for religion. But it must be a 'natural religion', free from obscure dogmas and inhuman rites; one that should 'help men to be good without making them absurd'. To him, all historical religions were absurd, against reason, and schools of intolerance. Christianity was no better than the rest: it was barbarous, 'good only for the *canaille*', and no less to be despised than paganism or Islam. The priests were 'rogues' who exploited the crowd's 'imbecility'; in their desire for domination they had to foster superstition and fanaticism, and even at the cost of bloodshed were bound to suppress every threat to their own authority. They were the worst enemies of free thought. Unless superstition — '*l'infâme*' — were extirpated, the tyranny of the priests would remain, and any peaceful and lasting civil progress must be rendered impossible.

With the generation that came after Voltaire, we find materialism and atheism in full flood. For La Mettrie (1709-51) and Diderot (1713-84) the heavens are empty, man's destiny is confined to this world, and morality must abandon all religious foundation and establish itself on a purely positive basis. *Timor fecit deos* repeated Diderot, with Lucretius: thought must be freed from the dead weight of the supernatural and the fetters of superstition (for Diderot all religious faith was superstition). The oppressive and unreasoning divinity was the enemy that man must destroy if he wanted to be finally free.

The anti-religious theory had its gospel in the *Système de la nature*, published anonymously, and largely written by the Baron d'Holbach, possibly with the collaboration of Diderot, who frequented the Baron's philosophical gatherings. Its chief weapon was the *Encyclopédie, dictionnaire raisonné des sciences et des arts et métiers*; a monumental work in thirty-four folio volumes edited, at first, by Diderot and d'Alembert, and then by Diderot alone, since d'Alembert was soon daunted by the undertaking. So comprehensive a publication could hope neither for widespread popularity nor systematic reading; moreover, the materialism and atheism of the editor and some of his collaborators, and the anti-clericalism of all, had often to be toned down or dissembled in order to avoid suppression by the ecclesiastical and civil authorities. Nevertheless, this dictionary, in which publicists, *dilettanti*, and persons of ordinary education could find all branches of human knowledge set out in alphabetical order and distilled to them through the medium of anti-Catholic thought, was the most efficacious weapon employed by eighteenth-century free-thinkers against the Catholic Church.

In politics Voltaire, Diderot and the other Encyclopaedists, though all steeped in humanitarianism and philanthropy, and liable — especially Diderot — to verbal excess in moments of exasperation, were not open revolutionaries, and still less democrats. Voltaire, the son of an attorney, regarded himself as a gentleman; he liked being courted by the great, and would never have dreamed of advocating a democratic republic. In his view, there was no need radically to change society: certain prejudices only, that marred it and impeded progress, should be done away with, and chief of these was religious prejudice. This work was to be accomplished not by 'cobblers and serving-women' but by an aristocracy of intellectuals: 'all is lost when the mob takes to reasoning'. In the same way d'Alembert wrote, 'Freedom is of no benefit to the people, which is like a small child that falls and hurts itself when left to walk alone, and then gets up to strike its governess'. And Diderot: 'The progress of ideas is limited: they cannot spread to the suburbs. The populace is too dull-witted. The number of *canaille* is always more or less the same, and the mob is always ignorant and stupid.'

They demanded reform of the administration, of taxation and of the laws. Voltaire's campaign against the use of torture, against the severity of penalties imposed for minor crimes, against confiscation of property, arbitrary courts, punishment for religious offences, and the venality of posts in the magistracy — and, also, in favour of freedom of the press — was one of the glories of his career. But according to him these reforms must be brought in by the Government, not won by revolution. 'It is not a question of making a revolution, as in the time of Calvin and Luther, but only of bringing one about in the mind of those who govern.' To those who were to hold the reins of government Voltaire and his followers were ready to concede the most despotic powers, provided that they let themselves be guided by the *philosophes*: provided they were 'enlightened'.

Yet to Voltaire, Diderot and the Encyclopaedists, each one of whom was, as has been said of Voltaire, 'conservative in all things save religion', common opinion has attributed a large share of responsibility for the Revolution. 'Your creative breath,' said André Chénier to Voltaire, 'has made us what we are.' In eighteenth-century France the clergy were great landowners and feudal lords, possessed of privileges and the right to levy imposts; they kept the civil registers, decided on matrimonial causes, and belonged to the higher magistracy and the King's Council. They crowned the monarch when he came to the throne, endowing his office with a sacerdotal character; and not only did they oppose reform with the strength of their own inertia, but, in the eyes of the people, they guaranteed— with all the prestige of a centuries-old religious tradition— the legitimacy of absolute and feudal rule. To shake Catholicism, therefore, was to shatter the whole fabric of the feudal monarchy. To destroy religious sentiment was to tear the veil from the eyes of the simple, revealing the mutable and far from divine nature of society. Everything that the anti-clericals achieved in discrediting the clergy was so much ground gained towards the overthrow of the lay authorities themselves.

IV

The Baron de Montesquieu (1689-1755), too, would have been greatly astonished to find himself unanimously included among the revolutionaries by historians today. Born of the old nobility of the sword and the robe, he had for many years held office in the higher magistracy of Bordeaux, and had a passion for feudal privilege, often proudly recalling his descent from those whom he called 'our Germanic fore-fathers, who were warriors and free men'.

In his *Lettres persanes* he records the impressions of two imaginary young Persians travelling in Europe, who observe the customs of France and describe them from their own point of view to friends at home. The King is a man endowed with curious powers; 'he makes his subjects think as he pleases', and obliges them to believe one crown is worth two; 'he gives his preference to those who dress him or who hand him a napkin rather than to those who conquer a city or win a battle'. The Pope is a magician similar to the King: this 'old idol to whom the people, from habit, continue to offer incense', can 'make people believe that three is no more than one, that bread is not bread, and wine not wine'. The priests are 'a greedy and miserly sect'. The nobility would have become extinct were it not for the lackeys, who filled the gaps in it and served as a 'breeding-ground for great lords'. And so on, with reference to all other institutions of the time.

In composing such a book, Montesquieu had no subversive intention, political or religious. 'He saw around him the disintegration of social institutions that had existed for centuries', explains Albert Sorel; 'beliefs, habits and customs that had formed and sustained the French monarchy were falling into decay. He wanted to analyse this evil and to find a remedy; but he did not perceive that, in so describing it, he awakened in men's minds a wider awareness of its existence, and that his own work was the gravest symptom of the very crisis he believed he could exorcize. His warning was not simply a demand for reform: it was the signal for a revolution, the impulse for which lurked in all men's minds and the causes of which were everywhere manifest.'

The book sold 'like hot cakes', and in the course of a year four editions and four counterfeit editions were printed.

In the *Esprit des Lois*, published after thirty years of work and thought, Montesquieu's aim was to analyse the conditions determining the life of civil and political institutions, and to define the relationship between them and their physical, economic, moral and religious surroundings. It is a treatise on the philosophy of history, or what we should now call sociology. Though in some respects inferior to the *Scienza nuova* of Vico in its historical approach, it greatly surpasses the latter in wealth of material, variety of observation, and subtlety of analysis. The scientific value of the *Esprit des Lois* almost entirely escaped its contemporaries, as did that of Vico's *Scienza nuova*: because the fundamental principle of Montesquieu's theory, that of the relativity of political and juridical forms, conflicted with the total lack of historical sense that is an outstanding characteristic of the eighteenth century. The Revolution had to bring proof of much that Montesquieu intuitively understood, before students were able to appreciate this great thinker's genius at its true worth.

'If in a monarchy the prerogatives of the feudal nobles, clergy, aristocracy and cities are abolished, you will soon have either a democratic or a despotic state.' 'As soon as the army is dependent on the legislative body, the Government will become a military one.' 'There is no more absolute authority than that of a prince who succeeds a republic, for he will find himself heir to all the powers of the people, who did not know how to place limitations on it themselves.' 'If today a prince were to make such conquests [as those of the Romans in ancient times] the peoples, driven into the north, would remain on the confines of the civilized world until the moment when they could invade Europe and reconquer it once again.'

In these few maxims we seem to see the whole history of revolutionary France, from the night of August 4th to the abolition of the monarchy, to Brumaire, to the Russian campaign, and to the battle of Leipsic. Who, a century before these events had taken place, could have understood the profundity of Montesquieu's thought?

But if, for the time being, the book was not much understood, it was widely read, thanks to its brilliant literary form and the anecdotes and wit that enlivened the author's theme. In less than two years it ran through twenty-two editions, and was translated into many languages. It awakened in cultivated persons a taste for juridical and political studies, brought the social sciences into the field of literature, and helped more than any other work to create that atmosphere of sociological and philosophic dilettantism which enabled eighteenth-century revolutionary theories to prosper.

According to Montesquieu, 'the government most in conformity with nature is the one whose particular structure is best suited to the state of the people for whom it is set up'. From this it follows that he awards neither praise nor blame to any one form of government. But he does not cloak his deep dislike of despotism, which occurs whenever the same person or political body exercises legislative, executive and judiciary power together; in other words, when the ruling power can pass tyrannical laws, put them into execution, and enforce them through a servile judiciary. Montesquieu affirms his sympathy for what he calls 'monarchy', that is, for a political constitution in which 'one alone governs by means of fixed and stable laws', and, the authority being divided between different, autonomous bodies, 'power restrains power'. Under this form of government, the monarch's authority cannot degenerate into despotism, because it is limited by the privileges of the nobles and clergy, and by those of a free magistrature that preserves the fundamental laws of the realm and insists on their observance by the prince. The best form of monarchy was to be found in England: there, executive power was entrusted to the King; legislative power, with the right of voting every year on taxation and revenue, was exercised by two chambers, one formed by the people's representatives, elected by 'all citizens save those of so low a class that they are held to have no will of their own', and the other composed of hereditary members; while judicial power was in the hands of an independent body of magistrates. So far as France was concerned, Montesquieu would have been content with a limitation of the King's powers through the privileges of the hereditary nobility and the magistrature, who would maintain the fundamental laws of the monarchy. The States-General, or meeting of representatives of all classes in the country, did not seem to him desirable. The formation of big commercial, industrial and financial companies should, in his opinion, be prevented, so that the social hierarchy might not be disrupted by the growth of wealth divorced from landed property and political power. The nobles must be kept out of trade, in order that they should remain distinct from the commoners.

Since the privileged orders ought, according to Montesquieu, to use their privileges to unite the King with his people and to protect the latter from despotism, it followed that privilege would in effect prove useful and indispensable to the people themselves. This was a theory drawn from the history of England, where the nobles had often found themselves allied with the commons in resisting the growing powers of State officials. But even with this indirect and tenuous element of democracy it is clear that Montesquieu's ideas, far from pointing the way towards revolution, were really thoroughly reactionary: they would have led to replacing the absolute monarchy, not by democratic rule in the interests of the commons, but by an aristocratic government in which the feudal lords would have a monopoly of political power. It is a significant fact that the *Esprit des Lois* contains an apologia for those very feudal rights which the revolutionaries were later to assail with such ferocity.

Montesquieu, however, not only set forth the theory of monarchy founded on privilege, but also, with admirable acumen, analysed the principles — 'the spirit' — of republican democracy. He showed that this political form has as its basis equality of political rights and of wealth: freedom is not so essential in a democracy as equality. To maintain equality, the Government must have unlimited power, because 'the welfare of the people is the supreme law'. These powers must be used to prevent excessive growth in private wealth, to repress luxury, and to regulate dowries, endowments and the inheritance of property, in such a way as to bring about an equal share of the land among all citizens. The Government should also impose common ownership where no other way exists for preserving a democratic constitution.

It was Jacobin theory, neither more nor less: the revolutionaries took it over, lock, stock and barrel, for their own purposes, once the King's folly and resistance by the privileged classes had forced the commons to seek their own salvation in democracy. The *Esprit des Lois*, which, with serene and scientific objectivity, contained both the theory of an aristocratic monarchy and that

E

of a democratic republic, supplied the democrats with an outline of political and social reform. The arguments with which, from the point of view of the feudal classes, Montesquieu had attacked the despotic monarchy, served the *bourgeoisie* well in their own assault upon it, while the idea of popular sovereignty had only to be grafted on to Montesquieu's theory of the separation of powers, and his justification of aristocratic liberty to be supplanted by that of democratic equality, for Montesquieu, too, to pass as one of the greatest and most influential precursors of the revolutionary movement.

v

Not even among the 'economists' do we find ourselves in the company of revolutionaries.

The leader of this school of thought was the doctor Quesnay (1694-1744). Its principal writers were the Marquis de Mirabeau, Turgot, Dupont de Nemours, Le Trosne, and Mercier de la Rivière. Greatest of all was the Englishman, Adam Smith, who in 1776 published his monumental work on the Wealth of Nations. In France, these economists called themselves 'physiocrats' and termed their system 'Physiocracy' — a new word coined from the Greek by Dupont de Nemours — because they held that the production, circulation and distribution of wealth were controlled by natural laws analogous to those of the physical world, and that it was wrong both for the individual and the Government not to act in conformity with them.

According, then, to these theorists, it was a fundamental law of economics that the individual alone is competent to understand and procure his own advantage: when he is left free to dispose of his property, he will use it in the way he thinks best; production and consumption will thereupon expand, the population will increase, and the Government's power will grow proportionately: *laisser faire, laisser passer.*

But to this end, every man, they maintained, must have full use of his property. Property must not be regarded as a conventional creation of society, as Hobbes and Rousseau and the democratic writers claimed. As Locke had already shown, it was a natural right, in existence before society. Society must recognize this right and guarantee it. Certain sacrifices might be demanded from owners of property in the public interest; but society was not entitled to regulate or to limit this right in any way, still less to suppress it. Ownership of property, in fact, far from being an evil institution, was essential to the production of wealth, because the transformation of raw material presupposes control of the material itself. Such inequalities as it might entail— when not a result of disorder or artificial causes— are just and useful, because they are indispensable for abundant production, and an increase in general prosperity is the surest means of securing the welfare of all.

In our day, these theories seem conservative, but in the eighteenth century they were novel and revolutionary. The physiocrats disavowed the entire arbitrary tradition of the old régimes; they affirmed that even an absolute prince had no power to make laws, but must recognize natural laws and impose only what is imposed by nature itself; they condemned the whole mass of privileges and protective rights surviving from mediaeval times, which strangled individual liberty and the development of wealth; and instead of historical rights, they championed the 'natural rights' of the citizen to personal freedom and unfettered control of his property.

Furthermore, the physiocrats did not confine themselves to the elaboration of general formulae. They criticized every ancient institution in the light of their doctrine, and proceeded to indicate needful reforms. They demanded that production and commerce should be freed from control, the methods of levying and collecting taxes simplified, and taxation reduced to a single impost upon agricultural revenue — associated, at the most, with a proportional tax on income from investments. They also insisted that no further taxes should be imposed without the consent of those who paid them; that the administration should be decentralized and entrusted to locally-elected officials; that there should be an end to immunity from taxation; that all feudal rights should be revised and commuted, except those authorized by written title-deeds; that ecclesiastical tithes should be done away with; that new agrarian contracts should be drawn up to the advantage of the peasants; that uncultivated or badly-cultivated land belonging to the clergy, Crown or communes should be broken up and sold, so that the number of landowners with an interest in production might be increased; and that the right of primogeniture in feudal families should be suppressed.

Each of these proposals in itself was anything but revolutionary or dangerous. And indeed, the physiocrats, although they wanted unlimited freedom for the individual, did not foresee that, for its conquest, strenuous efforts would be needed. With a curious lack of consistency, explicable only as a result of centuries of autocracy, they hoped that political and economic freedom would be established by governments rendered far-sighted through philosophy, and were ready to confer very wide powers on the King provided that they were used in upholding natural laws. Some even preferred the absolute government of France to English constitutionalism, since, as one of them, Le Trosne, explained, 'in France, reforms that can change the face of the whole country can be effected in a moment, whereas in England even unimportant measures may be obstructed by party spirit'.

In time, experience was to prove their hope fallacious. The doctrine of physiocratic liberalism then revealed itself, together with the theory of the separation of powers, as a formidable weapon in the hands of the commons. Numberless unimportant reforms, proposed, individually, by writers who took little account of the work of others, led, all together, to the great revolution; and in the mass of material for research and study accumulated by the physiocrats, the revolutionaries found all they needed for solving the many problems of taxation, agriculture, justice, administration and finance that awaited them.

VI

In Jean-Jacques Rousseau (1712-78) we come to a really revolutionary thinker, who asserted the doctrine of popular sovereignty and democracy.

If, says Rousseau, we imagine man in his natural state, that is, without the artificial habits and sentiments with which social life has corrupted his native purity, we find a rough, ignorant being, with few needs, living a solitary life in the forests; simple and strong, without possessions, ambition, envy, vices or virtues; guided only by instinct, caring nothing for the future, unmindful of the past and content with the present. Unacquainted with suffering, he is happy.

This theory, which was to enjoy so great a popularity in the second half of the eighteenth century and during the Revolution, was derived from many originally diverse sources.

In the works of the jurists and political writers of the eighteenth century, the state of nature was an abstract hypothesis by virtue of which the material and spiritual conditions of men living outside any form of society could be investigated. That in a state of nature men were equal was accepted by all; but from this assumption different inferences were drawn. Hobbes affirmed that natural equality would produce savage internecine war and conditions under which, since might would be right, neither freedom nor private property could exist; and that an all-powerful ruler would be required to put an end to disorder. Locke postulated equality, liberty and property in a state of nature, all of which must, in the social state, be defended and preserved.

According to Christian dogma, too, man was, before his fall into original sin, an innocent and happy being. Christianity, moreover, affirmed the equality of all men before God, and condemned wealth and luxury as contrary to the ideal of moral perfection. In some ancient republics, also, and especially in that of Sparta under the laws of Lycurgus, an absence of private property had had beneficial effects, according to historians; while in the eighteenth century, glowing reports from American missionaries, and, in particular, from the Jesuits in Paraguay, describing the blessedness of natives converted to Christianity, had rendered the 'noble savage' — free and happy without civil institutions — a popular figure in fiction and on the stage. In literature, too, Plato's *Republic*, having produced in the Renaissance such imitations as More's *Utopia*, Campanella's *Civitas Solis* and Bacon's *New Atlantis*, continued to serve as a model for similar compositions. In the second half of the seventeenth century Varaisse d'Alais, in his *Histoire des Sevarambes* (1677), Fénelon in *Télémaque*, and other writers of romances, had portrayed hypothetical countries that owed their well-being to some form of common ownership. Later, under the influence of the *Lettres édifiantes* of the missionaries, and in imitation of the *Histoire des Sevarambes* and *Télémaque*, there were numerous descriptions of journeys into imaginary countries, or accounts of peoples in ancient times, amongst whom all property was held in common and who were therefore innocent and happy. These fairy tales, unsupported by any serious economic culture, served as a pastime for both writers and readers, or for moral edification: to demonstrate, for instance, that wealth should be despised. They propagated the idea that economic equality was the highest of social benefits, and helped to prepare the ground for Rousseau's famous theory of the 'state of nature'.

Rousseau, like the jurists, admitted that this hypothetical state of nature no longer existed, perhaps had never existed and probably never would exist; but he held that some precise idea must be formed of it in order to judge of contemporary conditions. With his vagabond life, his brilliant mind and lack of balance, his sensitive, ardent but impulsive character— aware of his own weaknesses but convinced that he was the best of men — Rousseau, who had largely himself to blame for the humiliation and adversity that were his lot, detested the society into which by ill-luck he had been born. The 'state of nature' was the ideal to which he turned in protesting against a social system that denied him the freedom and happiness to which he felt he had a right. He compared it with the present, used it as a standard by which to judge modern society, and invoked it in throwing responsibility for his own sufferings and errors upon the existing social order.

He did more: despite his own statement that it had never existed, he explained the corrupt social conditions of his time by turning the abstract hypothesis into primitive history and asserting that society had, in fact, arisen from this vanished state of nature. The change, he maintained, had gradually come about as men, in civilizing themselves, gave up being guided merely by instinct, and developed needs that were more specialized and difficult to satisfy; as they began to reflect, criticize and doubt, and to feel the need of combining for their own defence. When they built huts to live in they brought about the 'first revolution to make a distinction between one family and another, introducing a kind of property, from which perhaps much quarrelling and strife arose'. But no true society was constituted until private property emerged.

'The first man who, having enclosed a piece of land, dared to say: *this is mine*, and found men simple enough to believe him, was the founder of modern civilized society. How many crimes, wars and murders, how much misery and horror would have been spared the human race had some other, pulling down the fence and filling up the ditch, cried to his fellow-men: do not listen to that impostor; you are lost if you forget that the fruits of the earth belong to all and the land to none.'

According to Rousseau, the first effects of the possession of property were rivalries, conflicting interests, a desire to gain at the expense of others, and continual bloody struggles between the right of the stronger and that of the first occupier. This intolerable condition of things facilitated the appearance of yet another form of injustice: the rich induced the poor to accept a government which was to safeguard general security, on the one hand protecting the weak and on the other guaranteeing to each the possession of his wealth.

'This was, or must have been, the origin of society and of a system of laws that imposed new chains upon the weak, and gave new power to the rich; which destroyed natural liberty for ever and permanently established the law of property and inequality, turning a clever act of usurpation into an irrevocable right, and subjecting mankind to labour, slavery and misery for all time, to the advantage of a few ambitious men.'

To Rousseau, luxury, the arts, letters, science and philosophy were all evil products of this society, born of violence and fraud, corrupt and corrupting. Love was no longer serene and sincere, but disingenuous and influenced by self-interest, social prejudice and vice. The education of the young was hypocritical and immoral; the citizens were slaves of despotic governments, and the poor oppressed by the rich. All this was a result of many centuries of civilization; a lamentable state to which the human race had been brought through having abandoned the state of nature.

'Are not all advantages in our society reserved for the rich and powerful? Are not all lucrative employments held by them alone? Are not the public authorities entirely at their service? If an influential man defrauds his creditors or commits other villainies, can he not count on impunity before the law? If he is guilty of violence or murder, is not everything hushed up and after six months no longer referred to? But if this same man is robbed, the whole police is at once set in motion, and woe betide the innocent upon whom suspicion falls! Should this rich man have to pass through a dangerous place, he is provided with a large escort. If the axle of his carriage breaks, all fly to assist him. If there is a noise at his door, a word from him and all is silence. If the crowd incommodes him, a sign and all are scattered. If he finds a carter in his way, his servants rain blows upon him. All these conveniences cost him nothing, since the rich are entitled to enjoy them without expending their own wealth on such trifles. But how different is the spectacle of the poor man! The more compassion society owes him, the less he receives. All doors are closed to him, even when he has a right to have them opened. Should he, once in a way, obtain justice, he has to labour more for it than others for a favour. If a *corvée* is called for, or a military levy made, he is the first to be taken. He bears not only his own burdens but those his neighbour has managed to shift on to his back. At the least accident that befalls him, all leave him to his fate. If his cart overturns, he is unlikely to escape insults from the duke's servants, who hurry by. All gratuitous aid is refused him in his need, precisely because he has no way of paying for it. And woe betide him if he has the misfortune to possess an honest soul, a beautiful daughter or a powerful neighbour. He is lost. Let us, then, sum up in a few words the social compact between the two classes: You have need of me, because I am rich and you are poor; let us make an agreement, therefore, between ourselves; I will allow you the honour of serving me, provided that you give me what little you still possess, in return for my trouble in giving you orders.'

VII

We are clearly in an atmosphere of anarchical ideas, the logical consequence of which would be the destruction of all property and every form of government.

But Rousseau, though audacious in criticism, was much less subversive when it came to the practical application of his teaching. In modern societies, he explained, property was a necessary evil: 'humanity cannot retrace its steps, and it is impossible to go back to the age of innocence and equality once we have left it'. The abolition of property and government could only now be effected by 'substituting brigandage for corruption'. All, therefore, that could be done was to give men a true consciousness of their present condition and of the state of nature from which they should draw inspiration in checking the process of degeneration: 'When men are corrupt, it is better that they should be educated than ignorant.' This being agreed, the duty of political science was to excogitate a new 'social contract' in place of the existing system based on fraud and violence, and as far as possible to guarantee the freedom, equality and happiness which man had enjoyed in the state of nature. If the new social contract could be said to find a practical solution for this problem, then the social system arising from it might be accepted as a lesser evil.

To Rousseau, a government in which the citizens' rights do not depend upon the will of all but upon that of an aristocracy or a prince is not a free government, or one in conformity with nature. Kings, owing to the single fact of kingship, must be enemies of the people: 'Their own interest demands above all that the people be weak, wretched and unable to resist.' Even a representative régime is a form of aristocracy, in which the will of the deputies and not the general will is law. In other words, direct democracy, in which a whole population rules without delegating its powers to any sovereign or elective aristocracy, is the only government worthy to replace the state of nature. In this form of government, sovereignty rests in the 'general will'. The general will implies unanimity. There is no majority or minority. And this unanimous will is infallible, since it is guided by a moral law accepted by all. The government based upon it cannot be despotic, because under it the citizen obeys and commands at the same time, transfers all his individual rights into the collective right, and exercises sovereign power as a partner in collective sovereignty. 'The general will is always justified and tends towards the welfare of all,' while the individual will may easily be led astray and corrupted by private interests.

Such infallible agreement under a moral law accepted by all is due to a new education, given by the 'State'. 'Every people is what the State makes it.' It is not possible to understand Rousseau's theory of the general will apart from that of a new education.

Without the latter, his theory of direct democracy cannot hold together.

But what did he mean by 'the State'? To Rousseau, the State is something mystical which he never defines and in which individuals live, move and have their being. We, with our imperfect social systems, may ask of those who use this cabalistic word what they mean by it: a whole people, living within certain national and political boundaries? The network of governing bodies that provides for the collective needs of such a population? The central government which passes the laws to be enforced by this administration? Or the men at the head of the central government? It would have been idle to ask such questions of Rousseau. Where others put God or Nature, he put the State, just as mysterious, sacred and unchallengeable. Words that are left undefined have a fascination not possessed by those whose meaning is clear. The confusion of thought that was later to be found in the works of Hegel and the Hegelians had begun to produce its deleterious effects in Rousseau.

The sovereignty, then, of the general will is absolute and inalienable. No government is legitimate except in so far as it represents and enforces it. 'Hence it follows that those entrusted with executive power are not the people's masters but its functionaries; their duty is simply to obey the people, which can set them up and dismiss them as it sees fit.'

In a well-ordered government, laws established by the general will must 'protect and defend the person and property of each member by means of collective force'; but they must also 'strictly regulate the ownership of property and keep it always subordinated to the common good'. The laws must reduce economic and moral inequality to a minimum, for these are the basis of political inequality. 'If one seeks to discover in what precisely the greatest good consists, one finds it may be reduced to two main objects, liberty and equality; liberty, because all individual dependence is so much strength taken from the State; equality, because without it, liberty cannot exist.'

To restore liberty, as far as possible, to mankind, and to maintain it among them, the laws must suppress luxury, promote an average level of wealth, foster agriculture in preference to commerce, prevent depopulation of the countryside and too much drift towards the towns, regulate the inheritance of property, institute a graded tax on income and imposts upon luxury goods, and maintain a supply of foodstuffs by setting up store-houses for use in time of scarcity or famine. The laws must above all promote the moral education of the citizens, and imbue their hearts with virtue: since virtue is neither more nor less than 'conformity of the individual with the general will'.

To this end, says Rousseau, the concurrence of an official religion would be useful: a religion having nothing in common with Roman Catholicism, which subjects men's minds to the tyranny of princes and priests. It must also be opposed to the materialism of Diderot and his disciples: that sorry philosophy which likens men to beasts and with its arid doctrines undermines the true basis of society. The citizen must be taught to believe in a 'civil religion'; a kind of Christianity without dogma, without a God made in man's image, without Hell, and with a moral law all romantic tenderness and poetic philanthropy.

Montesquieu had said more or less the same thing, in explaining the kind of 'spirit' by which legislation should be inspired in a democratic republic. But although he admired the virtues of democracy, Montesquieu thought democratic institutions no longer a possibility, and gave his own preference to a constitutional monarchy. Rousseau, on the other hand, with his unbounded enthusiasm for the ancient republics, as those nearest to the state of nature, maintains that his particular brand of democracy alone can erect a barrier against social degeneration.

Today, Rousseau's 'social contract' has gone to join 'natural law' in the limbo of out of date and forgotten theories. We know that no society was ever set up by signing an agreed contract, and that no society can suddenly be done away with, and replaced by a new one based on another contract. But it must not be forgotten that this ingenuous theory contained a moral principle that is anything but out of date: the theory that no political system can maintain itself without consent of the governed, or at least without that of the more politically active among them, who can make their opinion felt. Replace the explicit 'social contract' by the tacit, daily plebiscite of the people, and the doctrine is no longer absurd; unless it is affirmed that whatever government is in power has a right to maintain itself by any means, against any opposition, even when it has lost the consent of the governed.

It is obvious that in his 'direct' democracy Rousseau awarded the general will unlimited control over the property, the lives, the very souls of the citizens; in other words, he carried the theory of absolutism to its ultimate consequences. But it must be remembered that in Rousseau's 'social contract' the absolute authority of the people replaced that of the prince. In this lay the novelty of his teaching, and its revolutionary nature.

On the other hand, the dangers implicit in Rousseau's 'general will' must not be forgotten. In it there existed no distinction between majority and minority: only unanimity, created by a mysterious State through an education common to all. Our modern democratic doctrine, when it succeeds in keeping free from totalitarian influences that can be traced back to Rousseau, has renounced the ideal of a perfect society and its infallible, unanimous will; it recognizes that all men — education or no education, 'State' or no 'State' — are liable to error, and teaches that what they can achieve in the way of freedom and happiness, given their own imperfections, is best secured under a political system in which the majority is entitled to govern but is obliged to respect the minority's right to criticize and, as occasion arises, to govern in its turn.

When the time came to overthrow the traditional order of society and to construct a new social contract, Rousseau's followers found themselves faced by an unforeseen cleavage between majority and minority, indeed, between a number of minorities. What was to be done, in the absence of any unanimous general will? They solved the problem by attributing the rights of 'infallible unanimity' to that section of the community nearest the state of nature, in other words, to the People. ('*Le peuple*' in eighteenth-century French signified the poor, who lived by their own labour, as opposed to the *bourgeoisie*, who were a well-to-do class though distinct from the nobility: the contrast between 'capitalism' and 'proletariat' was only to appear in the nineteenth century.) Rousseau's followers felt themselves the natural representatives of the *peuple*: a term which to them was interchangeable with 'State'. Thus the will of the 'People' and the 'State' becomes Rousseau's 'general will'; and the infallibility of the general will, transferred from Rousseau's 'direct democracy' to the 'People' of eighteenth-century France, brought about the despotism of those who spoke in their name. The liberty of all became the tyranny of the few and led to the Terror.

Had Rousseau any inkling of the consequences to which his general infallible will might lead, if usurped by fallible sections of an imperfect society? It is here that, after finding in him the enthusiast of direct democracy, we discover the moderate liberal. His 'social contract', he admits, was only suited to small countries, as were those of ancient times. 'Much has been disputed as to the best form of government, without considering that every form is best in some cases and very bad in others. In general, democratic government is suited to small states, aristocratic government to medium-sized ones and monarchical to great ones.'

Among the forms of aristocratic government suited to medium-sized countries — and France was numbered among these by eighteenth-century politicians — the most practical, according to Rousseau, was the representative régime. Under this system, the right of election should not be given to 'the ignorant and contemptible crowd'; the 'abject and brutish populace, easily swayed by agitators', ready to sell themselves, and caring more for bread than liberty. Sovereignty must be reserved for that part of the population which, though not very rich, can give its time to public work: in other words, to the middle-class, which is 'the most healthy element in a republic'. Reforms, moreover, must be made with caution, since widespread upheavals are dangerous. Revolutions that lead to bloodshed must be avoided, for 'nothing on this earth is worth acquiring at the cost of human blood'.

'Think of the danger of suddenly overturning the mighty structure represented by the French monarchy! Who, once it had started, could keep such a convulsion within bounds or foresee all its effects? Even when the advantages of a new system are incontestable, what man of good sense would dare to do away with ancient customs in order to renew the State, which is what thirteen centuries have made it? Whether an existing government is what it was in the past, or whether it has insensibly changed during the course of many centuries, it is always unwise to touch it. If the same, it must be respected; if fallen into decay, it must be reformed by time and events, and human reason can do nothing about it.'

If the work of reform could be carried out by a king or an intelligent minister without in any way changing the basis of sovereignty, Rousseau would gladly set aside his hopes of a republic. 'Give us a Henri IV and a Sully, and perpetual peace will become a reasonable programme.' 'Would that I might see the lands of Frederick [the Second], the just and terrible, filled at last with a happy people, to whom he would be as a father: then Jean-Jacques Rousseau, the enemy of kings, would go and die of joy at the foot of his throne.'

Even with this the sum of doctrines that we owe to Rousseau is not complete. In the often confused thought of that many-sided genius we can also find a rough indication of what was to become the nineteenth-century 'romantic' reaction against the 'enlightened' philosophy of the eighteenth. To the clear, well-ordered reason of the *philosophes*, Rousseau had opposed the obscure instinct that precedes all conscious thought: the feelings and sentiments that cannot be controlled. It is true that he did not make sentiment the custodian of tradition; rather, he employed it in combating tradition. But the *philosophes* of the eighteenth century, under Voltaire's leadership, sensed in him a double danger: that of a disciple who carried their own teaching to its ultimate, revolutionary consequences; and that of the precursor of romanticism, opening a way to the reaction against eighteenth-century thought. Thus they waged ruthless war on him.

So far, then, as his practical conceptions were concerned, Rousseau was no real revolutionary. Not without reason has it been said that if he had lived till the Revolution he would have died either on the scaffold or of heartbreak at the way in which his teaching was being applied. But in that oppressive, decaying society, where all were discontented, and where innumerable arguments could be found to justify revolt, it was natural that Rousseau's unobtrusive counsel in favour of caution should pass unnoticed, and that his longing for a better world, his vehement protests against the privileges of wealth and birth, and his poignant and paradoxical pages full of indignation at injustice and love for equality, should be greatly admired. As men lost faith in their traditional institutions and the citizens prepared for an inevitable struggle against the King and the privileged classes,

Rousseau's persuasive dogma of popular sovereignty, together with that of the separation of powers, disseminated by Montesquieu, became the battle-cry of revolution.

VIII

About twenty years before Rousseau had published his first *Discours*, Jean Meslier, the parish priest of a village in Champagne, overcome with despair at failing to obtain justice in a dispute with his feudal lord, starved himself to death (we do not know for certain whether in 1729 or 1733) after making his parishioners his heirs, and writing his religious and political 'Testament' in three copies.

The private ownership of wealth, says Meslier in this singular document, prompts each man to increase his share at the expense of others. The most greedy and skilful are more successful than the rest, and so 'some grow fat with food and drink, while others die of hunger'. What wonder that the poor have to struggle so hard to make ends meet? 'You have to bear not only the heavy burden of your kings and princes, who are first among your oppressors, but also that of the nobility, clergy, monastic orders, judiciary, armed forces, tax-gatherers, customs officials and in fact all the useless idlers in the world.'

These 'vermin' live on the labour of the poor, 'who nourish them with the good grain and wine they have toiled to produce'. The Christian religion, says Meslier, must be false, because it sanctions monarchy, property, inequality, and other unjust institutions. The idea of God has been invented by rogues to keep men quiet and prevent them rising against social injustice, just as the monarchy's task is that of protecting the rich by force of arms. The devil is merely a bogy to inspire men's minds with fear: 'Know, my dear friends, that you have no worse devils to fear than your enemies the great and powerful of this earth: it is they who grind you down and make you so wretched.'

Too long have the poor let themselves be oppressed by the rich. 'Seek to unite yourselves, you and your like, and to throw off the tyrannical yoke of your princes and kings.' 'Salvation is in your own hands, it depends on you alone, if you know how to agree among yourselves.' 'All the great ones of this earth and all nobles

should be hanged, and strangled with the entrails of the priests.'
'Set up common ownership of property in every parish, that you
may all enjoy the earth and the fruits of your labour.'

In the second half of the century, when men's minds became
filled with an urge for reform, Meslier's ideas began to spread;
numerous proposals were made for social reconstruction of a
communist type, in which, for the first time in the history of
political literature, economic equality is treated not as a flight
of the imagination but as a practical and possible basis for
reform.

The Abbé Morelly, in his *Basiliade* (1753) and his *Code de la
nature* (1755) maintained that such unnatural prejudices as make
of inequality a necessity must be done away with; and he compiled
a code of laws for a well-ordered society. Its fundamental principles were common ownership of property, the maintenance of
the people at the public expense, and a share by all citizens,
according to their ability, in production. From these were derived
a series of lesser laws, economic, sumptuary, political, administrative, matrimonial, educational and penal, for the purpose of carrying these basic principles into every branch of public life.

The Benedictine Dom Deschamps, in *La vérité ou le vrai système*
(1761), starting from the assumption of moral equality amongst
men, advocated the merging of the individual into society, and
common ownership not only of goods but of women. This order
of things, which he termed the 'state of good customs', could not be
attained, as Rousseau wished, by a return to nature, but by bringing to perfection the existing 'state of laws'. He advised that an
experimental 'state of good customs' should be tried out beyond
the seas in a communist colony of 10,000 people.

The Abbé Mably, in his *Discours de Phocion* (1763), his *Doutes aux
économistes* (1768) and *De la Législation* (1776) declared that 'inequality of fortune perverts the natural sentiments of the human
heart', and proposed sumptuary and agrarian laws in conformity
with communist ideas and with those of the ancient republics.
Although he doubted whether any remedy remained for the evils
of private ownership, he did not despair of circumstances arising
in which his ideas might prove useful, if only in a revolution or a
civil war, either of which would always be preferable to slavery:
'It would be better if only a million happy men were left on the

earth, than this great multitude of miserable, brutish and half-clothed slaves.'

Rétif de la Bretonne, in *Le paysan perverti* (1775) and *Vingt épouses de vingt associés* (1782) planned and re-planned a state on communist lines, embellishing it with a glorification of the Catholic religion and with the most unbridled pornography.

Besides these writers, who may be looked on as the champions of intrinsically socialist beliefs, were others who did not go so far as to propose an entirely new distribution of property, but who, inspired by their own dislike of private ownership, criticized some aspect or other of the existing social order. For instance, Brissot, in his *Recherches philosophiques du droit de propriété*, etc. (1781), asserted that theft should not be punished by death, since it was not, like homicide, a crime against natural laws; in a state of nature all goods are common property, and therefore 'the real thief is the rich man, who has a superfluity'. It is only when private property is created that 'he who robs the rich becomes a thief'. In certain cases theft was not only not punishable, but legitimate. 'At your doors, O rich man, are a hundred starving wretches; and you, satiated with luxury, believe that you have a right to your property. You deceive yourself: the wine in your cellars, the food in your store-rooms, your furniture, your gold, all belong to these poor people: they are the owners of everything; such is the law of nature.' And again: 'Property is theft.'

The lawyer Linguet, in his *Théorie des lois civiles* (1767) and *Annales politiques* (1777-92) frequently deplored, with a force of language and analysis recalling Karl Marx, the appalling conditions of the proletariat. In a 'society born of violence' and under a régime of 'ownership based on usurpation', the working-man was still the slave of ancient times, though worse off in not having a master whose interest it was to feed him. Constrained by need, he sold his labour on such terms as the capitalist imposed: 'At all costs he must work today, or tomorrow die of hunger.' The freedom of those who 'are guilty of possessing a stomach and no money' was 'the freedom to starve'. The laws were 'a defence accorded to the rich against the poor'.

'The poor are born and brought up in the service of wealth, just as game is reared for the rich to kill on their estates, at no cost to themselves.' 'Never has privation been so universal, or more deadly for the class condemned to it, than it is today; never, perhaps, in its apparent prosperity, has Europe been nearer to total upheaval. The more desperation increases the more terrible this upheaval will be.'

What importance has this socialist literature, and in what way does it resemble or differ from the ideas of modern socialism?

The socialists who came before the French Revolution lived in an economic world in which a proletarian class, distinct not only from the artisans and small independent peasant-proprietors, but from the chaotic mass of beggars and vagabonds, was not as yet clearly defined. Consequently, eighteenth-century socialists had no idea of working-class organization as it was to develop in the next century. Whereas the aim of modern socialists has been to lead an economically and politically organized proletariat, those of the eighteenth century did not look — if an exception be made for Meslier — to the working-class in particular, more than to other social classes. Their socialism was not so much an economic and political doctrine aiming at the suppression of working-class poverty as a moral system intended to make all men virtuous, and through virtue, happy. Mably declared that the American republic 'was degraded' by the political prevalence of the 'workers' and warns legislators against entrusting power to the working-class; while Linguet, after demonstrating the dangers of social revolution, ends by thus addressing the working-man: 'Die and suffer in chains, it is your destiny. Society lives by the destruction of freedom, as the carnivora live by killing weaker beasts. Be content with your fate, since it is wrong to hope for any other.'

What theory could be found less socialist than this?

Furthermore, the eighteenth-century socialists, as was natural at a time when industrialism was in its infancy, had an exclusively agrarian approach. That is to say, they saw the problem only in terms of a better distribution of landed wealth. Their attitude towards the new phenomenon of industrial and commercial capitalism was both hostile and alarmed: they thought, not of conquering, but of destroying it. With their pseudo-Spartan foibles, their hatred of luxury and all the most exquisite products of civilization, these theorists, far from being revolutionaries, would have been reactionary had their ideas not been wholly outside the realm of reality.

In any case, socialism occupies a very restricted space in the political literature of the eighteenth century, and went almost entirely unobserved.

The communist and anarchist *Testament* of the *curé* Meslier remained unknown for a century, since it was not published until 1864, except for some anti-religious extracts printed by Voltaire in 1762. The old parish priest remained as though isolated from the history of thought, and contributed not so much towards the birth of modern socialism as to our knowledge of the plight of the martyrized rural population. The work, too, of Dom Deschamps remained unknown and unpublished until 1865. Mably, who alone among communist writers enjoyed great notoriety in his own day, owed his fame not so much to his communism as to that part of his work in which, following in Rousseau's footsteps, he appealed for political liberty, civil equality, the reform of taxation, and all those other legislative measures which were in fact demanded by every innovator of the time.

Finally, it must be noted that before the Revolution no clear distinction as yet existed between the conception of wealth and that of feudal privilege. The conflict between rich and poor was more or less identical with that between the privileged orders and the commons. Even the invective against bankers, so frequent in writings of the time, was political rather than social in origin: for the bankers were regarded less as capitalists and financiers than as agents for collecting the taxes, who, in so doing, enriched themselves at the people's expense. Criticism of private ownership was usually, in effect, directed at the oppressive system of feudal property. So soon as theoretic sympathy for economic equality found definite expression, it was always merged in the demand for political equality: while denunciation of the social order and of private ownership was, as a rule, only a preamble to demands for anti-feudal, judicial, financial and administrative reforms.

If, however, no genuinely socialist attitude existed, there was, even among writers and readers who were anything but eager for revolutionary change, a very general sentimental tendency — due largely to Rousseau's influence — to side with poverty against wealth. Man's original innocence and the state of nature, the 'good savage' and the Spartan republic, were all idealized; equality was praised, tyrants and luxury denounced, bankers and financiers condemned and the sufferings of the poor deplored; while the right of all to work and bread was loudly proclaimed. Moreover, the reform of charitable institutions, especially of hospitals, was studied, and plans discussed for co-operative and mutual aid societies based on equality between the members; while there were demands that the penal laws should be lightened for those shut out from the joys of life. In other words, there existed a sort of socialistic trend: the traditional rights of property had fallen into discredit. This pre-disposed men's minds to regard the coming revolutionary assault upon the property of both Church and nobles as legitimate. Criticism of private ownership was to serve, not to abolish private property itself, but to facilitate the handing over of feudal property to the commons.

Naturally, when the time came for this transfer of property to take place, physiocratic doctrines had to be set on one side. But once expropriation was completed, and the victorious middle-classes had to give legal form to regulations governing what was now their own property, physiocratic teaching returned to favour, and was called in to combat the egalitarian logic of the extreme revolutionaries, who now extended their criticism of the property-rights exercised by the privileged orders to all forms of private ownership, without respect of class.

CHAPTER III

ATTEMPTED REFORM AND THE
REVOLT OF THE PRIVILEGED
CLASSES

I. The heritage of Louis XV. — II. Louis XVI and Marie-Antoinette. — III.
Turgot. — IV. Necker. — V. Feudal reaction. — VI. New attempts at reform. —
VII. The revolt of the Privileged Classes.

I

WHILE the new ideas in philosophy, politics and economics were undermining all the ancient institutions of
France, the King's irresponsible rule was becoming
increasingly harmful in its effects. Drawn by different factions of
the court and *parlements* into disputes between the Jansenists and
Ultramontanes, Louis XV embittered the religious question
while failing to solve it, and only helped to bring discredit upon
religion itself. The alliance with Maria Theresa of Austria had
dragged France into the disastrous Seven Years' War (1756-
63). The *taille, capitation* and *vingtième*, the taxes on tobacco and
salt, and the *octrois* on foodstuffs had all been increased. In 1754 the
annual deficit was 100 million *livres*; it was estimated at 63 millions
for 1770, but there were 110 millions of payments in arrears, and
153 millions of future revenue had been spent in advance. In
January and February 1770, the Abbé Terray, Comptroller-
General of Finance, reduced the interest on a number of loans and
suspended payment on 200 millions due for redemption. To those
who complained that he was taking the money out of their
pockets, he retorted: 'Where the devil would you have me find it?'

The King's discredited authority, in addition to the financial
confusion and general discontent, was exploited by the *parlements*
in an endeavour to enhance their own power. Of these thirteen
supreme courts of justice, the Paris *parlement* ranked first in
importance, owing not only to its antiquity but to the extent of its
territorial jurisdiction and activities; and also because, its seat
being in the capital, it was attended on great occasions by Princes

85

of the Blood and eminent feudal nobles. The *parlements* combined the functions of a supreme judicial magistrature with that of 'registering' royal edicts: an office that today would correspond with promulgation and publication of the laws. This, little by little, had become associated, through the weakness of many French kings, with a right to scrutinize the decrees, to make remonstrances, and even to reject them. The King could, if necessary, override such opposition and enforce registration of a law by holding a special session of the *parlement* known as a *Lit de Justice*; but this procedure was not without disadvantages, especially in times of popular unrest.

Magisterial office in the *parlements* was purchasable, and carried ennoblement with it. For this reason the Paris *parlement*, in particular, was a centre for all the arrogant pretensions not only of the higher clergy and nobility but of the upper ranks of the bureaucracy. In Carlyle's words: 'Were the King weak, always (as now) has his Parlement barked, cur-like, at his heels; with what popular cry there might be. Were he strong, it barked before his face; hunting for him as his alert beagle.'

The reign of Louis XV was one of continual conflict between the absolute monarchy and its insubordinate *parlements*. In 1770 the Paris *parlement*, supported by those of the provinces and by public opinion, repudiated the validity of the *Lits de Justice* and raised a clamour about financial disorder. They proclaimed themselves authorized by the nation to control expenditure and to see that the kings observed the fundamental laws of the monarchy. Louis XV, in a *Lit de Justice* of November 1770, issued a decree forbidding the *parlements* to regard themselves as representatives of the nation and denying them any right to supervise the work of other governing authorities. The members of the Paris *parlement* thereupon resigned in a body. On being invited to resume their functions, they refused. The Chancellor Maupeou promptly banished a hundred and fifty magistrates from Paris and abolished the *parlement* altogether. When the provincial *parlements* came out in support of the Paris body, they too were suppressed. The *Cour des Aides* (a tribunal empowered to levy indirect taxation) made common cause with them and demanded that the nation's representatives should be convened in the States-General: it was immediately dissolved.

Apart from the accompanying circumstances, it must be admitted that these were among the very few wise measures ever carried out by Louis XV. The resistance of the *parlements* and their show of adhering to the doctrines of the *Esprit des Lois* were prompted not by a desire for the country's good, but by hope of increasing their own political influence. Their aim was to impose their will upon the King, and to bring to completion the return to feudal domination that had begun, after the death of Louis XIV, with the Regency of the Duke of Orleans. Furthermore, the tribunals set up by Maupeou to replace the *parlements* administered justice in a simpler and less expensive way, and far more speedily, than formerly. This is why Voltaire, then at the height of his fame, so warmly defended Maupeou and denounced the ignorance, corruption, intolerance and inhumanity of the *parlements*.

Unfortunately, the reform had to be carried out by the Abbé Terray, the hated Comptroller of Finance, and was directed at ancient institutions engaged in a struggle with the Government at a time when the latter was unpopular with everybody. The Paris *parlement* declared that laws were 'conventions between governors and governed': whom, precisely, they intended to indicate as governors, or governed, was by no means clear, but the equivocal formula served to sum up the general discontent. The *parlement* was proclaimed the 'Mount Sinai of the Nation', and there were loud protests by the 'patriots' against the Chancellor's 'despotism', and in defence of 'liberty'. The terminology of the Revolution was already beginning to be fashionable. To make matters worse, the Abbé Terray took advantage of the disappearance of the *parlements* to increase both direct and indirect taxation, and to declare the Exchequer bankrupt once more, reducing annual payments on life annuities by one-tenth and those on perpetual annuities by a fifth. In so doing he demonstrated all too clearly how necessary it was to deprive the King of absolute authority, and to set up independent assemblies capable of curbing the power of his ministers.

On May 9th, 1774, Louis XV died of smallpox. Thirty years previously, when he had fallen ill at Metz, the citizens of Paris had caused six thousand masses to be said in the churches for his recovery. In 1757, after a madman had made an attempt on his life, the masses in thanksgiving for his escape numbered six hundred. During his last illness only three were said for him in Notre Dame. No sooner was he dead than his already putrefying corpse was hurried by night and without ceremony to the royal burying-place of Saint Denis, amidst the jeers of such passers-by as saw the bier carried through the streets.

'At Court,' wrote the Austrian ambassador at Paris, Comte de Mercy, to the Empress Maria Theresa, 'there is nothing but confusion, scandals and injustice. No attempt has been made to carry out good principles of government; everything has been left to chance; the shameful state of the nation's affairs has caused unspeakable disgust and discouragement, while the intrigues of those who remain on the scene only increase the disorder. Sacred duties have been left undone, and infamous behaviour tolerated.'

II

The new king, Louis XVI, was twenty years old. He at once dispatched Madame du Barry, last mistress of Louis XV, to the convent of Pont-aux-Dames. He abolished the Accession Tax, amounting to 24 millions, which the French people were accustomed to pay, and he promised a further decrease in taxation and a reduction in Court expenses. Furthermore, he dismissed Terray and Maupeou, and appointed as Comptroller-General of Finance the noted physiocrat Turgot, a friend of Voltaire and other leading *philosophes*. 'No greater fortune could befall France or the mind of man,' wrote Voltaire, at Turgot's nomination. The Parisian populace characteristically demonstrated its satisfaction by forming processions more than ten thousand strong, by hanging the former ministers in effigy and by attempting to throw the Abbé Terray and his carriage into the Seine.

The hopes of the progressives, however, were doomed to disappointment. Louis XVI was a well-intentioned and good-hearted young man, without vices, and animated by a sincere desire to repair his predecessor's misdeeds. But he was no hero-prince, capable of overcoming the immense difficulties that he had inherited with the Crown. Brought up in the strict observance of religion, his political education had been much neglected; and he had no practical experience whatever of State affairs, since Louis

XV had never allowed him a share in the administration. Though endowed with a certain degree of natural good sense, he was lazy, lacking in self-confidence, slow-witted and coarse in his tastes. His good intentions were not prompted by well-defined ideas, and he was very weak-willed. Thus his decisions were made at random, according to impulse and the influence of those near him; and being mistrustful of his own powers and disconcerted when he found in others the resolution lacking in himself, he was ever ready to retrace his steps or to accept the *fait accompli*. To combat his growing stoutness he went hunting, and practised the locksmith's craft. After the effort of following the chase all day or of filing a lock, he would sit down to dinner, over-eat himself, and often fall into a heavy sleep at table.

Queen Marie-Antoinette did not even possess her husband's crude common sense. Beautiful, witty, vivacious, but very vain and empty-headed, she gave herself up to an endless round of balls, fêtes and riding excursions, in the company of persons often unworthy of her; with a mixture of caprice and arrogance that irritated those courtiers not in her favour and gave rise to malicious slanders which persisted long after her unhappy death. She understood little or nothing of State affairs. Her political activity was for the most part confined to procuring advancement for her favourites or to directing reprisals against those who had incurred her displeasure. At such times she would exert all her energy and skill to gain her ends; she would implore, weep, take offence, insist — and always succeeded in having her own way with the King. For her husband, she had a kind of affection mixed with pity, calling him *le pauvre homme* and, among her intimates, laughing at his simplicity.

'If she continues in this way, my daughter will bring ruin upon herself,' wrote Maria Theresa in 1775 to the faithful Mercy. And the Emperor Joseph II, Marie-Antoinette's brother, in drafting a letter which, it seems, was too outspoken to be dispatched, but which is of value as testifying to his private opinion of her behaviour, expressed himself as follows:

'Let me, my dearest sister, address you with a frankness justified by my affection for you and my interest in your welfare. From what I hear, you are becoming involved in a great many matters that are no concern of yours, and of which you know nothing, led on by intrigue and flattery that excite in you not only self-conceit and a desire to shine but jealousy and ill-feeling. This conduct may well impair your happiness and sooner or later must provoke serious trouble between you and the King, which will detract from his affection and esteem for you, and cause you to fall into disfavour with the public . . . Why should you, my dear sister, employ yourself in removing ministers from their posts, in banishing one and giving office to another, in seeing that some friend of yours wins his law-suit or in creating a new and expensive Court appointment: in brief, in discussing affairs in a manner that is little suited to your position? Have you ever asked yourself what right you have to meddle in the affairs of the French Government or monarchy? What studies have you made, what knowledge have you acquired, that you believe your opinion of value, particularly in matters calling for such wide experience? You, a charming young woman, who think only of frivolity, of your *toilette*, of your amusements; who do not read books or listen to serious talk for more than ten minutes in a month; who never stop to reflect, or to give a thought to the consequences of what you say or do? You simply act on the spur of the moment, prompted by the favourites in whom you believe . . . Listen to the advice of a friend, give up all these intrigues, have nothing whatever to do with public affairs and think only of deserving the King's affection and confidence . . . For the rest, do some reading, improve your mind. After all, that is the rôle of every woman in her own home.'

When, on coming to the throne, Louis XVI had won such popularity by banishing Madame du Barry and her acolytes and by remitting the Accession Tax, he had been moved by a genuine desire to have done with the moral and financial scandals of the past and to inflict no further burden upon his long-suffering people. But in his other actions he gave little evidence of realizing the grave responsibility of his task. Turgot was called to office not because the King approved of his ideas but because he had been recommended by the Abbé de Véry to Maurepas; and Maurepas, who was Louis' principal adviser, put forward his name. Louis thereupon appointed Turgot as Minister of the Marine, and, later, Comptroller-General of Finance, after very little discussion concerning his intentions or his programme, but simply giving him a free hand and an assurance of support. It was with Turgot's advice that Louis recalled the *parlements*, while imposing a number of restrictions upon them as a condition of their return.

'So at last,' wrote that witty sceptic, the Abbé Galiani, to Madame d'Épinay, 'at last M. Turgot is Comptroller-General! But he will not hold office long enough to put his ideas into practice: he will punish a rogue or two, make some stir, fly into a rage, try to do good, and will encounter rogues, thorny problems and difficulties on every hand: his prestige will suffer, he will become disliked, it will be said that he is no good, and his popularity will vanish. Then he will retire or be dismissed, and there will be an end to the anomaly of entrusting such an office, under a monarchy like that of France, to so wise and worthy a man!'

Turgot himself had no illusions about his task. 'In taking office,' he wrote to the King on August 24th, 1774, 'I foresee that I shall have, single-handed, to combat abuses of every kind and those who profit by them; and that I shall also have to oppose the good nature and magnanimous feelings of Your Majesty and of those dearest to you. I shall be feared, indeed hated, by the greater part of the Court and by all those who sell or solicit pensions, who will blame me for every refusal; and in persuading Your Majesty that it is not lawful for favoured individuals to become enriched at the expense of the poverty-stricken populace, I shall be accused of hardness of heart . . . To deprive me of Your Majesty's trust and confidence they will have resort to calumny, and perhaps appearances will be against me. Then I shall give up without regret an office that I did not expect, since I am ready at any moment to retire when I no longer see any hope of being useful to my country. . . .'

III

In 1774, with an expenditure of 325,300,000 *livres* and a revenue of 276,700,000, the deficit amounted to 48,600,000. Turgot's programme was to avoid both bankruptcy and further borrowing, to allow no increase in taxation, and to cut down expenditure. By suppressing various useless court posts, simplifying the financial administration, restricting the profits of tax-collecting syndicates and, further, by inducing the King to keep pensions and grants within the strictest limits, he succeeded in obtaining a surplus over expenditure of 5 millions in 1775.

Turgot also had in mind a vast plan of social reform on physio-cratic lines. On his advice, the King decreed free trade in grain within the country, removed all restrictions on the wine trade, and abolished the *corvées* and the trade-guilds. These edicts were accompanied by preambles justifying such innovations, and explaining the advantages of free trade, the injustice of construct-ing roads for rich landowners by forced labour, and the self-interest of the privileged trade-guilds in denying non-members a right freely to exploit their own work.

Moreover, he prepared a plan for extensive reform in local government. There was to be an independent municipal body in every commune: this was to consist of the richest and most prominent local landowners, without distinction of birth, and of representatives of the rest, who, divided according to their degree of wealth into groups of up to six, might nominate one from each group. These communal assemblies were to elect deputies to the provincial assemblies, which were to levy imposts and replace the *intendants*; and the provincial assemblies, in their turn, were to nominate a 'General Municipality' for the whole kingdom. The latter would apportion taxation and expenditure on public works between the different provinces. A 'Council for National Educa-tion' was to direct public education and to foster patriotic senti-ment and civic virtues.

Those in favour of reform were already hailing the dawn of a new era. Both workers and peasants were unexpectedly impressed by the Government measures, which to them were genuine lessons in practical affairs, since it was the priests' duty to read and ex-plain the decrees and their preambles at Sunday mass. Many obscure desires, hitherto unrecognized, began to take shape in the minds of the common people. The first reforms were greeted as fore-runners of greater benefits to come. There was much rejoicing among the peasants at the abolition of the *corvées*, and the Paris workers illuminated the streets to celebrate the end of the trade-guilds. A number of disputes arose between employers and workers.

At this point, Turgot was dismissed. The financiers had been infuriated by his reforms in the collection of taxes, hitherto carried out by private syndicates or other time-honoured methods. At Court, his economies had aroused intense indignation. Moreover, the military nobility wanted intervention in the war between England and the American Colonies, which Turgot resolutely opposed on grounds of expense. The clergy feared that he would tax Church property and allow free exercise of the Protestant faith. The edicts freeing commerce in grain and wine struck at many deeply-rooted vested interests. High food prices in the spring of 1775 were attributed not to the previous bad harvest but to the new corn law, and led to serious riots, particularly in Paris. In the summer of 1775 Marie-Antoinette joined the Minister's adversaries because he had refused some favour to the Chevalier de Montmorency, and had opposed the creation of an unnecessary post— that of Superintendent of the Queen's Household, with an emolument of 100,000 crowns a year— for the Princesse de Lamballe. The Queen was roused to fury when Turgot obtained the recall from England of the French Ambassador, the Comte de Guines; an amiable trifler who was accused of speculating in the London money market, but who was defended with might and main by the Queen. Turgot's enemies at Court went so far as to produce forged letters in his name, containing slighting references to the ambassador and the Queen, and to bring the correspondence to the King's notice.

At the beginning of 1776 opposition and intrigue had increased owing to the suppression of the trade-guilds and the *corvée*. The merchants and manufacturers, who stood to lose by the abolition of the guilds, denounced 'the chimaera of liberty'; while the replacing of the *corvée* by a territorial supertax— admittedly a light one— imposed without distinction upon both rich and poor, seemed to the upholders of social privilege nothing short of a scandal.

'All public financial burdens,' explained an important member of the Paris *parlement*, 'should be borne by the lower orders. These are subject by virtue of their birth to the imposition of the *taille* and, without any limitations whatever, to the *corvée*. The nobles, on the contrary, are exempted by birth from the imposition of all taxation.'

And the Paris *parlement* made the following official declaration: 'The first rule of justice is to conserve for each individual that which belongs to him. This is a fundamental rule of natural law, human rights and civil government: a rule which consists not only in maintaining the rights of property but also those vested in the individual and derived from prerogatives of birth and social position . . . When the serfs were freed they still remained, as commoners, subject to the *corvée* . . . To make the nobles subject to imposts levied in compensation for abolishing the *corvée* infringes the rule that no one can be subject to the *corvée* who is not subject to *taille*; and would be equivalent to declaring the nobles subject to the *corvée* as well as the labouring-classes.'

The disputes which arose in Paris between employers and workers after suppression of the trade-guilds, and the anti-feudal risings that occurred in some peasant communities, where the law on the *corvée* was accepted as heralding an end to all feudal dues, only strengthened opposition to the Comptroller's policy. Turgot — true type of the optimistic eighteenth-century theorist — was generous-minded and had the public welfare at heart, but lacked a sense of reality and was incapable of compromise. He therefore pressed on without allowing for inevitable resistance, disregarding every sort of vested interest and heaping up difficulties for himself that might have been avoided by proceeding more cautiously.

Louis XVI defended his minister against growing hostility until April 1776. But at last, pressure from the Queen, higher clergy, and *parlements* won the day. On May 10th the Comte de Guines was made a Duke in compensation for his recall from London. Two days later Turgot received his dismissal. 'At last we shall have some money to spend!' exclaimed the Comte d'Artois; while Marie-Antoinette was so incensed with the minister that she wanted him sent, without more ado, to the Bastille. In some places the bishops ordered prayers of thanksgiving to be said in the churches. The 'philosophers' party' had met with a resounding defeat.

'It is a disaster,' wrote Voltaire. 'I see nothing before me now but death. I am struck to the heart by this blow, and shall never be consoled for having seen the beginning and end of the golden age that Turgot was preparing for us.'

Under Clugny, the new Comptroller of Finance, Turgot's reforms were revoked.

'Even the ablest of men,' said Clugny, 'would not know where to begin; but so far as I am concerned, I can at least overturn from one quarter what Turgot has overturned from the other.'

Those who wanted war with England now had their way, and the Court officials plundered the royal Treasury to their hearts' content. When, on October 18th, 1776, after five months of office, Clugny unexpectedly died, the deficit had again mounted to 37 millions, while 60 millions of future revenue had been spent in advance. Participation in the American war imposed a further enormous burden upon the national exchequer: it has, in fact, been calculated that the cost of this war was 2000 millions. At all events, it gave the *coup de grâce* to the nation's finances, and led inevitably to the final crisis of 1788-89. The only reform introduced was the institution of a state lottery, to be drawn once a month.

A minister of proved financial ability was clearly required at the *contrôle général* to grapple with such a state of affairs. One was found in Jacques Necker, a banker originally from Geneva: a solemn personage, proclaimed a genius by his wife and those who frequented her famous Friday receptions, but an excellent man, both honest and disinterested.

Of Turgot's programme — no bankruptcy, no new taxation, no more borrowing, and strict economy in expenditure — Necker accepted the first, second and fourth parts, the last only to a limited extent. He rejected the third, having a blind faith in the power of credit. For that matter, given the universal conviction that increased taxation was not to be thought of, the only possible way of governing the country, in view of the urgent need of money for the war in America, was to go on borrowing. Necker calmly accumulated debt to the amount of 530 millions during the four and a half years of his administration. He was convinced that, when the war was over, the development in national wealth would automatically produce an increase in revenue, and thus allow of the extinction of debt. A not unreasonable hope, had the normal state of the Exchequer been good, and had borrowing been kept within bounds; but with a balance-sheet showing a deficit on ordinary expenditure of 40 millions (a part of the newly-borrowed money being used to mask the permanent adverse balance) the 500 millions of additional debt incurred by Necker so increased the gap between revenue and expenditure that the Treasury was faced with total bankruptcy.

For the moment, however, the war was in full swing and inflicting serious injury upon England; while the breathing-space accorded the country's economy was bringing about great progress in industry. All were persuaded that the Exchequer was in a flourishing state, and Necker was as popular as though he had discovered the philosopher's stone. 'Necker makes war without imposing taxation! He is a God!'

Being agreed upon the necessity for reform, although opposed to physiocratic theory and free trade, Necker abolished the remains of serfdom in Crown lands, but did nothing for the serfs of the nobles or the Church. He did not suppress tolls, but invited the toll-owners to produce their title-deeds, and reserved to the Government all right of commuting them — though, in fact, this was never done, for lack of funds. Furthermore, he ordered no further increase to be made in the *taille* without registration of the decree by the *parlement*, instead of, as formerly, by decision of the King's Council. As an experiment, he instituted local assemblies in five provinces, thereby to some extent taking over Turgot's plans, except that the representatives were nominated· by the King instead of elected. He suppressed many useless posts in the financial administration — with one decree alone, 417 were abolished in August 1777 — and replaced a number of tax-collecting syndicates by official boards of control. For a time he endeavoured to keep both pensions and Court expenditure within reasonable limits.

They were timely and useful reforms. But Necker was not as inflexible as Turgot, and had no wish to antagonize either the Queen or the Court. As soon as he met with resistance in making economies, he left the more important officials alone and turned his attention to the humbler, abolishing at a single blow 406 useless posts and wreaking havoc among cooks, washerwomen and ushers. Meanwhile the courtiers most closely surrounding the Queen — as, in the past, those around Madame de Pompadour and Madame du Barry — ruthlessly exploited the King's simple-mindedness, and succeeded, during Necker's four years of office, in raising expenditure on pensions from sixteen and a half millions to nearly twenty-two millions: the Polignac family alone securing from the Treasury an annual income of seven hundred thousand *livres*.

Nevertheless, Necker flattered himself that he had set the country's finances in order. In February 1781 he published his famous *Compte rendu* to make known his great work and at the same time to encourage new loans of private capital to the Government. Starting from the premise — in some measure justified — that France was passing through an abnormal period owing to the war, he compiled a largely fictitious balance-sheet, instead of rendering an accurate account of the financial situation. Thus he made it appear that revenue amounted to 264,000,000 *livres*, and expenditure to 254,000,000 leaving a surplus of 10,000,000. The truth was that in 1781 expenditure amounted to 526,500,000 *livres* and revenue to 437,000,000, and that therefore the adverse balance had risen to round about 90,000,000: to which another 129,000,000 had to be added to cover the deficits on preceding balance-sheets. But no one was in a position to check the figures, since this was the first publication of the sort to appear. The book met with a ready sale. Elegant ladies displayed it on their tables. Its readers, gratified at this apparent recognition of their right to be acquainted with the country's finances, and confirmed in their belief that 'the King's affairs' were in excellent order, continued to lend their money without qualms, and were full of praise for the great Minister.

But when Necker, by these somewhat dubious methods, had reached the height of popularity, the small group of court conspirators succeeded in overthrowing him, like his predecessor. The moving spirit in this intrigue was the minister Maurepas, who, jealous of Necker's influence, had been outraged by the publication of the *Compte rendu*, contrary as it was to every tradition of the absolute monarchy. To create difficulties for his colleague he circulated a private memorandum from Necker to the King containing criticism of the *parlements*, and thus roused the whole Paris *parlement* against him. The King's brothers joined in the campaign out of resentment at such meagre economies as the minister had succeeded in making.

Necker, believing himself assured of victory and anxious to quell all opposition, asked the King to admit him, though a Protestant, to the Council of State, as a resounding proof of confidence. Maurepas promptly seized the opportunity to play on the King's religious prejudices, and declared that he would resign rather than allow the rights of the Catholic faith to be violated. The King, not daring to override religious scruples, offered Necker other satisfaction. Unwilling to accept a semi-victory that would have been a moral defeat, Necker wrote the King a short and discourteous note, and resigned from office on May 19th, 1781.

V

Necker's resignation was looked upon as a national calamity. In the theatres and public resorts angry demonstrations were made against the Court, and it became the fashion among opponents of the Government to go in pilgrimage to the Minister's country home at Saint-Ouen, to which he had retired.

From now on, court extravagance and the restoration of feudal privileges went unchecked. On May 22nd, 1781, two days after Necker's resignation, an order — which the court officials were obviously holding in readiness but had not as yet dared submit for the King's approval — was made to the effect that all who desired commissions in the infantry or cavalry must give proof of titles of nobility dating from at least four generations back. Not only the *bourgeoisie*, therefore, but even the nobility of recent creation were shut out from military honours. The *parlements* agreed in secret to exclude from their own posts all candidates not possessed of at least two grades of nobility. Another secret decision taken at court was that of reserving all ecclesiastical benefices, from humble priory to wealthy abbey, to the members of noble families.

The nobles, assured now of support from both government and magistracy, applied themselves throughout the length and breadth of France to the enforcement of their seigniorial rights. They refused to recognize any rights on the part of their subjects that were not authorized by legal contract. They increased the *corvées* and feudal dues, and even insisted on payment of revenue fallen into arrears for the last twenty-nine years. Moreover, they renewed the tax-registers (making the peasants responsible for all expenses of compilation), laid hands on communal property, disputed the rights of the populace over forest-lands, and tightened up their monopolistic privileges.

The higher clergy were no less eager than the nobility to secure benefits for themselves. In the fervour of agrarian development that was spreading through France bitter legal disputes arose over the question of tithes, which the peasants maintained were due only on the traditional crops (oats, rye, barley and wheat), but which the collectors claimed also on those recently introduced, such as roots, potatoes and millet. The King upheld the clergy on this issue. The parish priests complained of their poverty and demanded an increase in their share of tithe, which was for the most part appropriated by the higher clergy. A royal ordinance of March 9th, 1782, forbade them to hold meetings among themselves without permission from their spiritual superiors.

Thus the hopes aroused when Louis XVI became king faded one by one. Deep discouragement prevailed.

'It is the end!' wrote Mably in 1784. 'We have fallen too low, we are too weak; the Revolution will never, never come!'

Necker's successor, Joly de Fleury, increased taxation on foodstuffs by 10 per cent. To placate the nobles he suspended revision of the property-tax (begun twenty years previously), from which it had been hoped to obtain an additional 27 millions a year through a better assessment of revenue owed by the privileged classes. In compensation, he created a new tax on property, leaving it, naturally, to those in authority to impose how and in what measure they pleased. He also re-established various posts at court that had been suppressed by Necker, and allowed the King to spend 14 millions on buying Rambouillet. Altogether, in two years of office, he ran up new debts to the sum of 300 million *livres*. As soon as he tried to check the Queen's extravagance, however, he was dismissed, on March 30th, 1783. His successor, D'Ormesson, after incurring a further 100 millions' worth of liabilities in seven months of office, though without showing himself sufficiently lenient towards court extravagance, was replaced, on November 2nd, 1783, by the *intendant* Calonne, a creature of the Polignacs.

By the end of 1783 there were 80 millions owing for war expenses and 220 millions of payments in arrears; 166 millions of future revenue had already been spent in advance and on current expenditure there was a deficit of 80 millions; altogether, an adverse balance of about six hundred millions. But Calonne was not the man to be alarmed at such a situation. Since money was lacking, recourse must be had to credit; to obtain credit, an impression must be given that things were going well, and to this end, considerable expenditure was necessary. In other words, according to Calonne, large sums must be spent in order to obtain more money.

Debts all along the line: 800 millions in three years. A large part of these had been consumed by the Court: 6 millions had gone to buy Saint-Cloud for the Queen; all the personal debts of the King's brothers had been paid; while to help the bankrupt Guéménée family, protégés of Marie-Antoinette's, the King had spent 12½ millions on a property worth only 4 millions, and had exchanged an estate bringing in an income of 70,000 *livres* for one producing only 33,000. 'If it is possible, it is done; if it is impossible, it shall be done!' said Calonne to the Queen, who in asking for ready money, had admitted that it was hard to find. 'Everyone holds out his hand,' explained a shrewd court official, 'so I hold out my hat.' Naturally, the wizard Calonne was idolized by the Court for three years. 'I knew perfectly well,' remarked a well-meaning observer, 'that Calonne would succeed in saving the State, but I never imagined he would do it so quickly.'

But with such methods Calonne could not continue indefinitely to 'save the State'. Distress was growing steadily, although public opinion had not as yet fully realized that its cause lay in the Government's spendthrift policy. Nevertheless, the Court's excessive luxury seemed a challenge to the people's want. The Queen's frivolity was provoking slanderous comment. Scurrilous pamphlets against her and the Polignac family were put in circulation, giving vent to the spite of those courtiers — including even the King's brothers — who were not in her good graces.

At a time when public opinion was so unfavourably disposed towards her, a serious scandal broke out concerning Marie-Antoinette. The fifty-year-old Cardinal de Rohan, who had incurred the Queen's displeasure, and whose wits were dulled by a life of debauchery, let himself be persuaded by certain shady characters that he could regain her favour by procuring for her a diamond necklace worth 1,600,000 *livres*. Forged letters were sent him, and a nocturnal meeting arranged in the grounds of Versailles with a woman impersonating the Queen, to whom he gave the necklace; which naturally remained in the tricksters' hands.

The jeweller, believing the necklace to have reached Marie-Antoinette and having received no payment, finally went to the King and gave the whole affair away. On the Day of the Assumption (August 15th, 1785), the Cardinal, fully robed and about to say mass at court, was arrested and denounced to the Paris *parlement* for *lèse majesté*. The *parlement*, always eager for an opportunity to gain popularity at the Court's expense, declared, on May 3rd, 1786 — after the scandal had lasted for eight months — that the Cardinal was innocent. The verdict was received with frantic applause by a large crowd which in this way was able to demonstrate its hostility towards the Queen.

The Treasury balance-sheet for 1786 showed a total deficit of 198 millions. A new loan was impossible, since the *parlement* would have been certain to reject it, and there was no hope of raising further capital, with debts amounting to 1,630 millions in ten years. Nor was new taxation to be thought of. A declaration of bankruptcy would have provoked universal execration. The only means of avoiding imminent ruin was to bring the privileged orders under taxation in order to augment the Government's revenue.

Calonne, between the devil and the deep sea, coolly adopted a new line, and discovered that France was 'impossible to govern' without the abolition of privilege. He proceeded to draw up a series of bold schemes for a universal land-tax that admitted of no exemptions, for suppression of the *dons gratuits* of the clergy and subjection of the latter to full taxation, for abolition of the *octrois* on foodstuffs, reform of the salt *gabelle* by making it simpler and less oppressive, and the institution of provincial assemblies elected without discrimination between nobles and commons, to administer local affairs. Having obtained the King's approval for this programme, it occurred to him that before presenting it to the Paris *parlement* for registration it would be advisable to assure himself of the necessary moral authority for winning over the opinion of those classes called upon to make sacrifices. He therefore suggested that it would be as well to summon an assembly of Notables, in other words, authoritative persons designated by the King to whom the Treasury's desperate plight could be explained, and from whom he could ask a vote of confidence in his plan for universal reform. He had no doubt that these Notables, flattered at the honour done them by the King, convinced that reform was indispensable, and desirous of the common good, would give the Minister their approval; all the more so, since the reforms were, broadly speaking, those demanded by the better part of public opinion.

VI

The summoning of the Notables aroused universally ironic comment. They were likened to a company of players who were to begin by acting a comedy entitled 'False Hopes', then one signifying 'Enforced Consent', and finally an allegorical panto-mime representing 'The bottomless cask of the Danaïdes'. A Paris shopkeeper, being burdened with a large stock of twopenny dolls that nodded their heads, labelled them 'Notables', and found a ready sale for them. The King's opening speech was summed up in the words: *Simulacra gentium argentum et aurum.*

However, contrary to expectation, the 144 archbishops, bishops, higher officials, nobles, magistrates and wealthy ennobled members of the *bourgeoisie* who met at Versailles on February 22nd, 1787, were in no mood to nod their heads in acquiescence. Seeing a fundamental threat to their privileges in the proposed reforms, they rose against them as one man. They declared themselves not altogether opposed to provincial assemblies, but held that the members should not be elected without distinction between the orders, as this method might in some cases result in the exclusion of both nobles and ecclesiastics, and thus 'destroy the hierarchy necessary for maintaining the King's authority'. They agreed that, in assemblies elected by the three separate orders, the *tiers état* should have half or even two-thirds of the total voting strength, and that the three orders should vote together; but they insisted that a nobleman or prelate should always preside over the meetings, 'since the assemblies would tend towards democracy if not directed by the superior enlightenment of the higher orders'.

The reform of the salt *gabelle* was declared inadequate, and endless objections were raised concerning abolition of the customs duties on foodstuffs. As to the reform of taxation, which touched them most nearly, they dared not openly take the line of defending exemption for the privileged classes; but they protested against wasteful expenditure and declared that the country, consistently deceived and now all but bled white, was entitled to know the true state of the national Exchequer. Having thus side-tracked the issue on to the ground of financial confusion, they asserted that it was impossible to make any pronouncement on the suggested reforms until the Government had clarified the situation. The boldest among them even demanded convocation of the States-General.

At the same time, not only the Government's creditors — who had lent their capital in good faith and now saw it endangered by enormous liabilities — but the tax-payers, threatened by new imposts, and even peaceable citizens, usually reluctant to assert themselves, were all outraged at the Government's chicanery. They pointed out that it was scarcely six years since Necker had announced a favourable balance of over ten millions, and no more than a year since Calonne, in launching a new loan, had declared the Treasury's affairs to be in excellent order; yet now this appalling deficit, of such long-standing growth, was sprung upon the country, and the people were called upon to submit yet again to fresh taxation.

The Notables opposed Calonne for reasons differing from those that prompted the *bourgeoisie* to protest. The *bourgeoisie* wanted an end to privilege and financial chaos, and saw in Calonne a representative of the old régime; the Notables resisted him because his reforms threatened their own privileges. Calonne tried to counter their equivocal policy by distributing pamphlets and memoranda to all the *intendants* and parish priests, explaining how his proposed reforms would benefit the poorer classes, and accusing the Notables of selfish conduct towards the people. But everyone had lost faith in Calonne. The court nobility itself turned against him so soon as it discovered that he was ready to sacrifice their prerogatives.

On April 8th, 1787, the King dismissed Calonne from office, and on May 18th, bowing to the all-powerful will of the Queen, he summoned Loménie de Brienne, Archbishop of Toulouse, to be Comptroller: a cynical ecclesiastic, ruined in health by youthful excesses, who posed as an economist and a *philosophe* and, as one of the Notables, had been among Calonne's most bitter opponents. To meet the immediate needs of the Exchequer, the new Minister issued a loan for 67 millions; transferred himself from the archbishopric of Toulouse to that of Sens, which carried with it an income of 678,000 *livres* a year; and endeavoured to apply, as minister, the very reforms which he had combated as a Notable.

The Notables continued their opposition, denying that they had any authority to agree to the Government's proposals. One of them, the Marquis de Lafayette, who had taken part in the American War of Independence, demanded immediate convocation of a National Assembly. On May 25th, Brienne dismissed them; but having eliminated this obstacle from his path he now came into conflict with the *parlements*.

The Paris *parlement*, assuming an air of sympathy towards reform, raised no difficulties over registering three edicts, laid before them by Brienne, providing for free commerce in grain, the institution of provincial and communal assemblies, and commutation of the *corvée*; but refused to discuss his decree on extension of the Stamp Duty to all private deeds, letters of exchange, legal documents, manifestoes, newspapers, etc., without first seeing a full account of revenue and expenditure, and ascertaining the necessity for such a tax.

The King, in a *Lit de Justice*, disallowed the competence of the *parlement*, as a judicial body, to exert any control over the administration of public affairs, and had the rejected decree registered. The *parlement* retaliated by passing a resolution to the effect that no new taxation should be levied without the approval of the nation's representatives; they rejected the edict providing for a new land-tax, repeating that only the States-General could authorize such subventions to the Government (July 30th); condemned wasteful expenditure by the Court; declared the *Lit de Justice* 'illegal, null and void' (August 7th), and the King's fiscal edicts contrary to the 'rights of the Nation'; and set up an inquiry into Calonne's administration.

Brienne hoped to subdue this resistance by drastic methods. He published a number of pamphlets attacking the Paris *parlement* for defending the privileged orders' immunity from taxation; and on the night of August 14th-15th he ordered the members to take their departure within twenty-four hours for Troyes, to which town the whole *parlement* of Paris was to be transferred. This was only adding fuel to the flames. In the streets of Paris the Comte d'Artois, the King's brother, was met by catcalls, and the names of the Queen and members of the Polignac family were the subject of lampoons and bitter execration. Every provincial *parlement* suspended registration of decrees and demanded a meeting of the States-General. At Troyes, deputations flocked in from all sides; a stream of addresses congratulated the 'Fathers of the Country' on their heroism, and demanded convocation of the States-General, now the watchword of resistance.

Once the first excitement had died down, however, the transplanted members of the Paris *parlement* began to feel that there were disadvantages attaching to heroism. In the small provincial city of Troyes, so far from the splendours and conveniences of the capital, they were bored and discontented. Moreover, they began to fear that the *tiers état*, whom Brienne was trying to arouse against the *parlements*, might end by seeing that they had some other part to play in the conflict between him and the privileged classes. How far might not Brienne go, if driven to extremes by the intransigence of the *parlements*? For his part, Brienne, with empty coffers and no possibility of raising money without parlementary registration, soon allowed it to be understood that he would willingly make peace.

On the one hand, therefore, heroism, and on the other, dignity, were renounced, and a compromise, for the moment, was effected. The King recalled the *parlement* to Paris and withdrew the edicts that had been the cause of so much trouble; while the *parlement* granted the 'prorogation of the second *vingtième*', in other words, the enforcement of a land-tax which was due to be abolished in 1790.

Relations between the *parlement* and Brienne became so amicable that the former undertook to register the issue of a loan for 420 millions, provided that the King would promise to summon the States-General in a few years' time. It was hoped that the recent agitation would meanwhile have time to abate, and that the Government would obtain enough money to continue for a while in peace and to prepare for election of the deputies. In any event, a meeting of the States-General would not, it was thought, constitute any serious threat either to the Government's authority or the privileges of the feudal nobility.

VII

A single incident was enough to start the trouble all over again.

On November 19th, 1787, during the session at which registration of the loan was to take place, the King, on the advice of Lamoignon, Keeper of the Seals — an arrogant, petty-minded official imbued with absolutist prejudices — refused to promise convocation of the States-General for 1789, as a number of *parlementaires* demanded, rather than for 1792, as Brienne had decided; and when the *parlement* came to vote on registration of the loan, the King ordered the edict to be registered forthwith, as though the session were a *Lit de Justice*. The Duke of Orleans, a Prince of the Blood, protested that registration in that form was illegal. The King, caught unawares, became flustered and stammered out: 'It is legal, because such is my pleasure.'

No sooner had the King gone than the councillors — some out of a blind desire to obstruct, others to escape responsibility for the new loan, which was bound to be unpopular, and others, again, in protest against the King's unfortunate and provocative attitude — unanimously declared the registration of the edict to be invalid.

Five long months of protests, threats, and mutual vituperation followed. The Government abused the *parlement* in demagogic terms, accusing it of hypocrisy in defending privilege and of a wish to transform the monarchy into 'an aristocracy of magistrates'. The *parlementaires*, supported by the other courts of justice and by public opinion, which was hostile to the ministers of state, denounced governmental tyranny, swore never to consent to any restriction of their own authority, and even reached the point of proclaiming, in a 'Declaration of the Principles of Monarchy' (March 3rd, 1788), that the King was bound to govern not despotically but according to the laws, and that no taxation was legitimate without the freely-expressed approval of the States-General.

In the end, the King gave the Council of Ministers power to

arrest Duval d'Éprémesnil and Goislard de Montsabert, who were prominent leaders of the rebellion. Warned in time of the threat to their liberty, the two parlementary champions, wearing their ceremonial robes, sought asylum on the morning of May 5th in their official premises and mingled with their colleagues, who had hurriedly gathered from every part. The *parlement* placed both councillors under protection of the King and the law, sent a delegation to Versailles to beg for justice and decided to remain in permanent session until their return. The envoys were kept waiting all day, and finally, at midnight, the King intimated that he was not going to receive them. Meanwhile, at eleven in the evening, the officer entrusted with the order of arrest had all approaches to the seat of the *parlement* occupied by troops. Entering the great hall, and taken aback at the presence of so many magistrates, he asked that the two guilty councillors might be pointed out to him. The president refused. The officer withdrew; then returned to repeat his request, but in vain. The troops lit camp fires around the building as though it were a besieged fortress, and dawn broke on May 6th with the *parlement* still in session. Towards midday, after thirty hours of suspense, the two councillors surrendered, amidst the embraces, lamentations and tears of all present.

On May 8th, at a sitting of the *Lit de Justice*, the King entrusted registration of the laws to a new Plenary Court. The courts of first instance were all reorganized, and forty-seven second-grade tribunals were created and placed over them. The functions of the *parlements* were reduced to dealing only with civil law-suits involving sums of over 20,000 *livres*, and to penal proceedings concerning the nobility and clergy. A number of judicial posts were suppressed, many feudal courts abolished, procedure simplified and the use of torture restricted. Between death sentences and their execution an interval of one month was made obligatory, to give the King time to examine the evidence and, if necessary, grant a reprieve. If condemned persons were found to be innocent, the right to a fair indemnity was recognized.

These were all good measures, which the revolutionaries themselves were to adopt in due course, and which in other circumstances would have been received with general approval. But at that moment they appeared as an expedient for throwing dust in the eyes of the public whilst the only remaining obstacle to the King's authority was being disposed of. The members of the Paris *parlement* refused to fulfil their duties under the new laws, and the twelve provincial *parlements* unanimously resisted the edicts. The provincial nobles, who had close ties with the *parlementaires* and whose interests were affected by the reforms abolishing feudal courts, rose in defence of the *parlements*.

In the Rennes *parlement*, on May 10th, two royal officials sent to demand registration of the new laws were insulted and maltreated amid scenes of violence. At Pau, on June 19th, a crowd of peasants, instigated by the nobles and lawyers, besieged the *intendant*, invaded the law-courts and demanded that the *parlement* should resume its meetings despite the King's orders.

Still more serious disturbances occurred in the Dauphiné. At Grenoble, on May 11th, the nobles of the vicinity nominated a permanent commission to maintain and direct resistance. The members of the provincial *parlement* met in private on March 20th, and declared that the province 'would consider itself wholly released from its allegiance towards the sovereign' if the decrees were not revoked. On June 7th, hearing that the parlementary councillors were to be sent into banishment, the municipal authorities sounded the alarm by pealing the church bells. Crowds barricaded the streets and attacked the troops: a detachment under Bernadotte, the future King of Sweden, who was then a humble sergeant, was ordered to fire and killed two citizens. On June 4th the nobles' commission summoned leading members of the nobility, clergy and *tiers état* to the Town Hall, where it was decided to set up a general assembly of representatives of the three orders in the Dauphiné, without the King's permission. Accordingly, 46 ecclesiastics, 165 nobles and 391 members of the *bourgeoisie* met on July 21st in the castle of Vizille. Here a unanimous resolution was passed demanding convocation of the States-General, failing which the province was to refuse payment of all taxation. The meeting also urged the King to revoke the edicts of May 8th, proclaimed any person accepting office in conformity with them a traitor to his country, and exhorted all France to imitate the Dauphiné in its struggle against governmental tyranny. The nobles, now far gone on the road to rebellion, and forced to accept help from the *bourgeoisie*, recognized the right of the *tiers état* to have as many representatives in the States-General as those of the first two orders together.

Thus began the intervention of a new element, that of the so-called 'nationals', in the struggle which, until now, had been confined to the Government and the privileged orders. The middle-classes, hitherto apathetic and distrustful, roused themselves, took heart from the nobles' example and, applauded by the feudal classes, took up their stand in the forefront of the battle. For the time being, this served them as a point of vantage in the fight against despotism; it was soon to become the position from which the commons were to launch an attack of another and more formidable kind against their then allies, the nobility and clergy.

Brienne, exhausted by overwork, assailed and abused from every side, found himself confronted with a bankrupt Exchequer. During the reign of Louis XVI the public debt had trebled, and now amounted to over four milliards. On June 15th the clergy, summoned to an extraordinary assembly, refused to make a *don gratuit* and demanded convocation of the States-General. Many army officers sided with the opposition, and showed no energy in quelling disorders. Even the court officials were dissatisfied with Brienne, because he had tried to effect some small economies at the expense of their sacred rights. 'It is frightful,' one of them remarked, 'to live in a country where what belonged to one yesterday may be taken from one tomorrow; such a thing used only to be seen in Turkey!'

The setting up of the new provincial assemblies had disrupted the administration. The old *intendants* remained, but without authority and reduced to acting partly as the Government's representatives and partly under the orders of the assemblies. Between the new administrators, suspicious and inexperienced, and the old officials who were jealous of, and ill-disposed towards them, there was constant friction. Thus the administrative machine was becoming more and more disorganized at the very time when the central government, if it were to survive the crisis, had most need to rely on it.

To allay the gathering storm no course now remained but to announce a hasty convocation of the States-General, to get rid of Brienne, who had become extremely unpopular, to call to office a man who could be relied on for an honest, liberal and progressive policy, and to revoke the May edicts. Louis XVI, on August 8th, 1788, summoned the States-General for the following May. On August 24th he suspended payment on the public debt, on the 25th dismissed Brienne, and on the 26th recalled Necker to office. On September 23rd he re-established the *parlements* in their former functions.

The absolute Monarchy had acknowledged defeat, and the Revolution had begun.

CHAPTER IV

THE FALL OF THE FEUDAL RÉGIME

I

THE whole opposition had solidly supported the *parlements* so long as convocation of the States-General had been the point at issue. But once the King and his ministers had yielded to this demand, the struggle of all classes against the despotic monarchy was promptly succeeded by a struggle for power between the classes themselves.

Should the sovereignty that was now slipping from the King's hands be allowed to return to the feudal classes, or transferred to the commons?

When the States-General had last met, in 1614, the representatives of the three orders had sat in separate assemblies, each voting as one body; and the two votes cast by the nobility and clergy had naturally always prevailed over the single vote of the *tiers état*. The question as to whether this procedure should be followed in 1789 was now vital. Since 1614 relations between the orders had fundamentally changed, and the former practice was no longer acceptable to the *tiers état*, who insisted on a single Chamber, like those of the provincial assemblies proposed by Calonne and set up by Brienne: a principle already accepted in the Dauphiné by the first two orders at the Vizille meeting. Furthermore, since the *tiers état* would obviously be at a disadvantage if, as formerly, the number of their representatives were the same as that of each of the other two orders, the commons demanded that they should be allowed as many deputies as those of the nobility and clergy together.

The aristocracy saw that to yield on this point would be to surrender the last remaining weapon in their hands. If the body that was to be the trustee of national sovereignty were a single one, and if the commons were to equal in number the combined strength of both nobility and clergy, they might at any time win over such deputies from the lower ranks of the privileged classes as were eager for popular favour, and thus gain a majority over the forces of conservatism. A single assembly of all three orders and double voting strength for the *tiers état* would mean an end to the traditional hierarchy and defeat for the feudal classes.

The Paris *parlement* had resumed its functions on September 24th, acclaimed by a crowd in which the voices of both nobles and commons were united. Believing themselves masters of the situation, the *parlementaires* hastened to secure the future Assembly for the privileged orders. On September 25th, in registering the declaration by which the King pledged himself to summon the States-General for the following year, they inserted a clause to the effect that the Assembly was to be constituted in the same way as in 1614. This move was suicidal. Instead of the cheering crowds of September 24th, a deathly silence reigned two days later. D'Éprémesnil, who, until then regarded as a hero, was returning to Paris from exile, had found himself at first enthusiastically acclaimed on his way; but his popularity declined day by day, until, when he reached his destination, he was met with jeers and insults. In travelling 200 leagues he had passed from triumph to ignominy. The 'nationals', who had joined in defending the *parlements* so long as the latter served the ends of the *tiers état*, turned upon them in fury when it became clear that the *parlements* only wished to destroy monarchical despotism in order to replace it by the tyranny of the feudal classes.

At Court, no one realized the gravity of the situation. Necker was a skilful financier, and, sustained by a general trust in his personal integrity, had succeeded in satisfying the more urgent daily needs of the administration; but he had all the vanity of a former bank official suddenly raised to the very pinnacle of power, and he tried both to curry favour with high society and the Court, and to preserve his popularity with the *bourgeoisie*. Lacking political education of any sort, he was incapable of realizing the importance of the problems before him. Indeed, he could only see the financial aspect of the social crisis that convulsed the nation and 'looked upon the convocation of the States-General as the summoning of an extraordinary meeting of shareholders'. By origin a Swiss, he was unaware of the deeply-rooted hostility dividing the social classes in France; and he assured the King not only that the commons would never dream of restricting the prerogatives of the first two orders, but that a satisfactory settlement would be reached through the disinterestedness and patriotism of the privileged classes. Louis XVI, by nature indolent and irresolute, was only too glad to share his Minister's optimism and consoled himself for the vexations he had to endure for his people's sake by hunting, or practising his craft as a locksmith. The Queen continued on her misguided course. Of the King's two brothers, one, the Comte de Provence, an egotistical, cunning and cowardly man, sought to avoid compromising himself with any party, in expectation of the time when he might step into the King's shoes; while the other, the Comte d'Artois, an arrogant wind-bag, was always making futile threats to 'unsheathe the sword' against the *tiers état*. The court officials, irritated by the rebelliousness of the provincial nobility and delighted at the sudden unpopularity of the *parlements*, intrigued against the first two orders and tended to favour the *tiers état*; but they always regarded the commons as incapable of action on their own account, and useful only as a kind of bogy that the King could use in bringing the erring aristocracy to reason. In fact, their whole outlook was conditioned by hostility towards all serious reform and stubborn defence of their ancient privileges. In the Government, some ministers supported Necker; the rest, under the leadership of the new Keeper of the Seals, Barentin — no less obstructive than Lamoignon, whom he had succeeded — opposed any decrease in the absolute power of the monarchy, and thanks to Necker's indecision were always successful in blocking such measures as they disliked.

Meanwhile, the King and his ministers allowed the question of a single assembly and double representation for the commons to be submitted for public consideration by a flood of books and pamphlets, in which not only the formation of the Assembly but a mass of historical, social, political and philosophical questions connected with it were debated. 'Public discussion has shifted its ground', wrote Mallet du Pan in 1789. 'The King, despotism, and the Constitution are now subjects of secondary importance; the conflict has become one between the *tiers état* and the other two orders.' When everyone had had ample opportunity for examining the respective merits of each possible solution, the Government — failing to end the uncertainty as to whether voting was to take place per head and in a single assembly, or by each order casting a single vote in three separate bodies — decided that the *tiers état* should have about six hundred deputies out of a total of 1155: in other words, as many as the nobility and clergy together.

Of all possible solutions, this was the most foolish. An equal number of commons' representatives and voting per head were two inseparable elements of a single solution. The *tiers état*, having conquered the first position, was forced to attack the second unless it were to accept defeat and ridicule. Had the King himself decreed that all three orders were to vote together he would without doubt have dealt a death-blow to feudal privilege: he would, in fact, have brought about the Revolution. But it would have been a revolution of his own making: one that, endowing him with popularity and moral strength, would have enabled him to control the *tiers état* after giving them the victory. The nobility and clergy, abandoned by the King, and impotent in the face not only of the *tiers état* but of the State officials, would have had no illusions about the possibility of regaining their position, and would not, through their blind, obstinate resistance, have provoked the fury and excesses of the revolutionaries. It is true that nothing, by then, could have saved the privileged orders or delayed the triumph of civil equality in France; but the monarchy itself might well have survived the overthrow of feudalism. Instead of which, Necker and the King gave the commons the numerical strength they required over their adversaries, without conceding them the power to use it for a legal victory. It was simply an invitation to help themselves to the rest, and it inevitably urged them forward on the way of revolution.

II

The electoral procedure consisted not only in the nomination of deputies, but also in the compilation of *cahiers*, or addresses to the Crown, in which each of the orders set forth their desires, complaints and grievances. The nobles and clergy could fill up their *cahiers* at a single assembly held in each constituency, and nominate their representative forthwith. The far more numerous commons, on the other hand, had to begin with preparatory assemblies of the inhabitants of rural parishes and city wards, or of the trade-guild members, in order to compile preliminary *cahiers* and nominate the first-grade representatives; the latter then had to meet in the towns or rural centres to draw up new and more complex *cahiers* from the original ones, and nominate other representatives; these last, having met the chosen representatives of every rural and urban electoral unit composing a constituency, had to combine all the local *cahiers* into one, and finally elect the deputy.

While this hierarchy of assemblies was slowly functioning, a further spate of pamphlets appeared to direct, enlighten and stimulate the ideas of the electorate. Those produced in support of the conservative cause were few and uninspiring; but the literature of the *tiers état* was copious and animated, ranging in style from academic restraint to unbridled violence.

'What is the *tiers état*?' demanded the Abbé Siéyès in a pamphlet that had a tremendous sale. 'Everything. What has it been until now in the political sphere? Nothing. What does it desire? To count for something.' But if the *tiers état* were everything, why should it merely content itself with counting for something? Thus, as the writer developed his argument, the relative discretion of the opening words changed into implacable enmity towards the 'caste of nobles', which existed as a parasitic plant on the nation's life.

'Ask no more what place the privileged classes should have in the social order: as well seek to assign a place in the diseased body for the malignant growth that corrodes and torments it, for a dreadful malady that devours the living flesh.'

The future Assembly, according to Siéyès, should in no way resemble the old States-General, which had been restricted in its powers. The new one would have to give France a political constitution. But a nation's constitutional charter must be agreed upon by the representatives of all its citizens, possessed of equal rights and equal duties. Should the aristocracy refuse to participate in the common work, so much the better! If the States-General could not be formed, the representatives of twenty-five million Frenchmen would set up a National Assembly without the privileged minority.

In view of the state of public opinion and the conflicting passions dividing the social classes — in view, too, of the discredit now attaching to the old, absolutist traditions — it is easy to understand the lines upon which the elections were carried out, and the results to which they led.

On certain points all the *cahiers* of the nobility, clergy and *tiers état* were in agreement: for instance, on the inviolability of private property and personal freedom, and on periodic convocation of the States-General to control taxation and expenditure and to frame the laws. They were also agreed on such questions as those of personal immunity for the deputies, full ministerial responsibility, a guarantee for the public debt, economy in Court expenditure, and the holding of provincial and communal elective councils: the end, in short, of absolute monarchy. But all these aspirations were merged in a single, universal stipulation: that the States-General, before proceeding with any other work and before approving new taxation, should draw up a constitutional charter of the realm. Several *cahiers*, even from the nobility, demanded that the States-General should formulate a declaration of human rights.

Except, however, for the stand made against the absolute monarchy, dissension was at once apparent.

It was not that the *cahiers* of the privileged classes were blindly opposed to reform of any kind. Even excluding such nobles and clerics as the Comte de Mirabeau, the two Lameths, the Marquis de Lafayette, the Abbé Siéyès and the Archbishops of Bordeaux and Vienne, who, out of a desire for popularity, out of opportunism, interest, or sincere conviction, supported the cause of the *tiers état*, it is a fact that the necessities of that historic hour had made themselves felt, more or less, by all: among the higher nobility and clergy in the guise of a dilettante philosophy, and in the minds of the humble parish priests and lesser provincial nobles as a more or less undefined desire for some new and better way of life. Nevertheless, whilst favouring reform in the abstract, they were cautious in committing themselves as to its consequences; or, to be more precise, in condemning privilege, they had in mind the privileges of others rather than their own.

The nobility demanded confiscation of Church property, freedom of conscience and religion, freedom of internal trade and suppression of the trade-guilds, an end to the venality both of official posts and noble rank, and reform of judicial procedure; they even went so far as to surrender their own immunity from taxation. But all these concessions to what was the mode of the time seemed to the majority the strongest possible justification for tenaciously defending all their other prerogatives; particularly their feudal rights and a separate vote for each order in the future Assembly.

In the clergy's assemblies, too, the parish priests, who outnumbered the rest, succeeded in keeping the high Church dignitaries chosen as deputies to as few as eighty-three out of two hundred and ninety-one. They cheerfully sacrificed all privileges of birth, renounced their immunity from taxation and even approved of the vote by head in the Assembly, or else gave their representatives power to decide on the question. But when it came to discussing the privileges or what they considered the legitimate rights of the Church, the clergy, too, became intractable: they insisted not only on keeping the censorship of the press and the monopoly of education in their own hands, but also on the exclusion of non-Catholics from public office, the prohibition of non-Catholic cults and of mixed marriages, and the inviolability of tithe and ecclesiastical property.

Thus the nobility were ready to strip the clergy of their possessions, and the clergy to sacrifice the nobles' privileges; the nobles of the sword tried to oust the nobles of the robe; the lesser nobility rebelled against the great; and parish priests made war on bishops and canons. It was an undisciplined and disunited army, heading straight for defeat before hostilities had begun.

The *cahiers* of the *tiers état* were very different. The commons certainly deceived themselves as to the ease with which reform might be achieved; they made a great show of paying homage to the King, and in every way betrayed an ingenuous optimism only too soon to be belied by the facts. But apart from their miscalculations as to the way in which victory might be achieved, their ideas on such reforms as they were explicitly charged to secure were clear and concise, and indeed anything but ingenuous. There was to be no regard for either privilege or privileged. The commons knew well enough that no single reform was possible without first abolishing the particular privilege that blocked its way; that indeed every reform they wanted could be achieved simply by suppressing privilege altogether and winning civil equality. The theory of popular sovereignty, which they had taken from Rousseau, and that of the separation of powers, borrowed from Montesquieu— even the Constitution, which all desired, as a check to the despotic power of both ministers and Court— were of value only in so far as they were guarantees of civil equality. The absolute monarchy had not seen fit to concede this civil equality, which, even if it were granted, might later be withdrawn; therefore the nation must conquer it for itself and safeguard it for the future by means of its legitimate representatives. For this reason the *cahiers* of the commons were as unyielding on the subject of the Assembly voting as were those of the nobles. They realized that this was the key-point of the battle, and they insisted, unanimously, on voting by head in a single assembly. With very rare exceptions (that of Mirabeau at Marseilles and at Aix, and of the Abbé Siéyès at Paris) the commons chose as their deputies only members of their own class. Some *cahiers*, echoing the arguments of Siéyès and anticipating events, affirmed that even without the presence of the privileged orders the representatives of the *tiers état* would suffice to interpret the nation's will, and that, if need arose, they must take it upon themselves to act as a National Assembly.

III

Not only the political pamphlets but also the final *cahiers* from the constituencies paid scant attention to the needs of the peasants, who, although they formed four-fifths of the electorate, were represented by very few deputies from their own class. For the most part candidates from the towns were chosen: professional men, merchants, owners of factories, men of letters, and above all, lawyers and legal experts.

It is easy to understand this neglect of the peasants' interests. The writers of political pamphlets were all town-dwellers. The city knew nothing about the countryside and its sufferings, and cared even less; while the peasantry had no means of making urban electors take their troubles into consideration. To compile their *cahiers* the peasants had met together in parish assemblies at the behest of the King— 'their good King'— and had drawn up long, careful and detailed lists of their grievances. For this reason, *cahiers* from the rural communities are precious documents of the time. But in subsequent meetings in the urban centres, among *bourgeois* electors who quoted the *De officiis* of Cicero and copied out the *cahiers* of neighbouring districts — or merely transcribed models furnished by the electoral committees — the peasant representative found himself at a loss: abolition of taxation and feudal dues meant more to him than all the theoretic rights of mankind. He might with difficulty succeed in having a fraction of his disproportionate grievances inserted into some collective *cahier*, and then returned home, bewildered and discouraged.

But the anonymous masses were far from bewildered and discouraged. Turgot's reforms had already awakened in them the first hopes of new and better things. The subsequent return to feudal domination had, in dashing these hopes, merely exasperated the old feelings of hatred towards the privileged orders; and in 1787 administrative reform had abruptly roused the rural population once again. Brienne, in fact, had instituted elective bodies for local government in the provinces and country parishes to which both the priest and feudal lord belonged by right, as well as the peasants' elected representatives. But since neither priest nor feudal lord paid taxes, it had seemed natural to exclude them from voting on financial matters — in other words, on all questions of importance. Thus the *seigneur* found himself in the company of his own peasants but with no authority over them; and the peasants were quick to seize the advantage. Moreover, early in 1778, several provincial assemblies, in making an inquiry into rural conditions, had invited the peasant communities to draw up reports in reply to a *questionnaire* on the number of privileged persons belonging to each parish, the character and scope of their privileges, the value of property exempted from taxation, the extent and value of Church property, the lines on which reform of taxation was desired, and so on. This was simply inviting the peasants to pass all their wrongs in review and to dwell upon the causes of their distress.

The harvest of 1787 had been bad; that of the following year even worse. In July 1788, a violent storm laid waste the whole of north-western and south-eastern France. Bread prices rose sharply, causing great hardship in the towns, without bringing any relief to the poverty-stricken rural producers.

Between 1773 and 1783 the grape-harvests had been poor, and in the latter year had reached a disastrously low level, after which conditions had improved. But whereas the peasant-cultivator of grain sold only as much of his crop as was not needed to feed his family, the vine-grower could not consume all his wine at home. The greater part of it had to be put on the market; and the market, impoverished by the high prices of foodstuffs of prime necessity, could not absorb all the wine available. The wine-trade, consequently, was suffering not so much from a crisis in production as in prices.

Consumption of industrial products was affected by the depression. The building-trade — always an index of economic well-being or of stagnation — became paralysed. In 1789 there was acute unemployment throughout France.

In such circumstances, tithes, feudal dues, direct taxes and the *octrois* on farm produce became an intolerable burden upon the wretched inhabitants of the cities and countryside. They were helpless against bad seasons; but they could turn upon the collectors of tithe, the feudal lords, the *gabelous*, in a word, upon the 'government'. And after all, they had good reason to do so, for it was the Government rather than the weather, to which they owed their misery.

Thus, the drawing up of their *cahiers* was, for the peasants, a final recapitulation of all their woes. The election of deputies seemed to them an assurance of better times to come. The 'good King' had invited them to set forth their grievances and desires: he would hear, consider and assuage the ills of his people. There would be no more taxes, no more dues, no more tithes, no more game laws and no more salt *gabelle*. Here and there they began forthwith to resist payment of imposts and feudal charges. For the time being these were isolated and almost negligible signs of rebellion, but at the first opportunity they were to merge into one general revolt.

Meanwhile, at the end of January, Breton nobles and young men of the *tiers état* had come to blows in the streets of Rennes over the question of voting in the Assembly. Similar riots took place at Besançon between March 30th and April 3rd. At Marseilles and at Aix the starving people rose, sacked the store-houses of grain and flour, killed the corn-merchants and broke up the toll-barriers.

At Paris there were repeated demonstrations, particularly in the great enclosure of the Palais-Royal, which was protected by the privileges of the house of Orléans and immune from police control. On Saturday, April 25th, a rumour spread that, in an electoral assembly, the industrialist Réveillon had 'spoken ill' of the people. What he had said, no one knew, but he was soon credited with the statement that fifteen *sous* a day were more than enough for a labourer with wife and children. During the Sunday, tension increased, but the police took no precautionary measures. On Monday attempts were made to sack Réveillon's house and next day there was a general assault upon it. Troops were called out and fierce fighting took place, with more than five hundred casualties in killed and wounded.

IV

The King and his ministers might well have accepted the *cahiers* and election results as grounds for associating themselves with the *bourgeoisie* and more liberal elements among the nobility and clergy. In so doing they would have made the Government a centre-point for the forces of a new conservative party which, though ready to abolish old, unpopular privileges, could have dedicated all its energies to preventing an outbreak of anarchy. But they would have had to face the fact that the time for self-deception and half-measures was long past: clear-headedness and resolution were now imperative. The King, however, had neither clear ideas nor firmness of will. Even Marie-Antoinette, as late as July 1789, was capable of replying to a trusted friend who attempted to explain the gravity of the situation to her, 'You see everything in gloomy colours, you exaggerate!' As for Necker, he was still dreaming dreams of universal concord in the best of all possible Arcadias.

When the States-General opened, neither the Government nor the Court knew which reforms to accept or reject. They had not even settled how the voting was to take place, a question bound to arise at the Assembly's first meeting. In compensation, the court ushers had decided that the commons' representatives should on all official occasions wear the black habit and slouch hat of the clerks, as in the States-General of 1614; a costume that, by 1789, had become an object of ridicule in all the theatres of France. At the reception on May 2nd at the Palace of Versailles the clergy and nobles entered the King's private apartment, the double doors of which, according to ancient custom, were thrown wide for the clergy, while one leaf only was opened for the nobles. The deputies of the *tiers état* had to pay homage in the King's bedroom, where only one side of the double doors was opened for them.

At the inaugural session on May 5th, the nobles and clergy took their places in comfort to the right and left of the King, while the commons had to remain for three hours packed together in a dark corridor, waiting to be introduced one by one through a small door at the end. When the King put on his hat the clergy and nobles followed suit; the deputies of the *tiers état* should, according to ancient custom, have remained bare-headed, but in spite of this they, too, defiantly placed their hats on their heads.

The King made a brief and colourless speech, referring neither to the Constitution nor to reform; he called for financial stability, deplored the general unrest, and promised carefully to consider such proposals as the deputies might put before him. A lengthy discourse by Barentin, Keeper of the Seals, intimated that the Government intended to take no initiative in changing the old method of debate in the Assembly and would leave this question to the three orders themselves. Then Necker, amidst growing anxiety, made an interminable speech on the financial situation: for three hours together he quoted figures until he became exhausted, and had to leave the latter part of his address to be read by a clerk. He glossed over the adverse balance of 105 million *livres* and, claiming that the deficit hardly amounted to 56 millions, indicated that it would be easy to raise this sum; with reference to the voting he admitted that no one could force the first two orders to vote in common with the *tiers état*, but he had no doubt that they would spontaneously join the latter when necessary. 'Why, then,' asked the bewildered commons and more daring deputies of the privileged orders, 'why summon the States-General?' It had been the financial situation that had forced the King to agree to their convocation: 'The deficit,' Mirabeau had said, 'is the nation's most valuable asset.' Now that the deficit appeared reduced to such meagre proportions there was nothing to prevent the King from sending the deputies home again; and then, farewell to the abolition of privilege and farewell to reform!

Next day the States-General met for verification of their credentials, and the question at once arose as to whether the three orders were to carry out this procedure in common or separately.

The clergy decided, in their own meeting-place— by 133 votes to 114— to verify their credentials as a separate body. The nobles took a similar decision by 141 votes to 47. To the *tiers état* the officials had unguardedly assigned the hall which was to be used for combined meetings of all three orders, and this endowed their gathering with the appearance of a general Assembly. After a long and confused discussion the commons decided to consider themselves a private meeting without official status so long as the 'dissidents' did not join them in the general meeting-place. Thus from the very first moment the question of voting by head or by class presented itself as a clearly-defined issue. It was also apparent that the privileged classes were far from unanimous, with the clergy divided into two nearly equal parts and a not negligible minority among the nobles.

Victory clearly depended on such skill as the *tiers état* might show in exploiting this tendency of the first two orders to split up, and in winning over dissident minorities to their side. Prolonged negotiations were therefore set on foot; but the clergy, paralysed by internal dissension, declared that they could come to no decision until the nobles and commons were agreed; and the nobles and commons were unable to reconcile their differences, since both sides realized that the fate of the whole battle depended on how this preliminary skirmish was to end. Meanwhile, unrest and irritation grew, both in Paris and other French cities. Among the clerical deputies, there were many parish priests who, incensed at the haughty attitude of the higher clergy, showed a readiness to desert; while discussions between majority and minority at the meetings of the nobles became increasingly acrimonious. After five weeks of futile debate it seemed time to bring matters to a head. On June 12th, at the suggestion of Siéyès, the *tiers état* decided to send the other two orders a final invitation to join them, and to begin verification of their credentials forthwith: designating as absent those deputies who did not respond to their summons.

The same evening the roll began to be called. On June 13th three *curés* from Poitou entered the hall and were received with wild enthusiasm. On the 14th, nine more parish priests joined the commons, and ten on the two succeeding days. Victory was already in sight. On June 17th the meeting, by 491 votes to 89, proclaimed itself the National Assembly. At the same time it unanimously declared illegal any future taxation not approved by the nation's representatives, and existing taxes payable only so long as the National Assembly continued in session. The public debt was given recognition and placed under the guarantee of the national honour. By such bold moves the commons at one blow assumed the powers of both King and States-General, and secured themselves from any attempt at a counter-blow: for if, in fact, the Court had wished forcibly to dissolve the Assembly it would have had to face not only resistance from the citizens, who were authorized to refuse payment of taxes, but also that of the Government's creditors, who, fearing a declaration of bankruptcy by the Exchequer, would have joined in defending the nation's representatives.

To the nobles and bishops, and to the Court itself, these decisions of June 17th seemed an outrage. Their resentment reached fever-pitch when, on June 19th, after a stormy meeting, 149 of the clergy, including 6 high prelates, determined, against tenacious resistance from the minority of 137, to join the *tiers état*. So these commons considered themselves rulers of the nation, and intended to crush the power of the nobles, while the lower clergy urged them on! They must be called to heel; the King must stifle these first attempts at rebellion and intervene to defend the threatened rights of his clergy and nobility.

On the morning of June 20th the astronomer Bailly, who was president of the Assembly, found the meeting-hall occupied by Royal Guards on the pretext that it had to be made ready for a Royal Session. Bailly, protesting, announced that the meeting would be held all the same, and, followed by the whole crowd of deputies, moved on, in the rain, to the nearby royal tennis court. Here, with only one dissentient, they all took an oath to allow nothing to interfere with the work of the National Assembly, to continue meeting wherever circumstances might dictate and never to separate until the constitution of the realm had been firmly established. On the following Monday the tennis court, too, was denied them. They therefore met in the church of Saint Louis; and it was here that the 149 clerical deputies and the first two nobles formally joined them.

At Court, the ministers anxiously debated what policy the King should adopt. Necker, as usual, was for compromise. Barentin demanded energetic action against the insubordinate commons, and, after three days of laborious sittings, had his way. On June 23rd, Necker being absent and the public excluded, the King, amid a great display of armed magnificence, read out his decisions regarding the three orders, who were gathered before him in the hall of general assembly: decisions clearly favourable to the privileged classes and equivocal concerning reform. He declared the decisions taken by the *tiers état* on June 17th to be null and void; agreed to joint meetings of all three orders, but only for business of common interest; and expressly excluded from such business 'the ancient and constitutional rights of the three orders, the powers to be awarded the States-General, questions concerning feudal property, and the ancient rights and prerogatives of office reserved to the first two orders': in other words, all matters of importance. He ended by ordering the deputies to adjourn and to meet next day in the three chambers assigned them.

When the King withdrew, the nobles and most of the clergy followed him, while the commons remained silently in their seats. The Marquis de Dreux-Brézé, Master of the Ceremonies, then returned and repeated the King's summons to adjourn. In conformity with ancient custom he was wearing his hat, since he came to speak in the King's name. Ignoring the uproar that this occasioned, he said to the Assembly: 'Gentlemen, you have heard the King's commands.' Bailly informed him that the Assembly had decided beforehand to continue its sitting after the Royal Session and that he could not therefore adjourn it without a debate. 'Is that the reply you wish me to give the King?' asked the astonished de Dreux-Brézé. 'Yes, sir,' replied Bailly, 'for I hold', he added, turning to the deputies, 'that no one can give orders to the assembled nation.' The Marquis thereupon retired, stepping backwards in his embarrassment and thus unconsciously observing a ceremonial required only in the King's presence. 'We have sworn to restore the rights of the French people,' declared

Siéyès, addressing the Assembly. 'Messieurs, you are the same to-day as you were yesterday: let us proceed with the debate.' Eighty members of the lower clergy then returned to the hall, and the National Assembly continued its business.

Tradition has it that Mirabeau took a dramatic part in the above colloquy, but his precise words are uncertain. Historians of the nineteenth century have handed on the version that he boldly intervened after Bailly had spoken, and eloquently addressed de Dreux-Brézé, intimating that the deputies were there by the people's will and could only be removed by force. It would seem, however, that Mirabeau, in recording his own words after the event, deliberately amplified and toned them down to suit the solemnity of the occasion; and that all he had, in fact, said, or rather, shouted, was: 'Go and tell those who sent you that we shall only leave here at the point of the bayonet!' Be this as it may, it was no small proof of courage to speak in so defiant a manner at such a moment.

More important from the historical point of view was the declaration of parliamentary privilege proposed by Mirabeau immediately afterwards, and passed by the Assembly by 493 votes to 34. This decreed that the person of every deputy was inviolable, and that whosoever should lay hands on any one of them would be acting with treacherous intent towards the nation and guilty of capital offence. The meeting, having also confirmed the decisions of June 17th and 20th, then adjourned until 9 o'clock the following morning.

Faced with a need for immediate action, Louis XVI gave way, as he always had in the past before opposition from the *parlements* or court intrigue. The Paris banks had closed at the announce-ment of a Royal Session. The *Caisse d'escompte* sent some of its officials to Versailles to advise against violent measures in dealing with the *tiers état*. Some deputies of the liberal minority among the nobles were threatening to defend the Assembly by force of arms. At Versailles the populace was seething with excitement and there were demonstrations of sympathy for Necker. The troops were restless and unreliable: lodged in unhealthy barracks, ill-paid and subjected to brutal discipline, they showed every sign of reluctance to fight on behalf of the privileged classes.

'They want to stay?' said Louis peevishly, on being told that the deputies had disobeyed his orders: 'then let them stay.' And he dissuaded Necker from tendering his resignation.

On June 24th a majority of the clergy came over to the commons. On the 25th, forty-seven nobles, among them the Duke of Orleans— a Prince of the Blood and one of the Queen's most bitter enemies — formally joined them. They were followed, the day after, by other nobles and clergy.

On June 25th and 26th, in Paris, the French Guards— picked troops for the personal defence of the King— disobeyed orders, and fraternized with the demonstrators.

On June 27th the King wrote to Cardinal de Larochefoucauld, who presided over the meetings of the clergy, and to the Duc de Liancourt, president of the nobility, commanding the two orders to unite with the *tiers état*. The defeat of the privileged classes was complete. 'Thus are kings led to the scaffold,' commented Mirabeau.

V

The Court intended the commons' victory to be of short duration. The nobles were encouraged to hold meetings on their own account, and rumours circulated that leading members of the Assembly were soon to be put under arrest. Meanwhile, despite repeated protests from the Assembly, troops were being concentrated round Versailles and Paris. Finally, on the afternoon of Saturday, July 11th, Necker, who, since his abstention from the session of June 23rd had been increasingly popular with the rebels and in bad odour with the court, was ordered by the King to lay down his office and to leave France.

Next morning— a Sunday— the news reached Paris. A crowd of 10,000 people who had gathered in the Palais-Royal enclosure began to riot. Busts of Necker and the Duke of Orleans were carried in triumph through the streets, gunsmiths' shops were looted and the troops assailed with stones and broken bottles. The French Guards made common cause with the populace. That night the Baron de Besenval, who was in command of the troops, but had received no definite orders, became alarmed at the French Guards' desertion and, fearing other regiments might follow suit, ordered a retreat to the Champ de Mars; thus leaving

the city to its own resources. Crowds of starving people and vagabonds thronged into the capital, broke up the customs-barriers
and sacked shops and food stores.

Early on the morning of the 13th a number of leading citizens,
alarmed at such disorder, met in the premises of the electoral
assemblies and began to organize battalions and companies of
town guards; others formed a committee at the Hôtel de Ville to
take command of the situation. They were, however, without
arms of any kind. Meanwhile the mob pillaged the grain-store at
the Saint-Lazare monastery, looted the royal armoury, broke into
the debtors' prison, and plundered the house of the Chief of Police.

Next day, the insurgents forced their way into the Arsenal of
the Invalides and seized muskets and cannon. They then surrounded the fortress of the Bastille, which was garrisoned by
ninety-five pensioners and thirty Swiss Guards, and towards five
in the afternoon succeeded in breaking in, leaving about a hundred dead and over eighty wounded on the ground. They killed
most of the garrison, hanged two gunners, insulted, maltreated
and finally murdered the governor, de Launay, and afterwards
carried his head through the streets on a pike. From the Bastille
the infuriated mob surged on to the Hôtel de Ville. Here they
seized Flesselles — *prévôt des marchands* and chief of the municipal
administration — ostensibly with the intention of taking him to
the Palais-Royal to answer charges of treachery; but on the way
there he was killed by a pistol shot, and his head, too, stuck on a
pike, was carried in triumph about Paris.

At Versailles the National Assembly, emboldened by the tur-
moil in Paris, demanded withdrawal of the troops and the creation
of a town militia. After passing a vote of confidence in Necker
they protested against any idea of the Government repudiating its
debts, again confirmed the decisions taken on June 17th, 20th
and 23rd, and decided to remain in permanent session.

Bewildered by such widespread and unexpected disorder, uncertain whether to attempt ruthless repression by using troops
of dubious loyalty, and above all paralysed by lack of funds,
which prevented them dismissing the Assembly, the Queen, the
Counts of Artois and Provence, Marshal de Broglie and the Baron
de Breteuil (who had succeeded Necker) consulted with one
another, not knowing how to control the monster they had un-

loosed. On the morning of the 15th the Duc de Liancourt brought Louis news of what had happened in Paris and of the decisions taken in the Assembly. 'But this is a revolt,' observed the King. 'No, Sire,' replied de Liancourt, 'it is a revolution.'

Surrender had to be faced. The King went in person to the Assembly and, announcing the troops' return to quarters, urged the deputies to exert a moderating influence on events in Paris. Next day he recalled Necker to office. On the 17th, amid a procession of deputies, city guards, military deserters and an immense crowd shouting *Vive la nation!* he went to Paris to acknowledge his defeat before the victorious city. Here he gave legal recognition to the municipal and military organizations formed during the crisis, with Bailly as mayor of Paris and the Marquis de Lafayette as commander of the National Guard. The preceding night he had parted in tears from the Comte d'Artois, the princes of Condé and Conti, Breteuil, the Polignacs and other faithful friends who, personally threatened by the revolutionaries, had been ordered by the Queen and himself to leave France. That morning, before setting out for Paris, he had heard Mass and made his will. On his return, the Queen and his sister hastened to meet him, breathless and in tears: 'I never thought,' said Marie-Antoinette to him, 'to have married a citizen of Paris!'

The capture of the Bastille aroused great enthusiasm among liberal-minded people throughout the world. The gloomy fortress, with its eight towers — where so many political prisoners had languished, and from which a resolute government could suppress any attempt at rebellion by the citizens of Paris — seemed a very symbol of the old, absolutist France. All who hated the past saw, in its fall, the now inevitable triumph of liberty.

After July 14th, the King of France was king in name only. In Paris, the mob, having once tasted freedom from restraint, was not easily to be subjected again to the rule of law. On July 22nd, the seventy-four-year-old Intendant of Finance Foulon and his son-in-law Bertier, Intendant of Paris, both of them contractors for the commissariat of the army concentrated near the capital before July 14th, were seized and brutally murdered. In other cities, the former state officials were by now reduced to impotence; many had fled, or gone into hiding, if they had not joined the ranks of the insurgents. Customs-barriers

were pulled down, grain-stores plundered, and the taxes left un-
collected. All those suspected of opposition to the *tiers état* went
in danger of death.

Even graver and more widespread was the convulsion in the
countryside. To the peasants, who cared nothing for politics but
were anxiously awaiting an end to taxation and feudal dues, the
Paris revolution and the lesser revolutions which broke out in
provincial cities were sparks setting off a train of powder that had
been prepared long since. At first, a sense of confused terror
filled their hearts: the *grande peur*, which left an indelible impression on the people's minds. They deserted their villages, took
refuge in caves and forests, gathered into bands and armed themselves against a danger which, in their over-heated imaginations,
was the more fearful for being undefined. Once their panic had
subsided they found themselves united and in arms. Then they
turned upon those evils that were familiar and near at hand.
There were to be no more taxes, no more feudal dues: the King
and the Assembly had decided; the law had been passed and
must be carried out. In eastern and central France, especially,
the peasants were not content with merely passive repudiation.
They imitated, in their own way, the taking of the Bastille, and
attacked *châteaux* and monasteries, burning manorial rolls and
the records of their feudal obligations, and leaving the buildings a
heap of ruins. If the noble or prelate resisted or was suspected of
opposing them they forced him to sign away all the rights of which
he stood possessed, and then, in many cases, murdered him with
his family or household.

VI

The majority in the National Assembly — commons, liberal
nobility and lower clergy — were themselves surprised at so vast a
landslide of events. Suspecting the Court of plotting behind their
backs they at first welcomed the revolt of the populace, which
seemed not inopportune, since it at least had the advantage of
disarming the Government. The Assembly, therefore, confined
itself for some days to passing harmless resolutions exhorting the
citizens to restore order and to show themselves worthy of the

freedom they had won. As time went on, however, news from the provinces grew increasingly grave, and the Assembly became alarmed.

'Property of all kinds,' declared a deputy at the sitting of August 3rd, 'is a prey to brigandage; everywhere the *châteaux* are being burnt, monasteries destroyed and farms plundered. Taxes and feudal dues remain unpaid, the laws are not enforced, the magistrates are powerless and justice is unobtainable in the courts.' He went on to propose that a statement should be issued condemning the disorders as 'contrary to the principles of common law, which the Assembly will never cease to uphold'.

At the afternoon session of August 4th, one of the Paris deputies, the lawyer Target, suggested the issue of another proclamation declaring payment of taxes and respect for feudal rights obligatory until such time as the law decided otherwise. But proclamations could avail little, so long as the Assembly had no effective means of imposing its will.

This was fully realized by the nobles, who had most to gain from a return to normal conditions. The Vicomte de Noailles explained that it was necessary to suppress the cause of the rioting and thus cure the evil at its roots; he therefore proposed that the Assembly should proclaim proportional taxation, an end of feudal dues, the opening of civil and military posts to citizens of every class, abolition, without indemnity, of the *corvées* and remains of serfdom, and free redemption of all other feudal rights. The Duc d'Aiguillon, too, one of the richest feudal lords of France, admitted that feudal charges and unjust taxation were a cause of the disturbances; but, he observed, if equality of taxation were to be introduced immediately, it would be wrong to abolish feudal dues without indemnity, since they too were a form of private property. He therefore proposed that they should continue to be paid, unless commuted by a capital payment corresponding to the annual value of each charge, multiplied by thirty. The same idea regarding commutation was put forward by a Breton deputy, Leguen de Kérangall, who wished to have the 'infamous title-deeds' preserving these unjust rights, 'acquired in dark and ignorant times', consigned to the purifying flames.

Surrounded in the great hall by an excited public and influenced not only by the philosophy and humanitarianism of the time but by genuine alarm at the course events were taking, the whole body of deputies became imbued, little by little, with a frenzy of enthusiasm. The Marquis de Foucault condemned the privileges of the court nobility. The Vicomte de Beauharnais demanded that all citizens should be eligible for public office. The Bishop of Nancy proposed redemption of the Church's feudal rights. The Bishop of Chartres wanted to abolish all privileges of the chase. The Duc du Châtelet proposed redemption of ecclesiastical tithes. The Assembly agreed and applauded. Thus one by one the privileges of the seigniorial hunt, the seigniorial pigeon-cote, and those of the feudal courts and trade-guilds were all done away with. Serfdom was abolished. Representatives from the provincial cities and country districts renounced their local municipal and fiscal privileges. Finally, the Assembly ordered a medal to be struck commemorating the great occasion, and endowed Louis XVI with the title of 'Restorer of French Liberty'. At eight in the morning, when the session adjourned amid acclamation and the deputies separated after embracing one another, the old feudal society of France had legally disappeared.

The Vicomte de Noailles, who had proposed suppression without indemnity of certain feudal charges and the redemption of others, was himself — as malicious tongues were not slow to point out — a younger son, possessed of neither property nor rights: indeed, he had been dubbed John Lackland. The Marquis de Foucault, who had attacked the privileges of the Court nobility, was a country gentleman. The Bishop of Chartres, who had urged abolition of the game laws, was no lover of the chase himself. And it is related of the Duc du Châtelet, who demanded redemption of tithes, that on hearing the Bishop's speech, he had laughingly said to those near him: 'He wants to stop me hunting; I'll make him give up something in return.' It is true that this is not the explanation of the famous night of August 4th; the whole body of deputies had, in fact, been carried away by genuine enthusiasm, and even those who were, in truth, only sacrificing the rights of others, sincerely felt that they were doing great things for their country. It is, however, undeniable that had the nobles and clergy surrendered their privileges a month earlier, their merit would have been morally greater, and they might well have prevented or at least lessened the gravity of the crisis.

As it was, they only gave legal recognition to destruction that had, in many places, already taken place.

Nor must it be forgotten that while certain relics of feudalism, such as immunity from taxation, the *corvée*, serfdom, and monopolistic and judicial privileges, were abolished without indemnity — which was the really generous aspect of these decisions — other feudal charges were declared commutable by capitalizing the revenue at about $3\frac{1}{3}$ per cent. The rural population could not possibly raise the enormous sums required for carrying out such an operation, which involved some four milliard *livres*: the Duc d'Aiguillon alone transformed his annual revenue of 100,000 *livres* from feudal dues into a liquid capital of 3 millions. It is obvious, therefore, that on August 4th the Assembly, in abolishing a part of the feudal rights, was hoping to safeguard the more important by forcing the peasants to redeem them.

Furthermore, so soon as it became necessary to embody these resolutions in legal form, every member of the privileged classes hastened to rescue what property he could from the wreck. The deputies of the *tiers état*, nearly all of whom were townsmen indifferent to the peasants' claims or else opposed to them because themselves possessed of feudal rights, put up no resistance to these manœuvres.

Feudal rights were classified as either personal or real; the former were abolished without indemnity, and the latter declared redeemable. Owing to the difficulty of making a clear distinction between them the Assembly instituted an extremely complicated schedule of individual cases, in the course of which very few rights were abolished altogether, and nearly all became redeemable. Redemption was hedged about with a thousand restrictions and formalities. All existing rights were assumed to be legitimate. In cases where this was contested the obligation to prove illegality was placed upon the peasants; and since proof was almost impossible to provide, the outcome of such disputes was a foregone conclusion. The original intention having thus been side-tracked, the provisions were embodied in the decrees of August 4th-11th, and subsequently developed and brought to completion in those of March 15th-28th, 1790: the first article of which opened with the words: 'The National Assembly has put an end to the feudal régime'; while the succeeding ones, by citing innumerable exceptions, re-established, to a considerable extent, the former order of things.

On one point only was the Assembly more generous than it had been on the night of August 4th: that of ecclesiastical tithes. The latter, which at first had been declared redeemable, were abolished without compensation for the Church, except that the Government undertook in future to maintain the clergy. The land was thus relieved of an annual burden of 120 millions. But these millions were for the most part swallowed up by the big land-owners — the nobles thus reimbursing themselves for loss of their feudal rights at the clergy's expense — while the farmers and peasantry gained little. On the other hand, the expense of maintaining the clergy, having been taken over by the nation, now fell on the taxpayers, whether they owned land or not.

This first attempt at legislation by the Assembly, therefore, was characteristic of all its later policy, and showed the contrast between its courageous intentions and the often petty meanness of its actions. The deputies, theory-ridden as they were and politically inexperienced, turned every question into one of principle: an absolute principle of equity and justice, or rather of what, in eighteenth-century opinion, stood for equity and justice. But so soon as concrete consequences had to be drawn from abstract principles, individual interests, habits and passions became involved, and led to the making of innumerable exceptions to what were intended as universally beneficent reforms. In this way, many contradictory and mutilated laws, of advantage only to the property-owning classes who formed a majority in the Assembly, were passed. It was a strange mixture of enthusiasm and prudence, of ingenuousness and cunning, that perplexes the historian and makes these early representatives of modern France appear, at one moment, quixotic doctrinaires pursuing unattainable ideals, and at the next, shrewd business-men, bent on extorting all possible advantage for themselves from the general ruin.

But the peasants, unable to follow distinctions and exceptions set forth by legal experts, cared nothing for the Assembly's decrees, just as they had not asked its permission before abolishing feudalism on their own account, after the Paris revolution. They accepted the one article declaring the feudal régime entirely suppressed, and refused to obey the rest. While the nobles and clergy, encouraged by the tortuous proceedings in the Assembly, insisted on respect not only for those rights declared legitimate, but also for those that had been abolished, the peasants would recognize none of them. They went hunting and fishing to demonstrate the end of the seigniorial game-laws, continued to attack abbeys and *châteaux*, and passed resolutions at their meetings to the effect that anyone paying feudal dues should be hanged. When National Guards were sent to check their destructive fury, they repulsed them by force of arms. Every law passed by the Assembly with the aim of breaking down their stubborn resistance was without effect: the havoc they wrought, or such restraint as they showed being the outcome, not of the Assembly's decisions but simply of their own needs, desires and passions.

VII

It was not, therefore, one revolution only but two independent revolutions: in the towns the aim of the commons was to deprive the privileged classes of their political power; and in the country-side, to root out every vestige of feudalism and to win personal freedom and full ownership of the land. The two revolutions at times became merged together, but were often in conflict; not seldom each disavowed the other, but in reality they gave one another mutual support. If the cities alone had risen, inspired by the philosophical and political theories of the time, we should perhaps have seen a third Fronde, in which the wordy strife of the *doctrinaires* would have replaced that of the *mazarinades*, and everything would have been reduced to the sterile efforts of un-satisfied *bourgeois* ambition. If the peasants alone had rebelled against feudalism we should have had a bloody *jacquerie*, and after inevitable defeat the insurgents would have retired discouraged, to brood over their wretchedness once more. But by taking place together and with converging aims, the two revolutions assailed the privileged orders and the Government from every side, bewildering and overwhelming them with a flood of revolutionary action impossible to stem.

Some historians exaggerate the duration and extent of this state of chaos. When we read the vivid description of 'spontaneous anarchy' given by Taine in his *Origines de la France contemporaine*, we are led to believe that all France was the scene during these years of such harrowing incidents. But the French *communes* numbered more than forty thousand; and although some, in varying degrees, were a prey to anarchy, the rest— indeed, it would seem, by far the greater part of them— passed from the old régime to the new in comparative tranquillity; while such excesses as occurred were of short duration, and afterwards life began at once to re-adjust to the new conditions.

In Paris the municipal administration arising from the revolution of July 13th-14th was well organized and began to function regularly. Elsewhere, once the former State officials had been dispossessed of their powers, the more influential, courageous or ambitous citizens met together, set up new communal councils, and organized battalions of National Guards, committees of *surveillance* and committees for the supply of arms. It was a spontaneous growth of new administrative bodies called into being not by the central authority but by local needs and impulses. They concentrated all power in their own hands and repudiated the former authorities: dealing, as best they might, with local affairs, making the necessary contacts with their neighbours and setting up a network of agreements and pledges for mutual support from one end of the country to the other. During the last months of this year, patriotic 'Federations' began to be held here and there, and soon spread throughout the country. These were solemn gatherings at which the National Guards of a country district or a group of cities, and later those of a province or an entire region, assembled together in open country and swore brotherhood amongst themselves and loyalty to the nation.

Slowly, imperceptibly, the great work of re-integration thus began; although at first unco-ordinated, it gradually filled the void left by the break-up of the former régime. But the middle-class, which was the dominating influence in the National Assembly and not only controlled the new municipal bodies but filled the ranks of civic guards, was inexperienced and impulsive. It found itself everywhere beset by formidable difficulties. The feudal classes, defeated but not destroyed, were still intent on regaining their rights: while the workers, whose help so far had been essential, and must continue to be so, if the *bourgeoisie* were to prevent the aristocrats from regaining power, were exasperated at the dearth of food and threatened to get out of hand. What was to prevent them changing from allies into masters? Furthermore, the dregs of society, the 'fifth estate' of beggars, vagabonds and criminals, who swooped on scenes of disorder like vultures on their prey, were everywhere spreading the contagion of their lawlessness.

Amid such dangers the new ruling class should have been able to count on the King's help. It was the King who could give their authority that stamp of legality required by every party, in the eyes of the country and even, to some extent, in its own, in order to obtain obedience or, perhaps, to enforce it with fewer scruples. This is more than ever necessary in the case of a revolutionary party, which must build up while it destroys. In supporting the commons, the King could have brought all serious resistance by the feudal classes to an end, for the latter would have been without a rallying-point from which to launch any new offensive. Finally, at a sign from the King, the former bureaucracy — now dislodged from the administration by the *bourgeoisie* — would have placed all their great experience in affairs at the service of the new ruling class; a most valuable asset in countering insubordination on the part of the populace.

Moreover, the middle-class, influenced by the old absolutist tradition that made of the King a being almost divine, still regarded the monarch with superstitious awe. Even when forced to oppose his will, they were always careful to distinguish between the King's personal intentions, which they regarded as good and wise, and the actions of his brothers, the Queen, the ministers or the Court. Had the King so wished, the whole middle-class would have thrown itself at his feet, ready even to augment his powers if he could have been trusted to use them against the privileged orders.

It is true that this King, the object of so much sympathy and respect, was a kind of idol in the possession of the faithful: obliged to obey their will if he did not wish to be broken. But even in times past, the King's personal will had never been omnipotent; when it had clashed with the interests of the feudal lords, they had never hesitated to oppose it. What difference was there between the oft-repeated resistance of the Paris *parlement* and the oath of the tennis court? So far as Louis XVI was concerned, it lay merely in the necessity from now on of upholding the will of the commons rather than that of the nobles and clergy; with the added advantage that the executive power would no longer be obstructed by all those privileges of *parlements*, orders, guilds, provinces and cities, swept away on the night of August 4th, which the kings and their officials had always tried to break down in order that the central government might have full liberty of action.

But it was precisely to this change that Louis XVI was unable to adapt himself. When in the past he had given the seal of legality to claims made by the privileged orders, these had seemed to him not unreasonable. He had approved them more or less willingly, and in so doing had felt himself his own master. But now the commons' behaviour appeared to him as bare-faced rebellion. To avoid worse evils still, he submitted to the *faits accomplis*; but he felt his hand forced and sought resentfully to regain freedom of action.

The *bourgeoisie*, who would have liked to rally round the monarchy and were anxious to avoid further disorder, though determined to countenance no return of feudal influence, found their advances coldly received or haughtily rejected by the King. They were also forced to defend themselves from the weakness of the Government's policy. And just as in their struggle against the King and the privileged classes they had been forced to accept help from any quarter available, so now, they found this help still ready to hand, in that of the mob. When good relations existed between the middle-classes and the King, the mob could be kept in control; but so soon as the *bourgeoisie*, incensed by the King's vacillation, slackened its restraint, the populace was swept by a new access of revolutionary fury, and another battle broke out.

VIII

The conflicts and uncertainties by which the country was distraught were clearly reflected in the National Assembly.

On the right sat the 'aristocrats': nobles and prelates of the absolutist tradition, equally inept in defence and attack. They did not listen to their opponents' speeches, but talked and laughed amongst themselves; interrupting, now and then, and leaving the hall when it was time to vote. At five in the afternoon they all went away *en masse*, since 'it was impossible to delay the dinner-hour'; and the Left took advantage of these regular absences to pass their own resolutions. The most violent among the deputies of the Right were Mirabeau's younger brother and Duval d'Éprémesnil, who had repented his past exploits. The only effective speakers were the Abbé Maury, who, the son of a shoemaker, was coarse and outspoken, but courageous: 'a grenadier disguised as a seminarist'; and Cazalès, a sincere and warmhearted army officer, belonging to the petty provincial nobility.

The liberal-conservative or 'monarchist' deputies gathered in the centre of the hall, under the leadership of the lawyer Mounier, the former *intendant* Malouet, the Comte de Lally-Tollendal and the Comte de Clermont-Tonnerre. Inspired by the theories of Montesquieu, they wanted to restore order and were ready to support the Government in so doing, provided that there was no idea of any return to despotism. They disliked the anti-feudal decrees passed in August because they saw in them a threat to private property, although the claims of the peasants were by no means met. At Versailles they felt ill at ease, with Paris and its seething democratic elements so close at hand.

The 'patriots' of the left, among whom were the so-called 'triumvirs' Adrien Duport, Alexandre de Lameth and Barnave, firmly upheld the August decrees and demanded that the King should sanction them forthwith. Although they disapproved of disorder, they feared counter-revolution more, and to prevent this were even ready to make common cause with the people of Paris and to renew the July revolution. Already the idea of safeguarding their recent victories from a royalist counter-blow by removing the King and the Assembly to Paris was being mooted.

On the extreme left were the democratic group: Pétion, Buzot, Dubois-Crancé and Maximilien Robespierre. They did not regard themselves as real revolutionaries, and not one of them was republican in his beliefs. But their attitude was uncompromising on two points: those of popular sovereignty and civil equality. They took the line that, if the aristocrats and Court were to give way over these, so much the better for everyone. Should they continue to resist, the worse for them. If they could only be brought to heel by violent methods, then violence must be resorted to: the means were not lacking, with a population that faced starvation whenever a crisis in transport paralysed the supplies upon which the cities depended.

With this group, which was numerically small and had but little influence, the followers of the Duke of Orleans were allied: men without conscience or honour, and ready to support any party hostile to the court, they hoped that the King's ineptitude would bring their master to the throne or at least to the position of regent. Forced to manœuvre behind the scenes, they were reduced to impotence by the lack of skill and energy shown by the duke himself, who, out of personal hatred for Marie-Antoinette, squandered millions in an attempt to create his own party, but who in reality had no plan or policy save that of indulging his own pleasures.

The rank and file of the deputies would have liked to follow the lead of the liberal-conservatives of the Centre, and were ready to support a strong ministry. But no ministers could be strong unless they enjoyed the King's confidence and support; and unfortunately the deputies were continually forced not only to distrust the King's intentions but openly to defy him. Thus the majority leaned towards the Centre when the conquests already made by the *bourgeoisie* were not endangered, and rallied round the Left so soon as reaction threatened. The result was that the Assembly was efficacious when bent on destruction and impotent and uncertain so soon as constructive effort was required.

Gabriel Honoré de Riqueti, Comte de Mirabeau — a son of that Marquis de Mirabeau whom we have already met among the writers of the physiocratic school — belonged to no party. In 1785 he had reached the age of forty. His penetration and practical sense, added to the powerful fascination that he exerted over all who came in contact with him, made him an outstanding figure; while his wide knowledge of history, economics and politics (gained in the course of extensive reading and long periods spent in Switzerland, Holland, Germany and England), his ability to recognize merit in others and to appropriate their ideas without scruple, and, finally, his brilliant oratory, should have marked him out for high office.

'Has the Government a plan?' wrote Mirabeau on December 28th, 1788, to Montmorin, the Minister of Foreign Affairs. 'It is

I who have a plan, monsieur le comte: it consists in a Constitution which will save us from the aristocrats' plots, from excesses by the democrats, and from the anarchy in which the King's authority and we ourselves are plunged. Do you wish me to communicate it to you? Will you show it to the King?'

According to Mirabeau, a strong and resolute government was necessary to bring order and prosperity back to France. Such a government must throw over the privileged classes and all those who dreamed of an impossible return to absolutism; it must accept, without reserve, all those reforms that could now no longer be put off, and must rely for support on the well-to-do *bourgeoisie*, who would return to a conservative policy so soon as they had obtained civil equality and adequate political guarantees to preserve it. In this way the spread of anarchy could be checked. The King should restore that alliance between the royal officials and the commons which in times past had brought his predecessors both glory and fortune. The King of France must no longer be King of the privileged orders; he must become King of the French. Failing this, nothing could stop the middle-classes from resorting to extremes in their resistance to feudal tyranny; and instead of a progressive monarchy, France would have a weak and unruly republic which would soon be replaced by the 'degrading slavery' of military despotism.

But a dishonourable past weighed heavily upon Mirabeau. Violent by nature, he had, from his earliest childhood, suffered acutely from his father's unreasonably harsh treatment of him; and indeed his whole youth had been a series of such disgraceful episodes that this paternal severity had become increasingly ruthless. The follies of his mother and sister, together with interminable family quarrels and scandals, had done nothing to calm or restrain his restless spirit. *Lettres de cachet* obtained against him by his father, imprisonment, escapes, seductions, trials, debts, fraud, duels, blackmail, sacrilegious and obscene writings — the memory of all these besmirched his name. His continual lack of means and the wretched expedients to which he had recourse in order to indulge his taste for riotous living frustrated every effort that he made to give his real talents full play.

During the electoral campaign, he had at first attended the assemblies of Provençal nobility. Despised and disowned by his own class, he retaliated by mercilessly castigating the pretensions of the dying feudal orders. He then formally joined the commons, succeeded in pacifying the mob when serious riots broke out at Marseilles and Aix, organized the *bourgeoisie* into armed bands — the first example of national guards — and restored order. Having been elected by the *tiers état* both of Aix and Marseilles as their representative, he opted for Aix.

'In all times and in all countries,' he wrote in a pamphlet of February 3rd, 1789, 'the aristocrats have implacably persecuted those who espouse the people's cause. And if by some caprice of fortune one of these arises from among themselves, they strike at him with especial force, in their wish to inspire terror by the very choice of the victim. It was thus that the patricians slew the last of the Gracchi, who, when he received the fatal blow, threw dust towards heaven, and called the avenging gods to witness; and from that dust was Marius born: Marius, less famous for having exterminated the Cimbri than for having overthrown the tyranny of the Roman nobility.'

When he appeared at the inaugural session of the States-General, with his 'lion's mane' of unruly hair, his short-sighted and imperious eyes beneath thick, arched brows, his ugly, pock-marked visage, broad shoulders and powerful frame, he was received with a prolonged murmur of hostility. The privileged classes detested him as a traitor; the commons were not yet accustomed to looking upon this deserter from the nobility's ranks as one of themselves; and all had a loathing for his infamous past. A flood of pamphlets denounced him as the 'new Erostratus', 'the deputy from hell', 'the verminous reptile'. Montmorin refused to enter into negotiations with him. Necker, whom he had mercilessly criticized as a charlatan, haughtily rejected his offers of help. Malouet was too honest a man not to distrust this 'conspirator' clearly destined for an end like Catiline's. His first proposals were rejected.

Mirabeau was not discouraged, being convinced that 'these imbeciles' would come in time to appreciate his true worth. He voted with the Left against the privileged orders, and with the Right and Centre in supporting the power of the monarchy. He raged at attempts by the nobles to re-impose their authority and was obsequious when he approached the person of the King.

In secret he offered to serve the Court, provided that it would adopt his proposals, but attacked it vehemently when he found them repulsed. Thus, while running up innumerable debts, taking bribes even from the Duke of Orleans, showing apparent indifference to accusations of immorality, ambition, double-dealing and treachery, he gradually obtained an ascendancy over the Assembly by the sheer force of his genius.

IX

A new clash between Louis and the Assembly occurred over the first articles of the Constitution.

As has been already indicated, many *cahiers*, from all three orders, had imposed on the deputies the task of drawing up a constitutional charter of the realm before undertaking any other work of legislation. On June 6th, 1789, the National Assembly had nominated a Constitutional Committee for the purpose of preparing the necessary material. Three days later the Committee proposed that the Constitutional Charter should be preceded by a Declaration of the natural and imprescriptible rights of mankind. 'In order that a constitution should be a just one', declared the Committee, 'it is necessary that it should be based on the rights of all men, and that it should openly protect them. To prepare a constitution, therefore, it is necessary to recognize those rights which natural justice accords to each individual; the principles upon which every kind of society are based must be restated; and every article of the Constitution should be the consequence of one of these principles.'

From August the 1st to the 4th, the moderates, under Malouet's leadership, made every effort to have this proposal rejected, or at least not put into execution until the Constitutional Charter was completed. They pointed out that it might at any time be necessary to lay down some practical juridical rule that would perhaps conflict with the abstract rights previously set forth in the declaration.

'No natural right exists,' they said, 'that is not found to be modified by positive actual right. If you set forth the principle together with the exception, that is law. If you indicate no limitations at all, why set forth in all their fullness rights which should not be enjoyed without proper restrictions? Why take a man up to a high mountain to show him his unlimited possessions, if he has then to descend and find barriers at every step?' — 'A declaration of rights without limitations would be eagerly received by the people, who would thereby be recalled to a state of equality and primitive liberty. But would not the people abuse their strength and disturb the general security, in a desire to recover those rights which should never have been lost? Let us, therefore, give the people back their rights, but with such reservations as private property, justice and public order may require. Let us beware of breaking down a dyke that has been preserved for centuries, without first ensuring our safety from the torrent which may well spread further than we foresee, and result in widespread consternation and damage to property.'

Many ecclesiastics proposed that a declaration of duties should, as a corrective, be appended to the declaration of rights.

On the afternoon of August 4th, the Assembly, before proceeding to discuss the feudal régime, rejected by 570 votes to 433 the proposal for a declaration of duties; it decided almost unanimously to draw up a declaration of human rights; and from August 20th to 26th it drafted the text, in which proposals by Lafayette, Siéyès, Mounier, Target and other deputies were merged, according to the inspiration of the moment, with suggestions that rained in from every side. Spurred on by shouts and applause, they improvised formulae and emendments, embodying in concise, forceful, and clear-cut maxims the whole of eighteenth-century revolutionary thought.

'1. Men are born free, and remain free and equal in their rights. Social distinctions can only be based on the requirements of the common good.

'2. The end of all political association is the conservation of man's natural and imprescriptible rights. Such rights are those of liberty, property, personal security and resistance to oppression.

'3. The principle of all sovereignty is vested in the nation. No form of collective power and no individual can exercise authority that does not directly emanate from the nation.

'4. Liberty consists in man's right to do as he pleases so long as his actions do not injure others; therefore the exercise of each man's natural rights has no limits save those that assure to other members of society the enjoyment of similar rights. These limits may be determined only by law.

'5. The law should only forbid actions that are to the detriment of society. No man must prevent what is not prohibited by law, and no one can be forced to do what is not demanded by the law.

'6. The law is the expression of the general will. All citizens have a right to take part in framing the laws either personally or by means of their representatives. The law must be equal for all. Every citizen, being equal before the law, is equally eligible, according to his capacity, for all dignities, offices or posts in the public administration, without distinction, save that due either to character or talent.

'7. No one may be accused, imprisoned or held under arrest except in such cases and in such a way as is prescribed by law. Those who solicit, give or carry out, or who cause others to carry out, arbitrary orders, shall be punished; but every citizen who is summoned or arrested in virtue of the law, must obey instantly; if he resists he is guilty.

'8. The law can only establish such penalties as are strictly and obviously necessary, and it can not be retroactive.

'9. Every man is presumed innocent until he is proved guilty. Therefore if his imprisonment is held to be indispensable, all severity exceeding that which is necessary for securing his person must be strictly repressed by law.

'10. No one may be molested for his opinions, religious or otherwise, provided that the manifestation of these does not disturb public order, as established by the law.

'11. Free expression of thought and opinion is one of the most precious rights of mankind: every citizen may therefore speak, write and publish freely, but must be held responsible for abuse of this freedom in such cases as are determined by the law.

'12. The defence of man's natural and civic rights renders a public police force necessary; this force is therefore constituted in the common interest and not for the particular use of those to whom it is entrusted.

'13. To maintain this public force and for the expenses of administration some common form of taxation is indispensable. This must be shared equally amongst all citizens in proportion to their means.

'14. Every citizen has a right to ascertain, in person or by means of his representatives, the necessity for this public tax, to approve it freely, to supervise its use, and to determine its amount, distribution, collection and duration.

'15. Society has the right to demand from its public servants an account of their work.

'16. That society in which there is no guarantee of rights, and in which the separation of powers is not determined, has no constitution.

'17. Since the ownership of property is a sacred and inviolable right, no person may be deprived of his property except with legal sanction and in the public interest, after a just indemnity has been paid.'

One right is not found openly affirmed in the Declaration: that of freedom of worship. It is an omission that may seem strange at a time when not only principles of tolerance but indifference to religion had become widespread owing to a violent anti-clerical campaign. But in August 1789 the *tiers état* still needed the lower clergy's help in its struggle against the privileged orders. To avoid alienating them it was advisable to abstain from any direct attack on the monopoly of the Catholic faith. The Assembly therefore confined itself to stating in a somewhat indirect manner that religious opinion should be free. Not until December 24th, 1789, did it proclaim civil equality for both Protestants and Catholics; and it waited until December 28th, 1791 — the very eve of its dissolution — to decree, after long uncertainty, civil equality for Jews.

This instance is a proof that the Assembly was by no means that gathering of pure metaphysicians, hypnotized by abstract theory, upon which Taine has poured such contempt. It is true that the Declaration is in form both abstract and metaphysical; and also that it is extremely doubtful whether the 'natural rights' of mankind can be said to exist at all. In all societies known to history, rights are the juridical formulation of existing relationships, and these relationships are not permanent, but alter constantly, since they are derived from the shifting balance of social forces and from changing moral ideas. But we must not miss the spirit of the Declaration in criticizing the letter. Each one of the rights which it designated as absolute meant, at that moment, abolition of some real abuse, and was essential to the commons' welfare.

'The guarantee of personal freedom,' the historian Janet has observed with acumen, 'was prompted by memories of the Bastille and of the power of arbitrary arrest; freedom to publish recalled the burning of *Émile* by the public executioner and Rousseau's banishment for having written one of the finest books of the century; while freedom of conscience was a reminder that the Protestants had been deprived of their civil rights and driven from the country. The declaration that possession of property is a natural right was aimed at the feudal charges levied upon it in the past; equality before the law denied jurisdiction to the feudal courts; equal eligibility to public office brought within reach of the commons all those higher posts formerly reserved to the nobles, and equality of taxation recalled the *taille*, to which the Third Estate alone had been subjected.'

Monod, too, declares with reason that 'every article in the Declaration of Rights has a concrete as well as an abstract side to it; it is in fact the affirmation of an abstract principle directed against a concrete fact'. Others have justly held that the Declaration, far from being a metaphysical composition, was 'a realistic, experimental document'.

The very form of the Declaration, so absolute in expression, originated from an intuitive awareness of practical necessities. With it the Assembly awarded moral justification to the battle against privilege, proclaimed its own victory a legitimate one, raised a doctrinal barrier against any return of the old régime, and formulated the 'national catechism' of the new *bourgeois* France.

If by a metaphysical work we mean one wholly confined to theory and out of touch with reality, then none could be found less metaphysical than the Declaration of Rights, to which the history of France and Europe has subsequently given ever wider application. The Rights of 1789 are certainly not 'natural' in a sense implying that all human society not in conformity with them must be considered 'unnatural': but they are 'natural' to us moderns in the sense that without them our own civilization could not exist, and we ourselves could not live. Every government in France from 1789 onwards has had to give fuller recognition and guarantees to the principles of the Declaration. It was the inspiration of all those peoples who in the nineteenth century rose against despotism and set up their own constitutional governments. All our civil and penal legislation is descended from the Rights of 1789. Oppressed nations, in gaining independence, have found in them moral justification for their efforts. Today the masses still invoke the same principles of equality and freedom, which, having served as weapons in the struggle that put an end to feudalism, have passed now into other hands and have become an instrument of yet wider change.

It must not be thought that the social conflicts of today have been produced by the Declaration of 1789. Many other factors have contributed to them: the great factories and workshops where the proletariat learns, through the close contacts of common work, to be aware of its own social function and its numerical strength; the complexity and delicacy of our modern economic structure, which causes a crisis at one point to dislocate all the rest; education and the press, both of which spread the ferment of thought into ever wider fields; and the franchise, through which the unpropertied classes can control their governments — all these have created a lack of equilibrium in modern life, prompting men to react against the traditional system of private ownership. But the proletariat is assisted in its struggle today by the same principles that upheld the *bourgeoisie* of 1789 and which they asserted to be primitive, absolute and common to all men: and the *bourgeoisie* can never now set them aside unless it wishes to bring the functioning of the social order to a standstill; unless, in fear of death, it wants to commit suicide. The class war, as Faguet rightly observes, had existed even before the Revolution; but at that time the commons had not had, at their service, 'a general ideal, a kind of dogma, that justified and consecrated the struggle, which was one of strength against strength, of attempts on the part of the weak to support one another against the strong.' Today this is so no longer. 'The Revolution, by proclaiming the dogma of equality, has given the class struggle not so much a reason for existing, as a reason for proclaiming that it exists by right; and a reason for appearing to have right on its side.'

The same may be said of all the other great national, constitutional and legislative achievements of the nineteenth century: they have not sprung directly from the Declaration of Rights, for they are a necessary product of the modern social order. But in the

Rights of 1789 they have found their theoretic justification; they have found a time-honoured system of ideas within which they themselves could be incorporated. If this is metaphysics, then all history is metaphysics.

X

When the Assembly had approved the Declaration of Rights, it went on to discuss the first articles of the Constitutional Charter, regarding the legislative authority.

Since Montesquieu's dogma concerning separation of the legislative from the executive power was immediately accepted by all present, and as there was no difference of opinion over the principle that the executive power should be monarchical, the question arose as to whether the legislative authority should consist of one or of two chambers, and, furthermore, whether the King should have the right of veto against its decrees.

The liberal-conservatives of the Centre, with Lally-Tollendal, Mounier and Malouet to the fore, wanted a higher chamber set up to restrain the actions of a single chamber that could lay no claim to infallibility, and that, left to itself, might easily be led into over-hasty decisions.

Objections were promptly raised on the score that this second chamber might become a haven for the privileged classes, and consequently an obstacle to equality and freedom. The whole Left supported Mirabeau, who, interpreting fears among the lower ranks of both clergy and nobles that a political monopoly might be created for high Church dignitaries and more powerful noble and *bourgeois* families, energetically opposed an upper chamber; and the project was rejected by 849 votes to 89, with 122 abstentions.

The Left also opposed the royal veto. 'It would be a *lettre de cachet* against the general will,' declared Siéyès. 'It would be a monstrosity, practically and morally inconceivable,' asserted Robespierre: 'the will of the representatives must be considered and respected as the will of the nation'; '*one man alone* must not have a right to set himself in opposition to the law'. Mirabeau, now that it was no longer a question of attacking the privileged classes but of defending the King's authority, was in open sympathy with the Right and the Centre: he made every effort to make the Assembly see that the popular vote might even be mistaken in its choice of representatives, and that it was unwise to endow the latter with unlimited power, which they might use to oppress the very people who had elected them.

But once power to limit and amend the work of the people's representatives had been denied to an upper chamber for fear of favouring the aristocracy, the question as to whether this function should be entrusted to the King, whom Robespierre had designated as 'one man alone', and of whose feudal preferences the deputies were only too well aware, became a thorny one. Obviously, this weapon would be used against the Assembly; but in defence of whom? The privileged classes or the commons?

The revolutionary press of Paris took up the discussion, and protested against any right of veto by the King. On the afternoon of August 30th a rumour reached the patriots of the Palais-Royal that most of the deputies were now in favour of the veto. A march on Versailles was at once proclaimed to bring the traitors to heel. Some two hundred of the more hot-headed gathered together with the intention of starting on their way, but the National Guard prevented their doing so and restored order without difficulty. Bailly refused to recognize the legality of a deputation that came to protest against the veto, and the ringleaders of the demonstration were imprisoned. But meanwhile Lafayette, who was anxious to preserve his own popularity, advised his friends at Versailles to take a middle course and to award the King a simple suspensive veto. Thus it was that on September 11th a resolution was passed, by 750 votes to 143, giving the King power to refuse his sanction to laws passed by the Assembly; it was then established, by 673 votes to 325 (11 abstaining) that the veto should be a provisional one; and on September 21st it was decided, by 728 votes to 224, that this suspensive veto should be valid for the length of two legislatures only.

At this point the King, thinking that the incidents of August 30th and the split between the Centre and Left over the veto indicated some abatement of revolutionary fervour, informed the Assembly on September 18th, in agreement with Necker and the leaders of the Centre, that he was unable to sanction the anti-feudal decrees passed in August. The majority of the Assembly at once joined forces with the Left, and on September 19th passed a resolution urging the King not to delay in promulgating the decrees. Two days later Louis replied that he would have them published, but not promulgated; and he also announced that, at the request of the National Guard and of the Versailles municipality, he was recalling the Flanders regiment from Douai. Very soon it became known that the King would also refuse to sanction the Declaration of Rights and the first articles of the Constitution. It was the signal for a renewed access of violence.

Throughout September the democratic press of Paris, the speakers at meetings in the Palais-Royal enclosure and the deputies of the extreme Left had all been urging that the King should be brought to Paris, out of reach of the aristocrats and their plots.

Alarmed at this propaganda, continually threatened by anonymous letters, and feeling themselves unsafe at Versailles, the principal deputies of the Centre held a secret meeting with leaders of the Right and on September 29th invited Necker to transfer the Assembly to Soissons or to Compiègne. The Council of Ministers debated the matter and the majority approved the idea. The King, tired after hunting, slept heavily through most of the discussion; when it was over he roused himself and declared that he did not like the suggestion: that he distrusted the deputies of the Centre no less than the other revolutionaries, and thought it undignified to give an impression of fleeing from Paris. He was sure the disturbances would die down of themselves and give him an opportunity to restore order: 'The remedy will come,' he said, 'from the very excess of the evil.'

Thus the discussions resulted only in a further concentration of troops round Versailles, which added fuel to the flames of revolutionary propaganda. On the evening of October 1st, the officers of the King's Bodyguard gave a dinner to their newly-arrived comrades of the Flanders regiment. It was a clamorous demonstration of royalism, attended by many ladies of the Court. The King and Queen, with the little Dauphin, came later to walk among the guests. Descriptions of the banquet, much exaggerated, were deliberately thrown by the newspapers into contrast with the people's poverty; it was alleged that the national cockade had been trodden underfoot, and the whole incident was represented as the sign of a coming *coup d'état*.

Goaded to fury by such provocation, a crowd of women, accompanied by men, too, in female attire, gathered early on the morning of October 5th to the sound of the *tocsin* and the roll of drums, and marched from the market-places to the Hôtel de Ville, shouting for bread. Having broken into the building they seized what arms they could find; and towards eleven o'clock, still to the cry of 'We want bread!', they set off for Versailles, brandishing pikes, pitchforks and pistols, and dragging two cannon with them. The National Guard, unsettled by rumours of a threatened counter-stroke, and favourably disposed to the idea that the King, Court and Assembly— 'the whole pack of them'— should come to stimulate the languishing trade of the capital, not only made no effort to oppose the procession, but gathered in the Place de la Grève after the women had left and informed Lafayette that they too wished to go to Versailles to fetch the King. After resisting their demands for five hours, Lafayette, feeling no longer able to control his men, and in his own heart not averse to the thought of the King's presence in Paris— since he too was suspicious concerning Louis' opposition to the Declaration of Rights— agreed to their departure.

The King was hunting, and the Queen walking in the Trianon gardens, which she was never, from that day, to see again. Hurriedly warned of the danger, she had scarcely time to return to the palace. The ministers debated what was to be done. Should resistance be shown or should the royal family escape while there was yet time? Louis, as usual, came to no decision; he disliked the idea of flight and he did not want to endanger the lives of his friends by leaving them behind. Resistance would be hazardous, and moreover he was too good-natured to approve the idea of killing women who were demanding food for themselves and their children: 'They only ask for bread,' he said: 'if I had my way, I would not have waited for their coming here.' He therefore gave orders that no use was to be made of force.

The National Assembly had been officially informed that very morning that the King would not accept the first articles of the Constitution without far-reaching reservations, and would suspend all decision concerning the Declaration of Rights. At this news the Left, with Mirabeau to the forefront, launched a furious attack upon the Court, without sparing even the Queen. They had just decided to send their president, Mounier, to invite the King to sanction the Declaration and the articles in question, when towards three in the afternoon the women, tired, hungry and soaked to the skin after their long march in pouring rain, arrived shouting, 'Long live the King! We want bread!' The Assembly decided that some of the women should accompany the president in a deputation to the King demanding recall of the Flanders regiment, punishment of those said to have insulted the national cockade at the banquet of October 1st, and measures to improve food supplies. In the darkening twilight the president made his way through the rain and the turbulent throng to lay the Assembly's resolutions and the mob's demands before the King. Meanwhile, the women went among the ranks of the Flanders regiment urging the men to desert, and noisily invaded the Assembly, devouring what little bread it had been possible to requisition for them in the city.

The King spoke kindly to the women, and gave his sanction forthwith to all that the Assembly demanded. When the deputation had gone, the question of flight was again discussed. The plan put forward was that the King should leave Versailles at once with his family and transfer the seat of government to Rouen. He was to go on horseback; one of the gentlemen of the Court was to ride with the Queen behind him, and another would carry the little prince in his arms. 'If you are taken to Paris tomorrow,' the Minister of War said to the King, 'the Crown is lost.' Necker opposed the plan. The King walked up and down the room repeating sadly, 'A fugitive King! A fugitive King!' At one moment it seemed that those in favour of flight would prevail, and preliminary orders were given. But Louis relapsed into his customary inertia, and finally the project was given up.

At ten in the evening Lafayette, with 15,000 men of the National Guard, arrived by torchlight. Fatigue, the lateness of the hour, hunger and the continual rain had had a quietening effect on the crowd, and it was easy for Lafayette to promise the King and Mounier that order would be maintained. He found what quarters he could for his men, and about five in the morning, exhausted with the exertions of the day, allowed himself, too, some rest.

Towards six, the crowd began to make its way into the palace by means of an entrance which, though normally unbarred, had, through unbelievable carelessness, been left open and unguarded that night. Some of the Royal Bodyguard hastened to intercept them. A scuffle ensued and a townsman and an officer were killed. The crowd rushed up the stairs, along the corridors and into the rooms, killing another soldier and sweeping aside all who attempted to oppose them. The Queen, startled by the clamour, had scarcely time to leave her room and take refuge, half-dressed, in the King's apartments. Lafayette hastened to the scene with his men, prevented a massacre of the Royal Bodyguard, and calmed the mob. Order seemed to have been restored when suddenly from the National Guard, the women, and the crowd swarming around the palace rose the cry: 'Bring the King to Paris! Bring the King to Paris!' It was both an order and a threat: the final seal of victory.

At two in the afternoon the great procession started on its way. The King and Queen, with the little Dauphin, went by carriage, surrounded by National Guards, workers armed with pikes, deputies from the Assembly, dragoons and Swiss Guards; behind came carts carrying flour and adorned with branches, and women riding astride the field-guns or dancing and singing along the route. The heads of the two soldiers who had been killed were carried upon pikes. Thus in the cold light of an autumn evening the King re-entered Paris, a prisoner.

CHAPTER V

THE CIVIL CONSTITUTION OF THE CLERGY

I. Exclusion of Mirabeau from the Ministry. — II. The new administration. — III. Confiscation of Church Property and the issue of *Assignats*. — IV. The Civil Constitution of the Clergy. — V. The conflict with the Clergy. — VI. Death of Mirabeau.

I

'WHAT are these people thinking of?' asked Mirabeau in a letter written towards the end of September to Comte de Lamarck upon the policy of the Court. 'Do they not see the abyss that is opening at their feet? All is lost: the King and Queen will perish, and, you will see, the mob will tear them limb from limb. You do not fully understand the danger: nevertheless, you must make them see it!' 'If you have any means of inducing the King and Queen to listen to you,' he urged, in writing again to Lamarck on October 7th, 'persuade them that they and France are doomed, if the royal family does not leave Paris.' He made every effort to explain to the ministers, Lafayette, and the triumvirs of the Left, how necessary it was to hold the Revolution in check and to create a strong government capable of taking over full responsibility for affairs. At the same time he continued to make a great show of revolutionary ardour, not only to increase his own popularity and facilitate his rise to power, but to impress upon the Court the wisdom of retaining his friendly offices.

In a secret memorandum which he drew up on October 15th for the Comte de Provence, he pointed out that the now all-powerful revolutionary forces in Paris would rise again at the first sign of dissension between the King and the Assembly; that they would then impose their will upon both, and reduce France to a state of anarchy. The King should safeguard himself and the country from this perpetual threat by retiring to one of the loyal provinces of western France, and gathering all the conservative forces around him; but at the same time he should unreservedly accept what had so far been achieved by the Revolution.

By thus openly approving the new principles of political freedom and civil equality he would win support from the majority of the nation, which only wanted to be left in peace to enjoy the benefits of reform. Thus strengthened, he could force the Assembly to leave Paris, or, in the event of a refusal, dissolve it and invite the nation to nominate another representative body better fitted to re-establish order and to give the new régime its final form. And because the emigration of the nobles, which had started after July 14th, was now increasing, and there were vague rumours that the *emigrés* would persuade foreign rulers to intervene in France, Mirabeau urged that the King should take every care to avoid encouraging such criminal intrigues. For this reason it was essential that in leaving Paris he should go, not towards the eastern frontiers of France, but to the central provinces of the west. Woe to him if he did otherwise! 'It would mean declaring war on the nation and giving up his throne. A King, the sole defence of his people, does not flee before them, but calls them to judge of his actions and principles; he does not put himself in the position of having to re-enter his kingdom with arms in his hands, or of begging help from foreigners. And who can foresee to what a pitch of frenzy the nation would be driven, on finding itself deserted by its sovereign, who in joining a few outlaws would become one himself? Would it not in its fury defy the forces thus gathered together by the King? I should be the first, in such an event, to denounce him.'

To prevent the inevitable crisis that a conflict between the King and the Assembly would provoke, and to preserve both the monarchy and the existing social order, Mirabeau stressed that an energetic and resolute man must be found to form a ministry which, chosen from the majority in the Assembly, would be assured of popularity owing to its known loyalty to the principles of liberty and equality. In thus showing his desire to acquiesce in the nation's views the King would find that ample forces for restoring order and for establishing the new régime would rally round him. Necker was a 'miserable charlatan', and must be got rid of.

In all this it was clearly implied that Mirabeau himself expected a prominent place in the strong government he envisaged. And the mere hint of such a possibility was enough to render his plan unacceptable to everyone concerned. The men of the Right detested him as a revolutionary. The Left feared his energy, brilliance and complete unscrupulousness, and had no wish to see these placed at the service of the Court. Lafayette was reluctant to assist in promoting a man who had often judged him harshly and who no doubt would outshine him in office. The Comte de Provence was too timid and the King too lethargic to welcome such ideas, while the Queen felt an uncontrollable repugnance for the terrible 'tribune of the people'.

At the same time, those who saw any imminent danger were very few. Most of the deputies, in that atmosphere of popular enthusiasm, were convinced that unrest was an inevitable but temporary consequence of passing from the old régime to the new, and believed that a period of tranquillity would soon supervene. The municipal authorities and Paris National Guard had taken energetic measures for maintaining order, now that, as Alexandre de Lameth observed, 'the King's officials were no longer to be feared, but popular outbreaks must be prevented'. When a baker, on the usual charge of withholding bread, was brutally attacked by the mob, his murderer was summarily tried and hanged; and on October 21st the Assembly, ignoring Robespierre's opposition, passed a decree of martial law against riotous meetings. A judicial inquiry was opened to fix responsibility for the rioting at the palace of Versailles on the morning of October 6th. The King and Queen, now that fear of a counter-revolutionary *coup d'état* was greatly reduced, were the object of frequent loyal demonstrations.

Most people, therefore, saw in Mirabeau's efforts to promote a strong government merely evidence of his thirst for power, or, worse still, of a desire for ministerial office in order to pay his own debts and the expenses of an irregular way of life. Mirabeau did his utmost to make the Assembly see the harm to the Government resulting from a complete division between the executive and legislative powers, and from the rule denying the ministers a right to share in the debates and resolutions of the legislative body; he strove in vain to show how disastrous and absurd it was that the King should be prevented from choosing his advisers from among the very men who, as the nation's representatives, enjoyed the trust of the majority in the Assembly; and, boldly facing the suspicions concerning his own motives, he proposed that the Assembly should exclude him, and him only, from the ministry, but should not deprive the King of the co-operation he needed from the ablest men among the deputies. But all parties were united in their opposition to Mirabeau, either from jealousy or dislike of his evil reputation. On November 7th a resolution was passed by a large majority debarring any deputy from taking ministerial office during the whole course of the session.

This was a grave blow to Mirabeau, who saw himself condemned to exclusion from the Government, deprived of any legitimate means of getting his programme adopted, and forced to intrigue in secret to obtain the formation of a ministry disposed to accept his clandestine advice. Furthermore, being unable to introduce the slightest order or economy into his extravagant way of living, the decision was financially disastrous for him, since he could no longer hope to settle his affairs out of the revenue, both official and illicit, appertaining to a post in the Government. Still more serious was the fact that this decision jeopardized the urgent political and administrative work awaiting the commons, if they were to check the growth of disorder in France. For if, as is customary in parliamentary government, the ministry had been drawn from the majority in the Assembly, the latter would have been forced to carry out its work of legislation with prudence; since the ministers would have possessed authority over their own supporters and could have directed and restrained them, while keeping in touch with administrative needs through the daily give and take of criticism in the Chamber. Such a ministry, moreover, could have always threatened to resign and hand over power to the opposition if necessary. Thus the executive would have found the requisite strength to oppose not only such efforts as the privileged classes might make to regain power, but also further revolutionary attempts on the part of the democrats.

'A revolutionary minister,' said Mirabeau, 'will not be a revolutionary minister at all; once placed in control of affairs, the most rabid demagogue, in contact with the evils that afflict the realm, will see that the power of the monarchy must be upheld.'

By prohibiting any deputy from entering the Government, for fear of corruption by the Court, the Assembly left itself wholly exposed to the influence of doctrinaire revolutionary theory. Moreover, even the most reasonable of the deputies were often forced to act as fervent revolutionaries; for they were confronted by a Council of Ministers chosen by the King without their approval, and — since they had no official contact with it except when imparting their decisions in the name of the nation — one that they not unnaturally regarded as hostile to the Assembly. Thus, instead of supporting the Government's authority, they had little choice but to work against it.

II

The country had now to be given an entirely new administrative system.

In the crisis following the fall of the Bastille and the *grande peur*, the whole centralized administration had been blindly destroyed by the populace. The *intendants* of the old régime had gone. France became a country of small, independent communal republics, between which only the moral bond of French national feeling remained: a bond that found expression in the ingenuous ceremonial of the *fêtes de Fédération*.

The Constituent Assembly sought to impose order upon all this chaos. It did away with the old, involved system of administrative districts, divided the country into eighty-three *départements* administered by a *directoire*, or standing committee with executive powers, and a Provincial Council, or departmental assembly; and it divided the *départements* into municipalities administered by a *maire*, assisted by municipal officials and a communal council.

It was clear that the departmental and municipal bodies would pay no heed to orders from above. No one intended to obey officials appointed, like the *intendants*, by the central government. The Constituent Assembly, therefore, did not attempt to re-establish direct control from the centre over provincial administration; it awarded the departmental authorities none of the powers that the *intendants* had once possessed; and it gave the municipal authorities not only control of local services (administration of communal revenues, public works, police, etc.), but also of others hitherto appertaining to the central administration: most important of which was the levying and collection of taxes.

The communal and departmental authorities were all declared to be elective; purchase of, or hereditary claims to, posts in public services were no longer allowed. Elections were to be held in the following manner: first, the electors, in preliminary assemblies, were to nominate the municipal authorities, and one second-grade elector for every group of 150 first-grade electors; the second-grade electors of each *département* were to nominate deputies for the National Assembly, and the district and departmental administrative authorities. The nation thus became the sovereign authority not only in the central government but also in local administration. Only the monarchy was to continue to be hereditary.

The question at once arose as to whether citizens of all classes should take part in these elections. According to the Declaration of Rights, men were 'born free and equal', and all citizens were entitled to take part in legislation, either personally or through their representatives. A principle inspired by Rousseau's ideas and implying no restriction of the franchise. But there was also the Encyclopaedist and Physiocratic theory that 'true citizens are those who own property'. The Assembly, ignoring demands by Robespierre and a few other deputies — over-logical followers of Rousseau — for universal suffrage, proceeded to divide all citizens over the age of twenty-five into two classes: that of 'active' citizens, who paid in direct taxation a sum not inferior to three days' wages, and who were allowed to exercise electoral rights; and 'passive' citizens, who were excluded from doing so. And since those qualifying as 'active' citizens under this law numbered 4,298,360, and the number of those over the age of twenty-five in a population of 26 millions must be calculated at about six millions, it followed that a third of the citizens of France were thereby excluded from the franchise.

The Assembly decided furthermore that second-grade electors and communal and departmental administrators were to be chosen from those paying in direct taxation at least the equivalent of ten days' wages. In the whole of France the second-grade electors hardly numbered 50,000: there were only from 300 to 800 in each *département*. The deputies of the National Assembly had to be chosen from citizens paying a sum equal to at least one *marc d'argent* (fifty-four *livres*) in annual taxation, and owning some kind of landed property.

When this law was passed, a chorus of protest arose from the whole democratic press.

'The *marc d'argent* decree,' wrote Camille Desmoulins in the *Révolutions de France et de Brabant*, 'hands France over to aristocratic government. To show how absurd this is, it is sufficient to point out that under its provisions Rousseau, Corneille and Mably would not be eligible for the Assembly, and Jesus Christ would be relegated to the *canaille*. Active citizens are those who have taken the Bastille, they are those who till the fields; while the idlers of Church and Court are parasitic plants that should be thrown to the flames, like the barren tree in the Bible. If, after this decision, the ten million [*sic*] disfranchised Frenchmen or their Paris representatives, the men of the Faubourg Saint-Antoine, had fallen upon Messieurs Maury, Malouet and company, saying: You have cut us off from society because you are the stronger in the Assembly, and we will cut you off from life because we are the stronger in the streets; you have taken our civic life from us and we will take your lives physically from you:— I ask Maury, who, when he likes, can reason well— would the people have acted unjustly? Where no equity exists and the minority oppresses the majority, I know of but one law upon earth, that of retaliation.'

When, in a subsequent decree of April 18th, 1790, it was laid down that the direct imposts of Paris were to be equalled by the tax on the rentable value of property, and it became apparent that to qualify for the *marc d'argent* tax in Paris it would be necessary to pay not less than 750 *livres* of rent, protests by the democrats grew still louder. The Paris Commune demanded revocation of the law. Marat, in the *Ami du Peuple* of June 30th— recalling that the Revolution had been made by the lower classes and that the Bastille was captured by workers of the Faubourg Saint-Antoine — appealed as follows on behalf of the 'eighteen million' disfranchised citizens:

'What, then, have we gained, in destroying the aristocracy of nobles, if it is to be replaced by this aristocracy of rich men? If we are to groan beneath the yoke of the *parvenus* we should have been better off with the privileged orders. We do not ask you today to give us a share of your property: those possessions which heaven has given all men to enjoy in common. But beware of driving us to desperation and of leaving us no alternative but to seek revenge in giving way to every kind of excess, or better still, by leaving you to yourselves: because, to take your place, we have only to stand with folded arms. Reduced, as you will then be, to working with your own hands and tilling your own fields, you will become our equals; but being less numerous than we, what security will you have that the fruits of your labour will be left to you?'

For the time being, however, protests by the democrats had no appreciable effect.

The 'fourth estate', as it was already beginning to be called, was not only as yet unprepared to demand the franchise, but gave no obvious signs of discontent when shut out from it. The democrats themselves had found this exclusion quite natural. Despite the verbal fury of Desmoulins and the threats of Marat (in whose words the idea of a political general strike is to be found, it would seem, for the first time) this dispute over the '*marc d'argent* decree' was, at bottom, only a conflict between richer and poorer members of the middle-class. In fact, few small shopkeepers or peasant proprietors had any thought of becoming the nation's representatives; and it is evident that limitation of the electorate was a matter of interest only to those lawyers, journalists and men of letters living, for the most part, in Paris, who, finding themselves not eligible as deputies, raised as great an outcry as possible.

Measures for judicial reform were on similar lines to those of the new administrative order. On November 3rd, 1789, the *parlements* were suspended and later abolished (September 6th, 1790). A justice of the peace was appointed to every commune or group of communes (*cantons*) to administer justice in rural penal proceedings and law-suits; in every district a civil tribunal was set up to try more serious cases and to act as a court of appeal against decisions of the *juges de paix*; while a penal court, with a jury, was to deal with criminal cases. Above these was the supreme Court of Appeal (*cour de cassation*). All these magistrates were elective: the *juge de paix* was chosen by the first-grade electors, and other magistrates by the second-grade electors. It was the end of all monarchical power, even in the functioning of justice. The Right, led by Cazalès, energetically opposed these reforms.

They were so alarmed by the stormy debates in the Assembly that they proposed an immediate dissolution, maintaining that the deputies had been elected during the previous spring for one year only. But the Assembly declared itself the Constituent body and on April 19th, 1790, confirmed the decision taken at the meeting of the '*Jeu de Paume*' that it would not break up until the Constitution had been completed.

In reorganizing the fighting forces, the Assembly — having, on December 12th, 1789, rejected Dubois-Crancé's proposal for universal conscription — decided to retain the old system of voluntary enlistment. It increased the pay of the lower ranks, reduced the number of higher officers, and made the rank of officer accessible to all, without distinction of birth. The King was declared supreme head of the army; but he was allowed to nominate only the Marshal of France (Commander-in-Chief of the army), half the number of field-marshals, half the lieutenant-generals and a quarter of the colonels. Otherwise, promotion into these ranks was to be decided by seniority. It was established that three-quarters of the nominations for officer rank were to be decided by competition; one quarter was reserved for non-commissioned officers chosen by order of seniority or on their colonel's designation. Non-commissioned officers were to be nominated by their colonel from a list of suitable candidates drawn up by the captains and non-commissioned officers themselves. Finally, local administrative bodies were given the right to requisition troops for their own purposes.

Thus the King, deprived of any control over legislation except for the suspensive veto, and no longer able to intervene in the functioning of the judicial and administrative machine, found himself with an army that was partly subordinated to the communal and departmental authorities: an army, moreover, in which the promotion of officers was almost wholly taken out of his hands. He was, in fact, reduced to almost total impotence.

Would the King, at least, be left power to direct foreign policy? Would he have a right to decide on questions of peace and war? Lameth, Barnave and Robespierre maintained that only the nation's representatives should decide on such grave issues and held it unwise to leave them to ministerial ambition and Court intrigue. Mirabeau's eloquence succeeded in obtaining from the

Assembly, on May 22nd, 1790, a decision to the effect that any declaration of war must first be proposed by the King, then discussed and approved by the Assembly and finally sanctioned by the King. Yet even this was only an expedient which would never have prevented the deputies, had they wished, from so arranging matters as to make war inevitable, by bringing pressure to bear on the King both to make the proposal and to give it his sanction.

Thus all the attributes of sovereignty — legislation, administration, justice and decisions on peace and war — were wrested from the King, and the principle, immortalized in the Declaration of Rights, that 'all authority resides in the nation and can only emanate from the nation' was fully applied: the nation's authority being exercised by the new elective assemblies, which were dominated by an oligarchy of 50,000 property-owning, 'second-grade' electors.

III

These debates on administrative and constitutional questions were accompanied by discussions on the financial problem, which was the gravest and most pressing of all.

So long as the Assembly was involved in a struggle to deprive the Court and privileged classes of their traditional authority, it had regarded the Government's financial embarrassments as a valuable asset; for the Government, continually harried by thought of the deficit and unable to raise further funds owing to lack of credit, was forced to give way to pressure by the Assembly, which alone enjoyed the confidence of public opinion and of financial circles. Indeed, the slightest danger of a return to absolutism was enough to make the *rentiers*, bankers, government contractors and, indeed, all those who normally form a conservative element in any country, rise in wrath and rally to defend the National Assembly, the only remaining guarantee of their threatened capital. But after the monarchy's final surrender in October, the nation's representatives found themselves endowed not only with unlimited power but also with the responsibilities of power. The public debt, which, when the States-General opened, had been 3 milliards and 119 millions, now amounted to 4 milliards and 262 millions; a sum requiring 262 millions a year in interest.

The Government's creditors could not always be placated with fair words, and solemn declarations placing the public debt in the trusteeship of the national honour were losing force through constant repetition. Furthermore, it was necessary to provide for daily civil and military expenditure; while at the same time arrears in the collection of taxes owing to recent disorders had to be added to the deficit.

Some radical remedy would have quickly to be found, as Mirabeau urged, if public administration were not to disintegrate and render all the Assembly's work abortive. But what remedy? It was impossible to continue the policy of borrowing, since owners of capital, far from being willing to lend more money, were clamouring for a return of the old. Two small loans of 30 and 80 millions, issued with the Assembly's approval, had not been fully taken up. No change could be introduced in the system of taxation without due care and consideration, and meanwhile the taxes were not being paid. When the Assembly, in a somewhat pathetic decree of October 6th, appealed to all French citizens to make a special patriotic contribution of 25 per cent of their income for the year, no one was in a position to estimate how much should be produced, and it was clear that every subscriber, despite the appeals to his patriotism, would pay as little and as tardily as possible. The practice of making private patriotic offerings, which had begun during the previous September, was touching, if ingenuous, but had no effect on the vortex in the national finances. The balance-sheet for 1789 ended with a deficit of 162 millions.

There was only one way out: a way almost always followed by Christian governments when in really serious straits. A way, moreover, which the French monarchy itself had not hesitated, more than once, to take, and which for the last half century had been proclaimed a necessity in France — that of laying hands on the property of the Church.

Talleyrand, Bishop of Autun, put it less crudely in the Assembly when, on October 10th, 1789, he moved the famous resolution to the effect that the clergy's possessions must be declared the property of the nation and converted to Government use in overcoming financial difficulties that otherwise must prove insuperable. The clergy, said Talleyrand, repeating what was now held by every innovator of the time, differed from other property-owners in that they could not freely dispose of their possessions, having received them as endowments not for their own benefit but for that of the Church and of charitable bodies. It followed, therefore, that as the promotion of charity and the practice of religion were in the national interest, all gifts to the clergy made with this aim were gifts to the nation; and for this reason the nation was the true owner of Church property, whereas the revenues appertaining to it belonged to the ecclesiastics. If, then, the nation undertook to provide directly, within due limits, for maintaining the clergy and for the needs of charitable and religious bodies, it could take over from them the revenue of what was in fact national property; after which, it could sell the property, and devote the proceeds, firstly, to Church requirements and then to other ends of general interest. In so doing, the nation would not contravene the wishes of those who had originally bestowed their possessions on the Church, nor would it in any way fail in strict observance of the rights of ownership.

In the debate on this motion, which became extremely animated, other deputies supported Talleyrand's proposal. The jurist Thouret, for example, affirmed that the clergy were a moral body, existing only according to a convention recognized by the law, whereas the physical individual was real, with an existence anterior to any law: the Government, therefore, although it could not encroach upon the rights of individuals — including the right to hold property — were entitled not only to take over the property of bodies such as the clergy but also to suppress them, after creating or tolerating them. Their suppression could not be regarded as a crime, and revocation of their right to hold property, accorded to them by law, would not be spoliation. Mirabeau, for his part, maintained that such property had been originally bestowed on the Church in one of three ways; by the Kings, in which case the nation could regain possession of it, since the sovereign had no right to alienate national property; by local bodies, who had presented it for Church expenses — in which case the nation, on assuming responsibility for maintaining the clergy, had a right to regain possession of their property; or by private individuals, whose gifts could not endow the clergy with rights superior to those of the State, and thus prevent the nation from organizing itself on sure foundations by suppressing such independent bodies as threatened to break up its homogeneity. For that matter, the wishes of these donors in times past should not be allowed to conflict with the common good. If religious foundations were never to be destroyed, they would so multiply with the passage of years that they would end by absorbing all privately-owned property: 'If the inhabitants of the earth had always been buried in tombs, it would have long ago become necessary to pull down these useless monuments to find space for cultivating the soil, and to move the ashes of the dead in order to sustain the living.'

Those who defended the clergy combated these arguments energetically. When, they asked, had donors of charitable endowments ever thought that they were making gifts to the nation, rather than to some particular church, convent or hospital? For thirteen centuries the Church had owned and cultivated its lands; it had put up buildings and made contracts, and the law had always recognized and defended its right of possession; but now, suddenly, it appeared that, being a 'moral' body, the Church had no right to own property at all. 'The ruin of the clergy,' proclaimed the Abbé Maury, 'is the financiers' most fruitful speculation': it was for this reason that they had refused to lend their money to the State; they wanted the financial situation to deteriorate, and 'were silently awaiting their booty'.

'But property is one, and sacred, both for us and for you. Our property is a guarantee of yours: today it is we who are assailed, but do not deceive yourselves; if we are plundered, you will be plundered in your turn. Your own immoral arguments will be turned against you, and the first disaster to overtake the State finances will involve and swallow up your own possessions. If the nation is entitled to seek in the origins of society a reason for despoiling us of our property, this new metaphysical principle will lead directly to all manner of claims for the common ownership of land: the people will take advantage of the existing chaos to obtain a share of property that even the most immemorial rights will not protect from invasion, and they will exercise over you those very rights which you claim over us: indeed, they will proclaim that they themselves are the nation, and are therefore bound by no prohibition.'

Such arguments did not affect the fundamental question of how to meet immediate debts. On November 2nd, 1789, the Assembly, by 368 votes to 346, with 40 abstentions, declared all Church property at the nation's disposal. Three hundred deputies of the Right were absent.

Having proclaimed this principle, the Assembly passed a decree on December 19th to the effect that a certain amount of Church property, together with the Crown lands, should be sold to the value of 400 millions. In order that so much property thrown suddenly upon the market should not bring down the price of land and attract too great a proportion of capital, thus upsetting other branches of economic life, it was decided, on March 17th and May 14th, at the suggestion of the Paris Commune, that all the property in question should be handed over to the communes to sell by auction, and that buyers should pay a part of the price within two weeks of the sale and the rest in twelve annual payments. Finally, as the money was required immediately, and sales and annual payments could not be waited for, a decree of April 17th ordered the issue of 400 million *assignats* (bills of exchange), which were declared legal tender, and were guaranteed by the confiscated property that was to be sold.

When part of the current debt and of the interest due on loans had been met by this sum of 400 millions, another 273 millions of payments in arrears were still outstanding. The Assembly continued to abolish now one tax and now another; while of those that theoretically remained, few were, in practice, paid. The deficit on the balance-sheet for 1790 amounted to 350 millions.

From every side came demands for economy. But it was easier to clamour for retrenchment than to enforce it. The hopes held out by the Finance Committee of reducing ordinary expenditure by 60 millions were clearly excessive, and Necker stated that a saving of more than 30 millions could not be effected. An inquiry into the pension list and into grants from the Exchequer resulted in a tremendous scandal. It was shown that during the reign of Louis XVI his two brothers had received gifts amounting to 28 millions; that the Duc de Polignac had in 1782 been given 1,200,000 *livres*, in addition to his pension of 24,000 *livres*, and that the Comtesse de Polignac had a pension of her own amounting to 13,000 *livres*. There were Court officials and favourites who received three, four, even six pensions each, and over 600 recipients of pensions of about ten millions a year. But these revelations and others equally shocking brought no ready money in to the Exchequer; while the suppression or ruthless reduction of many pensions, even of those honestly earned, did not effect a saving of more than twenty millions. The fact that the nobles and clergy had lost their immunity from taxation made little difference to the revenue, because the Assembly had decided that all direct taxes paid by the *tiers état* should be reduced by an equivalent amount.

It was soon necessary, therefore, to have recourse once more to the sale of Church property. On June 9th, 1790, the Assembly decided that all nationally-owned property should be put up for sale; and on September 29th a law was passed providing for the issue of another 800 millions' worth of *assignats*. A part of this huge sum went to meet the deficits of 1790 and 1791; with the rest, the more urgent debts of the State were paid.

Of all the Assembly's measures, the issue of the *assignats* was one that most contributed towards consolidating the new régime and preventing any form of counter-revolution. The *assignats* were, in fact, a paper currency based not on gold but on the security of Church lands. Should a counter-revolution enable the clergy to recover their possessions, the *assignats* would lose their guarantee; therefore their fate depended upon that of the Revolution. Whoever accepted an *assignat*— and everyone had to accept them, since they were legal tender— was committed to the revolutionary cause, if he did not want his money to become worthless through a return to feudal and ecclesiastical rule.

It is true that out of so many millions of revolutionary currency less than half went into liquidation of debt. For the most part it was employed in defraying current expenses and in making up for arrears of taxation. It is easy to liken the actions of the Constituent Assembly to those of a spendthrift, who, having sold his ancestral inheritance, pays off his most pressing debts and the interest on others, while he continues his extravagant way of life. Yet, in view of the social crisis into which France had been plunged after July 1789 through the crass stupidity of the King and the privileged orders, there was nothing else that the Assembly could do. In periods of tranquillity the monarchy had always administered affairs by piling up debts; it had avoided all financial reform and had, in fact, acted with criminal folly. The Assembly now found itself not only burdened with difficulties inherited from the former régime but forced to govern the country at a moment when the collection of taxes had been suspended and all the people's resentment was directed against the old financial system. It could not borrow more money; it did not want to declare a state of bankruptcy; and it had no wish to relinquish control of civil and military administration owing to lack of funds, and so open a way for a return of the old régime. It had no other means of maintaining its authority and concealing its own impotence save that of seizing what capital it could find and of doling it out wherever it was most urgently required.

IV

In abolishing tithe and expropriating ecclesiastical property the Assembly had pledged itself to provide for Church expenses and for the clergy's stipends. This being so, it was obvious that if the Government, by selling nationalized land, had succeeded, on the one hand, in liquidating a part of its debts, thereby saving a corresponding payment of annual interest, it had, on the other, been forced to incur considerable additional expenditure: the amount of which, if confiscation of Church property were to prove really fruitful, would have to be greatly inferior to what had been saved. In other words, the new expenditure on the clergy would have to be considerably less than the Church's former revenue. This object would be impossible to attain so long as the old ecclesiastical organization was allowed to remain intact. The number of clerical posts would have to be reduced and a limit placed upon the income attached to each benefice.

This necessity gave rise to the law of February 13th, 1790, abolishing the religious orders, and the still more famous law of July 12th, of the same year, on Church Establishment (*la constitution civile du clergé*). The latter provided for suppression of the archbishoprics and for the institution of a bishop in each of the eighty-three *départements*; urban centres with fewer than six thousand inhabitants were made into single parishes; the bishops, with the exception of the Bishop of Paris, whose see carried with it emoluments amounting to fifty thousand *livres* a year, were to receive annual stipends of from twelve to twenty thousand *livres*, and the *curés* of from twelve hundred to four thousand. The revenue was thus distributed in equal proportions and total expenditure reduced by half. This reform was justified by the Exchequer's needs and also because it afforded an opportunity not only to end the corrupt and insolent luxury of the higher clergy, but to introduce some order into Church affairs, which were as chaotic as those of the former civil administration. In fact, apart from the obvious unjust discrepancies in income between the higher and lower clergy, it was absurd — so urged the reformers — indeed, it was illogical, that there should be dioceses as extensive as that of Rouen, with 1388 parishes, and others like that of Agde, with only 19; that there should be high ecclesiastical dignitaries with revenues amounting to 248,000 *livres* a year, as at Strasbourg, to 126,000 at Vienne, in the Dauphiné, and to 120,000 at Lyons; while there were dioceses, such as that of Vence, which brought their incumbents no more than 7000 *livres* a year.

Nor was this all: for while financial reasons forced the Assembly to reform the administration of the Church, other reasons of a political nature prompted them to introduce wholesale changes into its hierarchy and discipline. The higher clergy had always shown themselves so tenacious of their feudal privileges that it was clearly necessary to deprive them of the right to nominate their parish priests. Furthermore, it was felt that by allowing Papal intervention in episcopal appointments the way was left wide open for a foreign power, closely allied with conservative interests, to exercise an incalculable and highly dangerous influence upon internal affairs in France. The old centralized administrative hierarchy had been destroyed in order to weaken the power of the King (who, after all, represented only an internal threat to the unity of the nation); was, then, the centralized ecclesiastical organization, extending beyond the nation's frontiers, and ultimately controlled by Rome, to be left intact? The Assembly, influenced by such considerations, laid down, in this same law of July 12th, that henceforth the *curés* should be nominated by the electors of each district, and the bishops by the electors of each *département*. A *curé*, having been elected, would have to appear before his bishop, and a newly-elected bishop before one of the ten archbishops chosen for the purpose, to obtain canonical investiture, after an examination in religious matters; should this be refused, appeal could be made to a lay tribunal which would determine whether rejection were justified or not. The bishops were forbidden to ask for Papal confirmation of an appointment: their nomination was simply to be communicated to the Pope 'as visible head of the Universal Church, in witness of the unity of the faith'.

In passing this law, the majority in the Assembly was not moved, as has been thought, by eighteenth-century philosophic and anti-Christian ideas. The jurists and experts in canon law who framed the new ecclesiastical legislation were almost all Jansenists; they held that the civil authorities had a right to regulate ecclesiastical discipline and wished to give the Gallican Church an organization that should make it independent of Rome. But they were firmly opposed to the philosophic spirit, and persuaded themselves that in the course of national regeneration a civil constitution for the clergy, far from undermining religion, would lead the clergy of France back to 'the discipline of the early Church, and would turn Frenchmen into true Christians'. Several bishops co-operated in working out these new laws, believing that in due time the Holy See's approval would be given them. Those deputies who were free-thinkers or indifferent to religious questions readily supported the work of the Jansenists and reformist clerics, since it accorded with the theory that the Church must be subject to State control and must constitute, in a sense, a branch of the political administration; and also because its disciplinary re-organization would be a useful weapon against any possible attempt at restoring feudal authority. The great majority of deputies had no ulterior anti-religious motives; they considered that they were keeping to their legislative duty if they reformed the external organization of the Church without violating its dogma; thereby bringing it into line with the new administrative and political systems established in France.

The reform, they argued, was not without precedent. Fundamentally, it was only a continuance of the French monarchy's traditional policy against the independence of the Catholic Church. Without going back to the time of Philippe le Bel, it was possible to instance Louis XIV as having promoted the declarations of the Ecclesiastical Assembly in 1682 on the rights of the Gallican Church, and having used them as a weapon against the Pope. The French Kings, in accordance with the Concordat of 1516, always took part in nominating the bishops. Moreover, the monarchy had opposed application in France of certain decrees of the Council of Trent, and it was the King who had expelled the Jesuits from France in 1764, without previous agreement with the Holy See. Louis XVI himself had proclaimed the civil equality of Protestants and Catholics in 1778 without consulting Rome. The only difference between the Assembly's policy and that of the kings lay in the substitution of popular sovereignty for that of the monarchy. And what, in fact, was the latter, in eighteenth-century opinion, but a delegation of popular sovereignty?

It was logical reasoning. But if there were no difference in theory between the actions of former kings and those of the National Assembly, there was a very great change in practice. The kings had encroached, step by step, and almost imperceptibly, upon the Church's rights during many centuries. Each single conquest had appeared as an exception to a religious and disciplinary system the foundations of which remained intact, and had in the end been accepted by the ecclesiastical authorities, who, though in theory unable to make concessions, have always been ready to come to terms with necessity. The policy pursued by the Assembly, on the contrary, was a sudden and wholesale onslaught upon the Church. It repudiated the basic canonical doctrine according to which the civil authority had no jurisdiction whatever in matters concerning the Catholic hierarchy and Church discipline. It made changes in the centuries-old diocesan and parochial division of the country; suppressed all pontifical influence over the Gallican Church by removing the Pope's control over recruitment of religious personnel, together with any means of enforcing respect for his own supremacy in religious matters; and, in destroying the bishops' authority over the parish priests by giving the people power to appoint them, it overset the whole hierarchy of the Church. Like the country's civil administration, the spiritual administration of the Church was completely subjected to the nation's will; and by allowing the people to choose their ministers of religion, the stability of doctrinal observance and the unity of the faith were placed at the mercy of an electorate that included Protestants, Jews, and free-thinkers, and in which even the faithful could not be relied upon always to adhere to the clear-cut official dogma of the Church.

This anti-clerical legislation, however, did not at once provoke such reaction on the Pope's part as might have been expected. At that time the kingdom of France included a third of the whole Catholic population of the world. To condemn the new laws forthwith would have meant assuming responsibility for provoking a schism which, in that over-wrought nation, might well have had serious consequences. Not that the Holy See could legitimize revolutionary theory; but it seemed advisable to gain time and to circumvent difficulties rather than to come into direct conflict with the enemy. The more conciliatory French prelates set about finding canonical *formulae* by means of which the Holy See might 'baptize' the newly-born Civil Constitution. And by seeking subtle interpretations and precedents it seemed that conciliation might indeed be reached without great difficulty. For example, the people's election of their ministers of religion could be interpreted as a presentation of the candidate to his ecclesiastical superiors, before whom, as the Civil Constitution itself laid down, he had to appear in requesting canonical investiture; the electors would be exercising something analogous to the rights of patronage which the Pope had formerly tolerated in the hands of kings, feudal lords and communes. The new diocesan boundaries might be accepted by the Pope as a 'delegation' of authority between neighbouring bishops, in places where parts of a former diocese were transferred to a new one. Ecclesiastical diplomacy has always given proof of inexhaustible *finesse* in compromise, when it has had a motive for showing compliance and good will.

The Pope, in favouring counsels of prudence, was also influenced by dangers now threatening the pontifical domain of Avignon and the Comtat Venaissin. These districts, situated in southern France, had been subject to Papal sovereignty since the fourteenth century. They were badly governed, and were not only a refuge for smugglers and brigands, but a perennial obstacle to communications between Languedoc, Provence, the Dauphiné and the principality of Orange. The kings had for long been tempted to occupy them in order to remove a hot-bed of unrest from the life of the South, but the Pope's moral authority had always prevented such a conquest. The risings that occurred throughout France in the summer of 1789, after the capture of the Bastille, had had repercussions also in this little Papal domain. Most of the inhabitants of Avignon supported the revolution and wanted union with France, while the inhabitants of Carpentras, divided from Avignon by centuries of enmity, were faithful to the Pope. Bitter fighting ensued, in which political principles served as a pretext for the criminal elements of the population to plunder and ravage the countryside.

The revolutionaries of Avignon laid a petition before the National Assembly demanding release from the ecclesiastical yoke. The Assembly, at the session of November 12th, 1789, refused even to discuss the matter. It had no wish to break long-standing treaties or to exploit the difficulties of another government in order to make territorial conquests. Indeed, the lust for conquest, which had prompted the former monarchy to wage so many wars of evil memory, was considered, in those early days of faith and enthusiasm, as an inhuman sentiment that should be purged from the hearts of all who formed the new society based on principles of justice, freedom and brotherhood. On May 22nd, 1790, the Assembly, amidst great enthusiasm, passed an article of the Constitution declaring that the French nation would never wage a war of conquest, and would not employ its forces against the liberty of other peoples.

Disorder in Avignon, however, continued, causing unrest in every neighbouring province. In the end, the city revolutionaries drove the Papal Legate out and set up a new municipal administration, which on June 11th, 1790, demanded union with France. The extremists in the Assembly urged that this request should be complied with, and invoked 'the natural and inalienable right of all peoples' to dispose of their own destinies. If the Pope's subjects voted for union with France, annexation of their country would not represent a conquest, but the recovery of what, in times past, had been wrongfully taken from the nation and handed over to Papal rule. The moderates contested the Avignon municipality's right to speak on behalf of all citizens in the *comtat* and, recalling the treaties between France and the Holy See, maintained that a simultaneous breach of international law and of the constitutional principle renouncing conquest could not be countenanced. The majority, wavering between traditional territorial ambitions presented in a new guise, and newly-adopted philosophic principles that seemed to enjoin respect for the *status quo*, confined itself, on June 17th, 1790, to nominating a commission of inquiry and sending troops to keep watch on the borders of the *comtat*. What inquiries the commission was to set on foot, or what the troops were to watch was not clear; but the Assembly, without realizing it, had taken the first step towards intervention and annexation. Meanwhile, time was gained and open rupture with the Holy See avoided. There were even some who hoped to gain concessions from the Pope over the Civil Constitution, in return for such help as the French Government might render in restoring order in the rebellious cities.

The Pope, on his side, refrained from any open show of intransigence over the religious question, being unwilling to provoke a break that would cause the Assembly's intervention in Avignon affairs. He therefore confined himself to issuing a secret Allocution on March 29th, 1790, condemning as impious the Declaration of Rights, the abolition of religious orders, and in general, the Assembly's whole policy in so far as it aimed at subordinating Church to State. When it appeared that application of the Civil Constitution was imminent he sent the King a Papal Brief, also secret, entreating him to refuse his sanction to so schismatic and heretical a measure. In public, he maintained an attitude of reserve.

v

The more uncompromising prelates, however, and those royalists who were most active, lost no time in organizing energetic opposition to the new ecclesiastical laws, in a hope of forcing the Pope to come out openly on their side. The lower clergy, who until now had favoured the revolutionary cause, were deeply perturbed. The Assembly had improved their economic condition by giving the parish priests a minimum stipend of 1200 *livres* a year, but the upheaval in ecclesiastical discipline troubled the conscience of all sincere believers. Anxiety increased when the Assembly refused to accept a proposal made by the Right, on April 13th, 1790, to declare Catholicism the State religion.

In Alsace the bishops ordered prayers to be said, as in times of national calamity, and publicly condemned the 'predatory laws' dispossessing the clergy. In southern France, at Montauban and Nîmes, the age-old hatred between Protestants and Catholics flared up and led to riots and bloodshed during the whole period from April to June.

Agrarian disorders still continued here and there. The army's mood was openly mutinous, and in April 1790 revolutionary forces and aristocratic regiments came to blows at Lille.

The lesser nobility, too, went over to the cause of counter-revolution in the spring of 1790. Until then, only the great lords had been directly and seriously affected by the destruction of the *châteaux* and the campaign against Court extravagance. The humbler provincial nobles had remained uncertain which cause to espouse, since the loss of their feudal dues had been fully made good by the suppression of tithe, and their hostility towards the great aristocrats was so pronounced that they were ready to welcome anything injuring the higher ranks. Two of the Assembly's decrees brought their uncertainties to an end. By the first, passed on March 15th, 1790, the rights of primogeniture and of male succession in feudal inheritance were abolished, and all heirs were given equal rights, without distinction of age or sex. With the second, enacted on June 29th, titles of nobility were suppressed. It meant an end to the whole centuries-old system of the feudal family, and a challenge to all the pride of the old nobility: the aristocracy, as a class, were to disappear, submerged by the plebeian flood, just as the clergy had disappeared as an independent class by being absorbed into the new elective civil hierarchy.

But a great majority of the people still remained favourable towards the revolutionary parties. Abolition of tithe, the end of feudal dues and the breakdown in tax-collecting, represented an annual saving for the rural classes of more than 300 millions, and freed the land from innumerable obstacles to agrarian development. High food-prices made such development a matter of urgency, and the sale by auction of Church lands was awaited with impatience. An enthusiasm for work and an optimistic faith in the future were spreading throughout the countryside. The beneficial effects of the revolution had not so quickly been apparent in urban centres, where the crisis of 1787 and 1788 had continued well into 1790: but here too, hatred for the privileged classes and hopes of benefiting from the sale of Church property made almost every city a centre of revolutionary resistance.

In the spring of 1790, the electors were called upon to set up new communal and departmental administrative bodies. Middle-class representatives were elected almost everywhere. Organized on military lines in the National Guard and masters of the local administrative bodies, they found in the novel exercise of power all such satisfaction to their *amour propre* as had been denied them when authority belonged to the privileged orders. Revolutionary faith and enthusiasm had its outlet in fêtes, in swearing oaths of fidelity and in taking part in the municipal, departmental, ecclesiastical and military elections; in other words, through full exercise of those powers which had passed from the absolute monarch to the nation.

To gain some idea of the state of exaltation prevailing at this time — when, in fact, the first great internal crisis of the revolutionary movement was maturing — it is enough to recall the Fête of Federation on July 14th, 1790. These '*fédérations*', or meetings of voluntary patriotic associations, had lately increased, and on June 5th the Assembly, to encourage them, had accepted a suggestion by the Paris commune that on the anniversary of the Fall of the Bastille a local Federation should be held in the chief town of every district and *département*, and a National Federation in Paris, to celebrate the indissoluble unity of all Frenchmen. While the provincial National Guards and land and sea forces were choosing those who were to attend the ceremony and take the civic oath on their behalf, from eight to ten thousand labourers were at work in Paris, excavating and levelling the Champ de Mars, and raising a high terraced ramp round it to accommodate the crowd of spectators. Since it was feared that the work would not be finished in time, two hundred thousand citizens hastened to the scene of operations to give voluntary help: monks and soldiers, well-dressed gentlemen and ragged beggars, rich *bourgeoises* and women of the people, workmen of every kind and peasants from the neighbouring countryside led by their *maires* or their *curés*. All these people laboured together for a week at excavating the ground, filling up ditches and making roads, singing: 'he that is raised up shall be humbled, and he that is humble shall be raised up'. Meanwhile the provincial *fédérés* were arriving at the capital in their thousands, having been not only enthusiastically greeted, but fed and housed free of charge upon their way.

On July 14th, two days after the Assembly had ended its debate on the Civil Constitution of the Clergy, a great altar was set up on the raised platform in the centre of the Champ de Mars, now transformed into a colossal amphitheatre. Fourteen thousand representatives of the provincial National Guard, from eleven to twelve thousand delegates from the army and navy, and the whole Paris National Guard, surrounded the altar. The King and Queen, with the little Dauphin and the rest of the Royal family, attended the ceremony. All the deputies of the Assembly were present. More than a hundred and sixty thousand spectators crowded the sides of the arena, and a still larger crowd took up its stand behind them. It was pouring with rain. But in those days little heed was paid to discomfort, and it would have taken more than rain to damp the general enthusiasm. After the Bishop of Autun, surrounded by about two hundred priests clad in white, with tricolour sashes, had said mass and blessed the banners, the National Guards and deputies swore loyalty to the Nation, the Law and the King; Louis XVI took an oath of fealty to the Constitution; and while the Queen held up the little heir to the throne as though to associate him with his father's words, four hundred thousand voices, to the roll of drums and the roar of cannon, joined in, shouting 'Long live the King, long live the Nation!' An ingenuous display of a people's hopes and illusions, to which Talleyrand, the cynical Bishop of Autun, added an ironic note by celebrating the mass in which he did not believe and in taking the oath that he was so soon to break. The clamorous joy of so great a crowd could not lighten the heavy hearts of all those on the royal dais. Yet it expressed a whole nation's hopes, and it was to be an ill day for the King when he was accused of betraying them.

Naturally, once the celebrations were over, disputes and disorder broke out again. Indeed, they became intensified. The soldiers, returning to their provincial regiments from the Fête of Federation, imported 'patriotic' propaganda into quarters which their officers had until then succeeded in keeping free from contagion. In August 1790, there was a mutiny at Nancy; the Marquis de Bouillé restored order with severe repressive measures, but discipline was already undermined throughout the army, and no military leader could any longer depend upon obedience from the rank and file.

In the Comtat Venaissin tension daily increased. The Pope was too weak and too far away to restore order; but his right to reject interference in his domains condemned the French Government to inaction. Once again, on August 27th, 1790, the matter came before the Assembly. But the deputies dared not decide on intervention.

Confiscation of Church property and the closing of all monasteries and religious foundations affected many interests and caused much unrest. Moreover, it gave full play to reactionary propaganda. On August 17th, 1790, twenty thousand royalist National Guards met at the castle of Jalès, in southern France, with the Cross as their banner, and nominated a permanent committee, declaring that 'they would not lay down their arms until they had reinstated the King in his glory, the clergy in their property, the nobles in their privileges, and the *parlements* in their ancient functions'. The moderates among the clergy, perplexed by the silence of Rome, were losing ground, and soon found themselves in no position to effect any kind of conciliatory move.

Irritated by such unexpected resistance, the Assembly decided on November 20th, 1790, to send French troops into the Comtat Venaissin to keep order. This was not only a step towards annexation, but open rupture of relations with the Pope. On November 27th the Assembly decreed that all priests in office must swear loyalty to the Constitution, including the new ecclesiastical laws: those who refused were to be regarded as having resigned their livings and would be punished for 'disturbing the peace' if they attempted to continue in their former functions.

On January 4th, 1791, the clerical deputies in the Assembly were enjoined to carry out this law themselves. The public galleries were packed, and an excited crowd surrounded the Assembly hall crying 'Death to those who refuse the oath!' The Bishop of Agen rose to declare, with the perfect manners of an aristocrat, that 'he had no regrets for office or for wealth; but he would grieve at the loss of his colleagues' esteem, which he hoped to deserve, and he therefore begged the Assembly to accept the expression of his sorrow at being unable to take the oath required of him'. The parish priest of Puy-Miélan, who was called next, replied that 'he took pride in following his bishop's example, as the deacon Laurence had followed Pope Sixtus, his pastor, to his death'. The Right applauded warmly. The Left, furious, insisted that those who were called upon should simply declare whether they wished to take the oath or not, without explanations. In order not to prolong so discordant a sitting the Assembly decided that all remaining clerical deputies should be asked collectively whether they would take the oath or not, and that those who promised to do so should have their names recorded in the Minutes. The Bishop of Poitiers, applauded by the Left in the belief that he was about to take the oath, rose to speak: 'Gentlemen,' he began, 'I am seventy years old; I have been a bishop for thirty-five years, and I have tried to do such good as has been within my power. Though bowed down with age and infirmity, I will not dishonour my grey hairs. I will not take an oath . . .' He was not allowed to continue, and could only add: 'I await my fate in a spirit of penitence.' Out of forty-nine bishops, only two took the oath, and two-thirds of the *curés* refused. Of the French clergy as a whole only seven bishops, and about half the *curés* swore loyalty to the Constitution; but many *curés* afterwards regretted having done so, and retracted.

The French clergy's attitude led Pius VI at last to make a public pronouncement on March 10th, 1791, condemning the Civil Constitution of the Clergy as schismatic and heretical; and with a Papal Brief of April 13th he suspended *a divinis* all those priests who had taken the oath and who did not retract within forty days.

Thus open war broke out between the clerics who remained loyal to the Pope and those who supported the Civil Constitution. The former were secure in their moral influence over the faithful, especially in country districts; the latter, under canonical law, were acting in a sinful and unlawful manner, but they enjoyed the support of the revolutionary parties and recognition by the political and administrative authorities.

Henceforth the higher clergy and nobility were able to relegate their own worldly interests in the conflict to a secondary place, and to appear before the world as defenders of the Catholic faith and of Church discipline.

From what happened in the Assembly it is easy to imagine the effect produced in the provinces by the law of November 27th, especially among the peasants. Violent outbreaks occurred in Alsace, Brittany and the south. All those formidable means of moral pressure— the preaching of sermons, the influence of the confessional and the withholding of the sacraments— which the clergy know so well how to bring to bear when they find themselves engaged in any serious struggle were now employed against the revolutionaries. Religious schism thus became involved with the already bitter passions of the civil conflict.

VI

The religious crisis finally roused the King from his torpor.

In May 1790 he had decided to enter into secret relations with Mirabeau. A fundamental element in their understanding was Mirabeau's explicit refusal to countenance any attempt to restore the former régime. The permanence and electoral nature of the National Assembly, the new administrative division of the kingdom, free justice and liberty of the press, ministerial responsibility, the sale of Church property, the end not only of feudal rights, privileges and immunity from taxation, but of the *parlements*— all these were reforms, Mirabeau insisted, which it would be madness to touch: the country would never renounce them, even after a long and bloody war waged with foreign support for the King. In compensation, unity and authority must be restored to the central government, together with all such powers as were necessary to enforce the law, maintain order, and provide for national defence. The Assembly should only pass laws and proposals for taxation: it would therefore be necessary to rescind all those decrees with which, in its mistrust of the King and his ministers, it had disorganized the civil, judicial and military administration of the country.

The undertaking, Mirabeau admitted, was undoubtedly difficult, owing both to Court blunders and revolutionary passions. But the radical destruction accomplished by the Assembly had by this time so compromised the interests of the commons— who were fundamentally conservative and had only become revolutionaries out of desperation — that were the King to resolve upon accepting the social conquests of the new ruling class, the latter would gladly throw over the Assembly, and, in rallying to his side, would not even grudge him additional powers. The Assembly, meanwhile, should be allowed to continue its excesses, for by so doing it brought discredit upon itself. If, the ground being thus well-prepared, civil war were finally to break out between the King and the Assembly, the monarchy would have nothing to fear, so long as it could count on the loyalty of the middle-classes.

As the Fête of Federation drew near, he advised the King and Queen to seize this opportunity of displaying sympathy for the new order of things. They ought, he said, to take advantage of the presence of so many citizens from the provinces — much less extreme in their views than those of Paris — to turn the national ceremony into one of dynastic allegiance and to strengthen the bonds between the nation and the monarchy, in its new and constitutional form.

Necker, according to Mirabeau, was 'a clock always behind the time'; 'he neither knew what he could do, what he wanted to do, nor what he ought to do'. He and his colleagues in the Government merely paralysed all initiative. They must be sent packing. But first they should be discredited, so that the King, in dismissing them of his own free will and appointing more popular ministers, might raise his own prestige. For this reason Mirabeau launched a violent campaign against Necker and his colleagues. On September 3rd, Necker had to resign, amidst the indifference of all parties. One by one the remaining ministers, except Montmorin, were forced to follow his example.

At the same time, although convinced that the *assignats* were 'a circulating plague' and that their issue was 'armed robbery', Mirabeau made two powerful speeches (prepared for him by his collaborator, Reybaz) in the Assembly, supporting the proposal for a second issue of 800 millions. He explained to the King that this capital would represent a great source of strength to an energetic Minister, in enabling him to survive the crisis without resorting to further borrowing or to increased taxation.

To prepare the ground for the moment when he might exploit his favour with the populace for his own political ends, Mirabeau continued, in public, to stress his revolutionary beliefs, vied with the triumvirs of the Left— until then omnipotent in the Jacobin Club— in his democratic opinions, did his utmost to discredit Lafayette and made every effort to isolate the revolutionary leaders from contact with the army. By the end of 1790 he had become the idol of Paris. On November 30th he was elected President of the Jacobins' Club: on January 17th, 1791, commander of a battalion of National Guards; on January 20th, he entered the Paris departmental administration; and on the 29th, he was elected by a great majority to preside over that very National Assembly which in his own heart he intended to ruin.

The rock on which the Assembly must be led to founder was the religious strife stirred up by the law on the Civil Constitution of the Clergy. This anomalous situation, Mirabeau explained to the King, must be turned to advantage: on the one hand the Catholics, and in particular the rural population, must be encouraged in their resistance to the new law; and on the other, the Assembly must be spurred on to yet further outrage against the Catholic faith and even induced to pass laws allowing divorce, the marriage of priests and civil equality for Jews. When the scandal had caused the Assembly to become universally unpopular and complete social and political chaos prevailed, the King must leave Paris and take refuge in the provinces. From there, protected by Bouillé's troops and with the malcontents of all parties supporting him, he should dissolve the Assembly and summon another to re-establish the Catholic religion and the authority of the Government throughout France. By approving the law on the clergy's oath to the Constitution the Assembly had committed itself on the religious question and could not now turn back. The moment for action against it was approaching.

The one real danger which the King at all costs must avoid, according to Mirabeau, was any international complication. Were a war to break out at such a moment of military and administrative weakness, the King— in the only too probable event of a disaster— would become 'an object of universal hatred and suspicion'. France needed above all else a long period of peace to build up her internal administration and to consolidate the political power of the commons. When she had succeeded in stabilizing the new order of things, her liberal institutions would become

a powerful centre of attraction for the people of every neighbouring country. The monarchy would thus acquire immense
influence in Europe, and without striking a blow the frontiers of
France might well be extended to the Rhine and the Alps. War,
on the contrary, would at such a moment be fatal for the monarchy, and would lead to the collapse of the Revolution and to
military dictatorship. 'He knew everything and foresaw everything', wrote Madame de Staël of Mirabeau in her *Considérations
sur la Révolution Française.*

Apart from their cynicism, these tactics were altogether too
involved and contradictory for the King, with his limited mental
powers, or the Queen, with her prejudices, to adopt. Mirabeau,
whose private life and political past were far from reassuring —
who pretended, in secret, to serve the Court, but in public,
despite occasional support for monarchical ideas, never disavowed revolutionary violence — was not a man to be understood
by the two hapless prisoners in the Tuileries. In their eyes he was
merely an unscrupulous intriguer in whom it would be unwise
to trust and who would as readily betray them as he was now
betraying the revolutionaries; just as, renegade noble that he
was, he had been a traitor to his King in joining the revolution.
Moreover, he had deprived himself of all moral authority by
accepting a monthly allowance of 6000 *livres* from the King,
who was also paying his debts and had promised him a million
livres at the closing down of the Assembly. It was all very fine for
Mirabeau to tell himself that payment by the Court was not
bribery since, having renounced none of his ideas, he was leading
the King to adopt them; or to say, 'A man like me can accept a
hundred thousand crowns, but cannot be bought for such a sum.'
In the eyes of those who paid, he was selling himself; and the
transaction lowered the value of all his advice and transformed
him into a political turncoat whose pockets the King and Queen
were ready to fill simply for fear of having him as an adversary.

But in any event, agreement between the King and Mirabeau
on the religious question was impossible. Louis XVI had accepted
without demur every other decree of the Assembly, for he wanted
to be considered its prisoner, and nothing suited his lazy temper-
ament better than the attitude of a victim forced to sanction revolutionary enormities. 'One might just as well talk of matters

concerning the Chinese Emperor,' said one of his ministers, 'as discuss affairs with that inert being.' 'What is to be expected of a man,' wrote the American Morris, 'who in such a situation can eat, drink, sleep soundly, laugh, and enjoy the best health in the world?' But when the law on the Clergy was presented to him, Louis was appalled; his religious conscience was deeply troubled and he was forcibly roused from the fatalism into which he had slipped after the events of October. This law, which he was asked to approve, was not simply a political one; it was an ecclesiastical law, the sanctioning of which would involve him in an attempt against the unity of the faith, and would lead the nation into heresy, schism and the horrors of religious war. Terror-stricken at the dangers that threatened him and his family if he withheld his approval, yet loathing the diabolical measure that jeopardized the eternal salvation of his soul, he sanctioned the law on the clergy's oath on December 26th only after long and anguished uncertainty. But from that moment, the idea of escape, of saving his family and having done with the revolutionaries, took possession of him. Marie-Antoinette urged him on, for she wanted her children removed to safety; detesting the revolutionaries, whose hatred for herself she was well aware of, she longed to avenge the affronts that she had suffered at their hands.

But how? According to Mirabeau, the religious struggle itself would cause the forces required for re-establishing order to appear at the side of the monarchy, even though at the cost of civil war; he regarded nothing as more disastrous for the King and the nation than foreign intervention. For Louis, it was a question of preventing religious anarchy from continuing to torment France; but he lacked the forces to suppress disorder. No other way remained open to him, therefore, than to beg for that foreign aid the dangers of which Mirabeau had made every effort, in vain, to convey to him.

For this reason, Mirabeau's secret advice, in contrast, as it always was, not only with his public actions but also with the personal leanings of the King and Queen, fell upon deaf ears. The Fête of Federation passed without a single word from the King that might have touched the people's hearts, apart from the Constitutional Oath, which he could not refuse to take. After the dissolution of Necker's ministry Louis appointed another government of nonentities, no less incompetent than those driven out by Mirabeau. On November 26th, 1790, the King, without Mirabeau's knowledge, empowered the Baron de Breteuil, who had taken refuge in Switzerland after the fall of the Bastille, to open negotiations with friendly Courts for the restoration of order in France.

Thus, while Mirabeau was still doing his best to stimulate revolutionary passions so that the King might regain popularity by accepting the reforms and then restoring order, Louis never co-ordinated his actions with those of the revolutionary leader, and the latter's conduct only intensified the dangers of the situation.

'The Court!' wrote Mirabeau to Lamarck. 'What vacillation, what cowardice, what culpable negligence; what a grotesque assemblage of out-of-date ideas and new projects, of petty prejudices and childish inspirations, of wilfulness and lack of will, of abortive loves and hates! And when they have failed to follow any of my advice, when they have refused to profit from even one of my victories, when they have taken advantage of none of my achievements, they complain, they declare that I have not been able to help them, that they cannot count on me; and all because I will not thoughtlessly ruin myself by supporting ideas, schemes and people whose success would prove disastrous to themselves before all else!'

What would have become of Mirabeau — confronted, as he was, by suspicion and accusations, the shameful truth of which none knew better than himself — if his exasperation, his frenzied and consuming work, and the brutish pleasures in which he tried to drown his agony and discouragement had not struck him down in the prime of his stormy life: if he had lived, for instance, till the flight of the royal family from Paris had revealed the gulf between his ideas and the King's? Induced by the immorality of his private life to abandon the high road of politics, he had lost his way in the devious paths of intrigue; what, then, would have been his position, between the Court, which had pretended to use him without understanding him, and the revolutionaries who had followed him unaware of his real purpose? The brief and violent malady that carried him off on the morning of April 2nd, 1791, ended all the conflicts and dangers in which step by step he had become involved. He disappeared in the tragic last throes of a world that would not let itself be saved, after a life compounded of brilliance and baseness, of glory and dishonour.

CHAPTER VI

THE FLIGHT TO VARENNES

I. Repercussions of the French Revolution in Europe. — II. Attitude of foreign governments: revolutionary proselytism and the *emigrés*. — III. Revolutionary agitation in the spring of 1791. — IV. Reaction against the democratic and Jacobin movements. — V. The Flight to Varennes and the Massacre of the Champ de Mars. — VI. Revision of the Constitution.

I

BY instructing the Baron de Breteuil to agree with friendly foreign courts upon measures for restoring order in France, Louis XVI and Marie-Antoinette were at the same time inviting these sovereigns to protect themselves from the rising tide of revolution, which now threatened every one of them.

Towards the end of the eighteenth century, indeed, social and political strife not unlike that which produced the Revolution in France existed throughout Europe. It broke out in all feudal and priest-ridden countries, where taxation was oppressive, royal courts irresponsible and extravagant, or military expenditure out of all proportion to the population's resources; where the Exchequers faced continual deficits, and industry, commerce or agriculture were impeded by trade-guilds, restrictions, monopolies and feudal rights; in fact, wherever the citizens were exposed to arbitrary rule and ill-regulated or unjust laws.

France was, in fact — however paradoxical the statement may seem at first — better off than the rest. It was precisely because of the more favourable conditions prevailing in the social life of France that the revolutionary crisis broke out there rather than elsewhere in Europe. The French middle-classes — richer, more educated, in closer contact with the higher ranks of society than were those of other European nations, and divided from the nobility by less marked differences in their way of life — were more acutely conscious of the injustice that excluded them from political influence and honours; and being possessed of moral and material strength that others lacked as yet, they were first to win that place in public life to which they felt entitled. Furthermore, in other countries, as for instance in Russia, Germany, Denmark, or Hungary, the peasants, utterly ground down by feudal serfdom, were too wretched to grasp such ideas as those of civil equality and liberty. In France, on the contrary, every peasant proprietor felt himself a free man on the piece of ground he had won by the sweat of his brow: and it was to defend himself from what remained of feudal tyranny, and his property from ruthless taxation, that he had recourse to revolution. In no other country, moreover, had the lay and ecclesiastical nobles, as in France, deserted the provinces and flocked round the central authority in a scramble for favours; and there was nowhere so deep an abyss between the different social classes as that which the French monarchy, with its centralized State control, had created by removing local administration from the nobility's hands. Elsewhere, the nobles, brutal and semi-barbarous, lived on their fiefs, carried out their political functions, administered justice, and provided for the common weal. If the peasants were oppressed, they also felt themselves protected by the rough rule of their lord; and the noble's duties were some justification for his privileges. Finally, in France alone had the capital city acquired such importance as to become the centre of the nation's entire political and administrative life; so that, when the revolutionary forces had gained mastery over Paris, the whole country too succumbed to them. In other nations administrative centralization was as yet rudimentary or entirely lacking, and provincial life remained more or less autonomous; unrest that arose in one area did not necessarily disturb the rest, and disorder in the principal centre had little effect on the provinces, where those who carried on the administration were not forced to wait for all orders, assistance, reproofs and payment to come from the capital. In France, widespread trouble in the provinces had an almost paralysing effect on the capital; while disorder in Paris was a mortal blow to the whole political organism and had repercussions throughout the country.

But although the elements necessary for a revolutionary outbreak existed in France alone, men's minds were troubled everywhere by a sense of unrest and a desire for change. A European revolutionary literature had grown up that was, in part, a product of disturbed conditions in each country, but was also, in a large measure, an importation from France. This had been facilitated not only by the geographical position of France, but by the easily intelligible language; and by the frequent journeys abroad of French men of letters and of cultured persons of all nationalities to France. 'The whole of Europe', wrote Voltaire, 'is a great republic of cultured minds.' Italy and Germany, in particular, were conquered by the ideas of the *philosophes*, physiocrats and encyclopaedists, long before their own revolutionary wars broke out. The Italian writers, Genovesi, Beccaria, Verri, Parini, Galiani, Filangieri, and the Germans Lessing, Pestalozzi, Kant, Schiller, Goethe, Fichte, and Herder — to mention only the greatest — cannot be properly understood if isolated from that great European intellectual movement which had its most active centre in France.

'All Europe', de Tocqueville wrote, 'resembled a military camp that, when roused at dawn, is a scene of confusion until the way is lit by the rising sun. An internal impetus of unknown origin seemed to shake the whole social structure and to throw ideas and customs into the melting-pot; everyone felt it impossible that things should remain as they were, but no one knew where the crash would come. Europe had the appearance of a huge tottering mass about to fall.'

When, in this atmosphere of hope and aspiration the French Revolution broke out, it was enthusiastically greeted by all who longed for change. The years 1789 and 1790 were years of enthusiasm, acclamation, intoxication, for cultivated Europeans. In Germany, Kant saluted the triumph of reason; von Humboldt went to France to attend in person the inauguration of the new era; Klopstock declared that he wished he had a hundred voices with which to celebrate the birth of liberty; Hegel, Schelling, and Hölderlin, when students at Göttingen, planted a tree to commemorate July 14th. When news reached Petersburg that the Bastille had fallen, 'Frenchmen, Russians, Danes, Germans, Englishmen and Dutchmen embraced and congratulated one another in the streets, as though they had been released from chains'. Alfieri dedicated an ode to the fall of the Bastille, and made a pilgrimage himself to the place where the gloomy fortress had once stood.

'France,' wrote Pietro Verri, 'will give a sense of freedom to all Europe. Everyone will compare his own yoke with the liberty that lies at hand. Oppression will no longer be tolerated. The people, aware of their strength, will sooner or later follow the example of the French.'

Wherever the circumstances were favourable, popular risings and political conflicts were not slow to appear. Riots broke out here and there in Savoy and Switzerland. All the small German states along the left bank of the Rhine showed signs of intense unrest. In August 1789, the Prince-Bishop of Liège was forced to leave his city and take refuge at Trèves. The Austrian Empire, shaken to its foundations by the despotic and anti-clerical policy of Joseph II, gave signs of breaking up; nobles and ecclesiastics in Hungary, Transylvania, Bohemia and Galicia were all threatening rebellion. In Belgium, the Emperor succeeded in maintaining order only by means of ruthless repression; but on October 23rd, 1789, three thousand refugees re-crossed the frontier, defeated the imperial troops and entered Brussels, where, on January 10th, 1790, the free 'United States of Belgium' were proclaimed. In Ireland, the Catholic population was rising against the English. In Holland the prosperous commercial *bourgeoisie* (the 'Patriotic' party) and adherents of the democratic party, suppressed in 1787 by the Stadtholder William V with armed intervention by Prussia, took heart again and began to stir up agitation in secret and to make seditious agreements with exiles outside the country. In Tuscany, the ignorant and superstitious populace, which had already risen at Prato against Leopold's ecclesiastical reforms in 1778, rioted again, in 1790, at Pistoia, Leghorn and in the Val-dinievole against freedom of commerce in agricultural produce. The Venetian Republic, which had hardly emerged from the agitation set on foot by Carlo Contarini and Giorgio Pisani for reform of the Constitution (1790), was pursuing an uneasy course; undermined by the hostility of its subject cities, and without arms or alliances, it was a tempting prey to its neighbours. In Sweden, the nobility, brought to heel by Gustavus III after a *coup d'état* in 1772, was champing at the bit. In the Polish Diet, which met at Warsaw on October 6th, 1788, the 'Patriots' were fiercely con-testing the pro-Russian party in order to strengthen and modernize the country's social, administrative and political structure and to secure it against fresh dismemberment such as that of 1772, by curbing the nobles' power, strengthening that of the Crown and improving conditions for the commercial classes and rural serfs.

These contemporary and, in their external manifestations, inter-dependent movements differed profoundly from one another in character. Each country had reached a different stage of social and political development and had its own internal problems to solve. It therefore responded in its own way, and in accordance with local conditions, to the revolutionary influences by which all were affected. In France and the Rhineland the middle-classes were struggling to free themselves from oppression by the privileged orders. In the countries owing allegiance to the House of Austria, and in Sweden, the conflict was between rulers who supported reform and feudal lords who opposed all change: a situation similar to that in France under the ministers Calonne and Brienne. In Poland, an attempt was being made, after the nobles' defeat, to set up a centralized authority resembling that which Richelieu, Mazarin and Louis XIV had established a century and a half earlier in France, and which the National Assembly had only just succeeded in destroying. But revolutionary *bourgeois*, reactionary nobles, Polish patriots favouring centralized government, and Belgian supporters of local independence, were all, in fighting for their own ends, convinced that they were on the side of absolute justice. All paraded the same philosophic maxims, all invoked the rights of mankind in their own defence, and all expressed the most varied and contradictory of aspirations in French revolutionary language. It was no wonder that every ruling prince and respons-ible minister felt a sense of unknown, approaching doom. So that while on the one hand they took hasty measures against the spirit of rebellion that was breaking out within their own borders, on the other they began to ask themselves whether it would not be wise to supplement such isolated action by seeking a general alliance of all States, in face of the common danger.

II

Reasons for war between Europe and France were not lacking.

The question of Avignon and the Comtat Venaissin offered a pretext, were one needed, for intervention in defence of the Pope. Another that might easily develop into cause for war was that of the Alsatian feudal princes.

In the Treaty of Westphalia, of 1648, under which the House of Austria and the princes of the Holy Roman Empire had ceded Alsace to France, the sovereign rights that the King of France might exercise over those princes who, though confederate members of the Holy Roman Empire, held a part of their domains in Alsace, had never been clearly determined. Louis XIV had claimed that they were his subjects, in virtue of the lands they owned within the French frontiers, and obtained recognition of this theory by the Empire in the Treaty of Ryswick. But although the German princes, under this treaty, renounced their attributes of full sovereignty, he was forced to confirm all the privileges and lesser feudal rights that they had enjoyed when Alsace had been part of the Empire.

These privileges, like those of the French nobles, were swept away by the anti-feudal decrees of August 1789, the confiscation of Church property and the new administrative system of France, which thus completed the work begun by Louis XIV. But since these reforms conflicted with the Treaty of Ryswick they revived the old question at issue between France and the Empire. The National Assembly tried to avoid an open clash, and on October 28th, 1790, authorized an approach by the Government to individual German princes with a view to compensating them for such injury as they might suffer in Alsace from the reforms. At the same time they affirmed the principle that 'within the French dominions no sovereignty exists other than that of the nation'.

'The Alsatian people,' proclaimed Merlin de Douai during the discussion, 'has clearly shown its desire to become one with France. What do they or the French people care about compacts made with the aim of uniting them in the days of despotism? Their unity has not come about owing to these conventions. The Alsatian people is joining the French by its own wish, and this alone preserves and legitimizes the union.'

In coming to terms with the French Government, the Alsatian princes would have given their sanction to the theory of national sovereignty, in conformity with which the Assembly had despoiled them; they would have recognized the abolition of feudalism as legitimate, even outside France; they would have given their approval, in advance, to anything their German subjects might attempt in imitation of the French revolutionaries, and they would

have torn up the charter of their rights in Germany as well as in
Alsace. Louis XVI, by means of a secret envoy, urged them not to
give way. They thereupon protested against violation of the
treaties, refused to offer any concessions to the French Government, and denied the right of individual action to those among
them who, out of greed or lack of money, were disposed to compromise. They proclaimed that, since France had broken the
Treaty of Ryswick, the Empire was no longer bound by the Treaties
of Westphalia; and they asserted the Empire's right to Alsace,
invoking intervention by those reigning monarchs who were
guarantors of the treaties — chief of whom was the Emperor himself. Thus, not only the three hundred princes of the Holy Roman
Empire, but the Emperor, the King of Prussia and the King of
Sweden became involved in the dispute. The ancient rights of
feudalism as personified in the princes, and the new conception
of the rights of the people represented by the French *bourgeoisie*,
thus encountered one another in the field of international relations,
and complicated the question at issue between the French social
classes by an external question between the new France and the
old Europe.

Fortunately for the French revolutionaries, the reigning
monarchs of Europe were too much concerned with their own
problems between 1789 and 1791 to think of making war on behalf
of the Pope or the Alsatian feudal lords. Their attention was
chiefly claimed by the war that Austria and Russia had been
waging ever since 1787 along the lower Danube and the Black
Sea against Turkey. The British Government were apprehensive
of too great an expansion of Austrian and Russian power in the
Balkans; while the King of Prussia hoped that eastern complications might produce a favourable opportunity for armed mediation
on his part between the belligerents, to his own advantage.
England and Prussia, meanwhile, were urging Gustavus III of
Sweden to attack the Russian Baltic provinces, and encouraging
patriots in the Polish Diet to throw off the yoke imposed upon
their country by Catherine II, at the treaty of 1772. With the
Austro-Russian war against Turkey, therefore, were interlinked a
war between Sweden and Russia in the Baltic, a war between
Sweden and Denmark (Russia's ally) on the western frontiers of
Sweden, Anglo-Prussian intervention in favour of Sweden against

Denmark, anti-Russian manifestations by the patriotic majority in the Polish Diet, revolution in Belgium, and a revolt of the Hungarian overlords, which distracted Joseph II from his war against Turkey. And finally, to all these conflicts was added the threat of war between England and Spain for possession of the Bay of Nootka in California. Who, amidst such confusion, could trouble about the King of France, the Pope and the petty princes of the Holy Roman Empire?

But on February 20th, 1790, Joseph II died. His successor, Leopold of Tuscany, a clear-sighted and level-headed man, skilled in the arts of compromise, threatened to cede Belgium to France, and thus detached England from Prussia. Taking advantage of the readiness always shown by Frederick William of Prussia to change sides and of his resentment at England's desertion, he induced him to come to an agreement on the preservation of the *status quo* in the East (Treaty of Reichenbach, July 27th, 1790). Having made sure of Prussia and England, he left Catherine of Russia to fend for herself, and on September 19th, 1790, opened peace negotiations with the Turks by the armistice of Giurgevo, which led to the Treaty of Sistova (August 4th, 1791). Meanwhile he revoked the reforms that had roused the Hungarian nobles to rebellion, and pacified the country. He then intervened in Belgium, and in a few days (November 22nd-December 2nd, 1790) succeeded in re-establishing his authority. In the meantime, Gustavus III of Sweden, weary of so long and fruitless a war, and left in the lurch by both English and Prussians, had made his peace with Russia, by the Treaty of Verelä, on August 14th, 1790. England, too, had come to an agreement with Spain on the question of Nootka in October 1790. At the beginning of 1791, therefore, Catherine of Russia was left alone to continue hostilities against the Turks. To all appearance, the Emperor Leopold and the King of Prussia, the King of Sweden, the King of England, the King of Spain and the King of Sardinia, indeed all the monarchs of the earth, had now plenty of time at their disposal for helping the French royal family in their distress.

If words alone could save men from destruction, Louis XVI would soon have found deliverance.

The most generous was Catherine II of Russia, who fulminated against the Paris revolutionaries and their crimes, exhorting all the powers of heaven and earth to rescue the unhappy King and Queen and put an end to anarchy in France. But in effect, neither the French royal family nor the suppression of anarchy mattered one whit to her. Her wish was to engage the Emperor and the King of Prussia in a war in the west while she set her affairs in order as best she might in the east: 'I am doing my utmost', she wrote, 'to spur on the courts of Vienna and Berlin to become entangled in French affairs, so that I can have my hands free.' Meanwhile, she continued her warfare with the Turks, and concentrated large forces on the frontiers of Poland. 'Each one of us,' she wrote enthusiastically to Vienna, 'will make his counter-revolution: the Germans at Paris and the Russians at Warsaw.'

Leopold II was too wary a politician to let Catherine fish alone in the troubled waters of the orient; he therefore delayed the conclusion of peace negotiations with the Turks as long as possible. As to Polish affairs, he had repudiated his predecessor's agreement with Catherine II, and being now a friend of the patriots, was, like Frederick William of Prussia before him, inciting them to resist the enemy from the east. At his instigation, the majority in the Diet transformed Poland's elective monarchy into an hereditary one on May 3rd, 1791, in favour of the House of Saxony, an ally of the House of Austria. These grave matters obviously could not be neglected for intervention in French internal affairs. Far from considering any such action, he was only too thankful that the distracted state of France left him free to keep careful watch on his crafty neighbour in Petersburg.

Similar satisfaction was felt by William Pitt, Prime Minister of England, occupied as he was with questions of internal policy, and particularly with financial reform. The international eclipse of the once formidable French monarchy allowed him to resolve the question of Nootka with Spain to England's advantage, and, without any likelihood of French intervention, to carry on the war with Tippoo Sahib in India, which had broken out early in 1790. Why hasten to restore order in France?

Frederick William, King of Prussia, a superstitious libertine, who believed in spirits and was surrounded by a secret society of crazy impostors known as Rosicrucians, made a show of deep distress at the misfortunes of Louis XVI. Having come away empty-handed from the settlement of eastern affairs, thanks to Leopold's adroitness, he now reflected that the prostrate French monarchy might well be persuaded to cede some border province to its rescuers, in recognition of benefits received. He grew enthusiastic at thought of the great task of social conservation to which fate had called him, and still more at the idea of such territorial gains as would assuredly be his. Leopold II, no doubt, would not let him be the only one to extend his frontiers within the very heart of central Europe. But in a counter-revolutionary alliance there would be booty for all, at France's expense. In order therefore to force his ally's hand he dispatched a Jewish agent named Ephraim to Paris, to foment hatred of Marie-Antoinette and Austria among the revolutionaries and thus to increase their thirst for war. Leopold II, wishing to keep on good terms with Frederick William in view of a probable break with Russia, declared himself always ready to conclude the proposed anti-French pact, but postponed matters from one month to another, and no agreement was reached.

The lesser ruling princes, German and Italian, more directly affected by the new revolutionary measures in France or threatened by revolutionary propaganda, were in no position to help Louis XVI, since they were themselves engaged in seeking assistance from more powerful courts in dealing with their own troubles. But each one of them distrusted the rest, and all were suspicious of Austria and Prussia: since it was only too probable that in the general *mêlée* the great princes would seize an opportunity for agreeing among themselves and even with the King of France, at the expense of their weaker neighbours.

It was Gustavus III of Sweden who really wanted to rid France of the revolutionaries; for he found himself deprived, thanks to them, of the annual subsidy of one and a half million *livres* which the French Court had always paid him for his support in eastern affairs, and which the revolutionaries had suppressed for lack of funds. Catherine II, who posed as his friend after the peace of Verelä, encouraged him in his crusade. He already saw himself leading a great army to restore the monarchy in France. His plan of campaign was ready: he would dissolve the National Assembly, outlaw the deputies, re-establish the former order of things with the exception of unequal taxation, and wipe Paris from the face

of the earth and from the minds of men. In reward for so magnanimous an enterprise, he reserved for himself — apart from the
glory that would redound to his name for centuries to come —
the more solid advantage of an increase of 3 millions in his subsidy,
and the renewal of the former treaties with France. But the army
existed only in his imagination. Catherine II, on whom he chiefly
counted, only made a mock of him.

Charles IV of Spain, too, would have crushed the Revolution, if
he could have had his way, and he proffered counsels of energetic
action to all concerned. But no one took him seriously, for all
knew him to be little better than an imbecile.

Such were the saviours to whom Louis XVI and Marie-Antoinette turned in their distress!

Their replies may easily be imagined. They all declared themselves ready to take action, but not one would make the first
move. Each, before committing himself, awaited the decision of
Leopold II, who, for his part, declared that he was unable to
resolve on his own policy before agreement had been reached
among the rest. The Comte de Mercy, writing to Marie-Antoinette from Brussels, explained that the uncertain state of eastern
affairs made any decision impossible, for the time being; but was
careful not to conceal the difficulty — even without this obstacle —
of obtaining any substantial help from these monarchs, for the
simple, if humiliating, reason that it was not their habit 'to do
anything for nothing'. Territorial sacrifices would be required to
gain the favour or at least the neutrality of England, and others
again to induce the King of Spain or the King of Sardinia to
adopt their cause. Only Leopold was really disinterested; but
even he could not move without agreement first with England
and Prussia; and since the King of Prussia obviously would not 'do
anything for nothing', it was hardly to be expected that Leopold II
should be the only one to follow the dictates of philanthropy.

The negotiations, therefore, were inconclusive. It was evident
that the King and Queen could not hope for effective help from
Europe, and for the time being no serious danger threatened
France and the revolutionary parties.

But it must be remembered that this is clear to us today only
because, after more than a century, we are able to reconstruct the
situation as it then seemed to the politicians of Europe, from the

many memoirs, letters, documents and secret decrees that have in the course of time come to light from public and private archives. The French revolutionaries were unable to see things so calmly and objectively. It was a commonplace to them that the new order in their country heralded similar change in every other: the time was at hand when no ruling prince would be able to resist France's example, and all would be forced to relinquish their privileges and ancient powers. Convinced that it was their mission to open a new era of liberty and happiness for mankind, the men of the Revolution were imbued with a great ardour for propaganda, and regarded themselves as the friends of all oppressed peoples and the natural allies of those who were ready to rise against injustice and to fight for freedom.

'O all ye usurpers of the world,' sang André Chénier in his Ode on the Oath of the Tennis-court, 'O ye kings, monsters of pride and self-indulgence, open your eyes and make haste to save yourselves; a divine whirlwind of vengeance is upon you.'

In these words he expressed the beliefs of every supporter of the revolutionary movement. But while on the one hand the revolutionaries uttered threats, on the other they felt themselves threatened, and went in fear of those very kings whose imminent ruin they predicted. It seemed obvious that these princes must resolutely resist the world-wide subversive movement envisaged by their enemies, and oppose the league of all peoples with a league of kings, in an attempt to stifle the movement in France before it spread throughout the world. The general armed state of Europe, with its troop movements and conferences attended by the various rulers — which arose, in reality, out of the eastern question — appeared to afford sinister confirmation of this universal counter-revolutionary alliance. Opposition by the aristocrats and non-juring clergy in the Assembly, too, was believed to be a result of plots set on foot by the royalists abroad. And since the King was only too plainly still in favour of restoring the former régime, it was natural enough to conclude that he had a hand in these conspiracies.

Those nobles who had found a haven among the small German courts of the Rhineland, or who gathered round the foolish and frivolous Comte d'Artois in Turin, certainly gave substance, by their irresponsible behaviour, to such fears and suspicions. To them, the Assembly's decrees had no conceivable legality; the destruction of feudalism, of the Church and the Monarchy, could not endow any government with legitimacy, and they owed no allegiance to this new France that was a home of anarchy and bloodshed — where all their ancient rights had been violated and all their past glory brought to nothing. To them, their true home was the land where they themselves held sway. They had left France, not as fugitives but as an army with colours flying, ready to cross the frontiers again under the banners of victory. They loudly demanded complete restitution of the absolute monarchy and the feudal system, and clamoured for due vengeance to be meted out to the rebels; and in the meantime they set about organizing their great counter-revolutionary crusade in broad daylight. In so doing, they felt assured of help from the nobility and courts of Europe, since the cause of the French nobles was that of all who were threatened by the revolutionary flood, and the French monarchy's fall would represent an obvious danger to every other European throne. The Prince de Condé declared, in a proclamation to all Europe, that 'notwithstanding his horror, as a descendant of Saint Louis, at the thought of plunging his sword in French blood, he would assume command of the nobility of all nations and, followed by every man who was loyal to his king, would hasten to deliver the unhappy monarch'. The Comte d'Artois, accompanied by Calonne, now appointed Foreign Minister of the 'true France', was making pleas for help on every hand. They all believed that the revolutionary frenzy in France would soon abate, and looked upon their exile as a brief sojourn abroad, during which, to pass the time as pleasantly as possible, they might continue to run up debts, make love, and wrangle with one another as though they were still at Versailles in the happy days when the incomparable Calonne was 'saving the State'.

It was childish bravado. The lesser princes who gave these illustrious refugees hospitality felt honoured by their presence for a time, but soon grew tired of their arrogance and their vagaries. Bouillé, to whom the Comte d'Artois had turned in the spring of 1790 for assistance in a plan to carry off the King, energetically condemned the folly of such a proposal. Leopold II, continually pestered by the Comte d'Artois, took no pains to disguise his complete indifference, and chafed at the difficulties created for him by this swarm of importunate idlers. Louis XVI and Marie-Antoinette themselves were filled with consternation at so much folly and impertinence, and begged the various governments in no way to encourage the *emigrés*, whose aim, they realized well enough, was to regain their own privileges and to impose their will upon the King. Marie-Antoinette, in particular, who was detested by the Comte d'Artois and Calonne, and who knew that their victory would mean an end to her political influence, had no wish to accept salvation at their hands.

All the same, the reckless provocation of these men — who, from the safety of foreign courts, insisted that it was their mission to save the King against his will — helped greatly to inflame passions and to destroy the last defences of the monarchy. Their intrigues, their insolent threats of vengeance and of armed intervention — when seen in relation not only to the large armies in being on the continent, but to royalist agitation in France and the King's insistence on posing as a prisoner — all gave credence to the belief that a ruthless counter-stroke was being prepared. There were continual rumours of the King's flight from Paris, of plots and of imminent invasion. At the thought that foreign aid might re-establish that feudal régime which the national will had overthrown, the most peace-loving of citizens were goaded to fury, and popular anger against the Queen, the royalists and all those who did not openly declare themselves enemies of the former régime grew daily more intense.

It was this atmosphere of increasing tension that gave rise both to the war against the allies and to the reign of terror in France.

III

It is easy to imagine the effect produced, in such an atmosphere, by the bloodthirsty propaganda of Jean-Paul Marat. In the *Ami du Peuple* he urged the citizens to keep watch on the King and royal family to prevent their flight from Paris, to be on the alert against treachery, and to deal ruthlessly with the plots of the aristocrats and refractory priests. In his hatred for everything that recalled the former régime Marat saw dangers, conspiracies, and enemies of the Revolution not only among open supporters of the feudal classes but in all those who did not oppose the old order as fanatically as he did himself. According to him, the deputies were 'born servitors of the Court, who deserved to be stoned, hanged, burnt alive, impaled and buried beneath the smoking ruins of their meeting-place'; Bailly and the Paris administrators were scoundrels who plundered the public revenues, Lafayette 'a hypocritical fiend whose throat should be cut', the National Guard 'hired assassins of the King', and the King himself a 'brainless automaton' and a 'treacherous dissembler': all were traitors, plotting with foreign courts or with the *emigrés*. In his fevered imagination some 4000 refugees became ten times that number, all in league with innumerable hidden accomplices in Paris. How strange that (on May 30th, 1791) Robespierre and Pétion should have proposed abolition of the death penalty to the National Assembly! It was as well that a measure offering too many obvious disadvantages for serious consideration had been rejected. 'Death, death is the penalty of traitors.' Marat demanded the heads of the ministers, of almost all the deputies, of Bailly and Lafayette, of the municipal councillors, the general staff of the National Guard, and the civil and military authorities. After the fall of the Bastille, he declared, 500 heads would have sufficed, and 'all would have gone well'. But later, the evil had increased. In December 1790 he wanted 20,000; in September 1792 he was demanding 40,000; six weeks later, 270,000. With the usual simple logic of the ignorant and fanatical, he clamoured for a dictator: a harsh and relentless dictator, in whose hands all power should be concentrated and who would put the people's enemies to death, together with all who were conspiring secretly for the return of tyranny.

'If I were tribune of the people, I guarantee that, with the support of a few thousand resolute men, I would complete the Constitution, set the political machine in order, and make the people free and happy within six weeks; in less than a year the country would be flourishing, and would remain so for as long as I lived.'

For a whole year his diatribes left the public unmoved; but he continued to execrate the citizens of Paris for failing to defend themselves from their foes, despite all his warnings.

Little by little, however, as the Court's demeanour and the indiscretions of the *emigrés* brought increasing disillusionment,

Marat's sinister denunciations acquired consistency and grew in force. He began to be referred to as 'the prophet'. The mob listened to him and anger was quickly kindled. Other democratic journals, such as the *Révolution de France* of Desmoulins, Fréron's *Orateur du Peuple* and Hébert's *Père Duchesne* vied with that of Marat in violence. As was to be expected, the National Guard, disconcerted at rumours of plots, resentful towards the King and the privileged classes, and fearing a counter-blow that now seemed not improbable, became less firm in putting down disturbances, and showed reluctance to carry out Lafayette's orders: in short, it returned to that attitude of apathetic tolerance towards popular outbreaks which in 1789 had opened a way to the October rising.

On November 13th, 1790, the Duc de Castries, who on the previous day had wounded Charles de Lameth in a duel, had his house sacked. Wild demonstrations were made in December to obtain the King's sanction to the anti-clerical decree of November 27th. In January 1791 the house of the Comte de Clermont-Tonnerre, president of the *'Amis de la constitution monarchique'* was also threatened. A scuffle between smugglers and customs officials in the Paris suburb of La Chapelle was at once interpreted as the effect of royalist plots, and serious disorders followed in the workers' quarter of Saint-Antoine, where barricades were promptly raised. In February there were disturbances at the departure of the King's two aunts for Rome; others were occasioned by a rumour that the King's brother, the Comte de Provence, was about to join the *emigrés*, and others again because some hot-heads wanted to destroy the Fort of Vincennes — said to be full of arms and ammunition and in subterranean communication with the Tuileries. Further outbreaks occurred because, hearing rumours of an attempt on the King's life, some hundreds of nobles had hastened to the Tuileries to defend the monarch, thus giving rise in their turn to new charges of plotting, and gaining for themselves the title of 'knights of the dagger'.

Matters became still worse when the Pope finally condemned the Civil Constitution of the Clergy, and declared that all those clerics who had taken the Civic Oath were guilty of schism and prohibited from administering the sacraments. On March 28th Clermont-Tonnerre's club was attacked by 400 persons, and dissolved by order of the municipal council. The churches in which non-juring priests were officiating began to close owing to public protest. Alarmed at the Pope's condemnation, the King dismissed his own chaplain, who had taken the constitutional oath, and in April made preparations to celebrate Easter at Saint-Cloud, where he could receive communion from non-juring priests. The wrath of the populace was now turned from the clergy towards the King. Camille Desmoulins wrote a violent article entitled 'The Great Betrayal by the King of the French'. The *Club des Cordeliers* denounced 'the chief functionary of the State and foremost subject of the law, the King himself, who resists the law of the realm'. The *Orateur du Peuple*, in recalling that 'the mouths of Kings are the abode of lies', affirmed the existence of a great counter-revolutionary plot directed by an 'Austrian committee' at Court, and warned the King that, if he went to Saint-Cloud, he would lose his throne. The effect of all this incitement to violence was such that, on April 18th, the King and his family were unable to take their departure from the Tuileries owing to hostile demonstrations not only by a large crowd, but by the National Guard itself: despite desperate efforts on the part of Lafayette, who for more than two hours tried to obtain free passage for the King. The idea of holding the royal family as hostages against the aristocrats and their foreign allies had taken root in the people's minds.

Thus while the masses were becoming more easily roused to violence, the resentment of the middle-classes against the Court grew more bitter every day, and many of them went over to the rebels. Of those who attacked the Duc de Castries' house, for instance, the greater number were well-to-do and well-dressed persons. In the minds of certain citizens, closely concerned with politics and favourable to the new régime, the doubt began, little by little, to take shape as to whether it were really possible to reconcile revolutionary aims with a continuance of the monarchy.

In 1789 there had been no republicans in France. The people were deeply attached to the King, who was their traditional defence against the nobility. The intellectuals, if in theory convinced that a republic was the best of political institutions — a commonplace that, in all times and among all civilized countries, has never done serious injury to any king — in practice did not dream of destroying the monarchy. Their programme was to reform it, to hedge it about with constitutional laws; to surround it, as was said at the time, with republican institutions. Even the stoutest upholders of popular sovereignty did not stop to consider that in such a theory the idea of a republic was necessarily implicit, nor did they suppose that the King's will might come into conflict with that of the nation. On the other hand, during the last days of the old régime a 'republican state of mind', as Aulard points out, already existed; and this led the followers of the revolutionary movement to act as republicans whilst sincerely believing themselves monarchists, and to destroy the last vestiges of royal power while showing every mark of filial devotion towards the person of the monarch. It was only necessary for the King himself to lose popularity and prestige for the idea of a republic to take immediate shape in the minds of the revolutionaries.

The first clear sign of republican propaganda appeared, it would seem, in a pamphlet 'On Kings and Peoples' published in September 1790. This was the work of an obscure man of letters named Lavicomterie, later a deputy in the Convention. His opinions were supported by the *Mercure National* of October 1st, a newspaper issued by a small group of literary men who used to gather in the *salon* of Louise Robert-Kéralio. It was this lady's husband, François Robert, a professor of common law, who was the author of another pamphlet, issued in December 1790, entitled 'Republicanism adapted to France'. In November 1790, Voltaire's *Brutus*, which was presented at the Théâtre Français, gave rise to noisy republican demonstrations.

The common people, who were regarded by so many eighteenth-century philosophers and physiocrats as beasts to be well-fed and on occasion well-beaten to make them work — that populace which had taken the Bastille and carried out the October insurrection — now seemed likely to be called on for further exploits if the resistance and plots of the aristocrats, priests, *emigrés* and court were to be frustrated. Every day the lower orders revealed themselves more clearly as a political force to be reckoned with, and their help would be no less necessary in defending the Revolution than it had been in destroying feudalism. It was indeed in them alone that, according to the extremists, the revolutionaries could safely put their trust.

'Expect nothing,' cried Marat, 'from the goodwill of the public officials: they are always instruments of despotism, and the greater their number, the more dangerous they will be. Hope for nothing from the rich and affluent, from men brought up in comfort and luxury, from the grasping men who love only gold. Free citizens cannot be created out of former slaves. It is only those who till the soil, who work as small tradesmen, artisans, craftsmen and labourers — the common herd, as they are called by the insolent rich — who can form a free people, impatient of oppression and ever ready to throw off its yoke.'

Since the distinction between active and passive citizens excluded the lower orders from full political rights, demands for universal suffrage increased as the democratic movement grew in strength. Protests not only against the tax-qualifications for candidates but against limitation of the electoral roll flowed in.

In this agitation for extending the franchise, Maximilien Robespierre naturally took a leading part. He was a lawyer by profession, and came from a lower middle-class family of Arras. Of slender build, with a pale face, receding forehead and thin lips, he was always meticulously dressed; but with his harsh, monotonous voice and somewhat laboured eloquence, he had little influence in the National Assembly, where he was regarded as a political theorist, unable to turn his unoriginal philosophical reflections into practical proposals. Robespierre, however, although embittered by the lack of effect produced by his studied orations, was always ready to speak in defence of the people's rights. Jean-Jacques Rousseau was his god, and he looked upon himself as Rousseau's prophet. The Genevan philosopher's eloquent invective against social and political inequality, his fascinating descriptions of virtue, reciprocal love and the perfect happiness that mankind had enjoyed in a state of nature, lost their artistic attraction when expounded by Robespierre, but were endowed for him with all the authority of divine inspiration. The 'people' were wise and good and generous; they could not commit crimes or excesses; they only asked for justice and the right to live their own lives. Their voice was the voice of nature and of the common good, and once they were freed from the corrupt oppression of a privileged minority, virtue and happiness would again reign in the world. All Robespierre's conduct was the practical outcome of these convictions. In the Assembly and the press he opposed the suspensive veto, the *loi martiale* on unlawful assemblies, the distinction between active and passive citizens, the '*marc d'argent*' qualification for political eligibility, and the King's right to decide in matters of peace and war.

As early as October 1789 he had begun to champion the idea of universal suffrage.

'If those who pay in taxation the equivalent of a labourer's daily wage have fewer rights than those who pay the value of three days', he said to Assembly, 'it follows that those who pay as much as ten days' labour have fuller rights than those who only pay three; therefore, those who have an income of a 100,000 *livres* have rights proportionately greater than those with an income of 1000 *livres*.'

In April 1791, he published a criticism of the '*marc d'argent*' decree, but included in it a condemnation of the whole electoral system set up by the Assembly.

'You say that the people, who have nothing to lose, should not exercise full rights of citizenship. People who have nothing to lose! How unjust and false this insolent language sounds in the ears of truth! These people, if they live, have the means to live. And if they have such means, they possess something to lose, or to preserve. True, the coarse clothes I wear, the humble abode in which I pay for the right to live in peace, the scanty wages out of which I feed my wife and children, are not the same, I admit, as lands, houses and carriages. My possessions are worth nothing in the eyes of those who live in affluence. But they mean something to humanity. They are a form of sacred property: just as sacred, doubtless, as the resplendent possessions of the great. But what am I saying? Freedom, life, the right to justice for myself and those dear to me, the right to resist oppression, and the right to free exercise of every faculty of mind and heart — all these dear possessions, the first of those bestowed on man by nature, are confided, no less than yours, to the protection of the law. Yet you say that I have no interest in the law! And you would therefore despoil me of the part that concerns me no less than you in the administration of public affairs: for the simple reason that you are more rich than I am!'

Doctrinaire in outlook and uncompromising in his attitude,

Robespierre almost always found his proposals rejected by the Assembly. But his voice went beyond the Chamber and reached the populace itself. It was warmly applauded at the *Club des Cordeliers*. Camille Desmoulins called him 'our Aristides', and Marat paid tribute to his 'incorruptibility'. He began to be an important personage in the revolutionary movement. 'That man will go far,' Mirabeau had once said of him, 'because he believes what he says.'

Not only political equality, symbolized by universal suffrage and republican government, but equality of other kinds had yet to be attained. These questions, too, were hotly debated, though the revolutionary atmosphere was ill-suited to the development of such premature social schemes.

In the *cahiers* of 1789 the only problem involved had been that of relations between the commons and privileged orders; no desire was shown for a general change in the existing system of property rights. The *cahiers* all demanded reform — reform of the constitution, the administration, the judiciary, and the system of taxation — but none raised doubts about the legitimacy of private ownership of property. Indeed, it was upheld, in contrast with the abuse of power permitted by the monarchical régime. Those who demanded confiscation of Church property did so in the name of the supreme right of ownership which they attributed to the nation itself. The lower orders protested against feudal rights on the grounds that they were not a legitimate possession of the privileged orders, and were therefore illegal as well as contrary to the general interest.

Such pamphlets as dared to criticize the existing order and to propose a different distribution of property cannot have numbered more than half a dozen, out of a flood of some four thousand issued between 1787 and 1789. A certain Gosselin, a Catholic and monarchist, declared in his 'Reflexions of a Citizen' that the land belonged to God; that men might use it according to their needs, but no further; and that no one could own it legitimately while any remained without property. Wealth should be divided 'in such a manner that all may support themselves by work'. Further, 'the speediest way of abolishing inequality would be to hold all property in common, and to share it out after the example of the Spartan legislator; each one would then be contented with

his lot'. Sylvain Mareschal, who later took part in the conspiracy of the 'Égaux', vehemently criticized inequality and
private ownership of property in his 'Modern fables for the use of
an hereditary prince'. The day would come in which the workers
would refuse to serve the rich and would say to them: 'We are
three against one. We wish to restore things to their original state,
that is, to a state of perfect and legitimate equality, for evermore.
We will put the land to common use. If there is amongst us one
who has two mouths and four arms, it is right that he should be
assigned a double share. But if we are all made alike let us divide
the cake in equal parts. At the same time, let us all lend a hand
in the work.' 'All this, at the time in which I am writing, is only a
fable; but in truth I tell you that it will become history.'

Babeuf, who was later chief of the 'Société des Égaux', claimed,
in the preface to a pamphlet on the *Cadastre perpétuel* of a certain
Audifred, that whoever did not content himself with what alone
was necessary to life must be considered as despoiling others, and
that whoever lacked such necessities had the right to go on demanding them till he was satisfied. In France, out of a total of
24 million inhabitants, there were 15 millions who possessed
nothing. Were these to die of starvation in gratitude to those who
had robbed them? The land must be divided up: each one must
have a share for his lifetime only, and this share must not be
transferable, so that 'the individual patrimony of each citizen may
be secure and not subject to sequestration'.

But little by little, as the Revolution proceeded, the scene
changed. Every class, every kind of interest, all private fortunes
became involved. Property to the value of many milliards was
transferred by law from the clergy to the middle-classes. Feudal
dues were no longer paid; the privileged classes protested that they
were robbed of their substance, and saw in the Revolution a step
towards collective ownership of the land. In reality, as Jaurès
observes, this great crisis, in abolishing the feudal régime, in
freeing property from arbitrary taxation, in securing the Government's creditors against defaulting finance ministers, in removing
the fetters of feudal serfdom from the land and in breaking up the
mediaeval collective property of the Church, not only extended the
rights of private ownership but made them clearly-defined and
secure instead of — as hitherto — ambiguous and subject to

arbitrary control by the public authorities. It was, in fact, the antithesis of socialism. But this was not to be apparent until the crisis was over and the Code Napoléon came into being. Meanwhile, owing to the rapid shift in social relationships, it was natural that the legislators should begin to seem endowed with unlimited power, even with regard to rights of ownership; and that aspirations towards some system of economic justice should take shape in men's minds.

The middle-class intellectuals of the democratic party, however, who had been brought up on the works of Rousseau and other eighteenth-century rebels, knew that the issue was not simply concerned with the commons' position in relation to feudal privilege or absolute monarchy, but was also one between poverty and wealth. And many of them rallied to the side of the poor. In the newspapers and clubs there were discussions on taxation of income, on laws of inheritance, on how to limit private property, curb luxury, and assure the working-classes a living wage. Wealth was condemned, legislation demanded to reduce inequalities between rich and poor, and the necessity for another revolution, to end the tyranny of the new plutocracy, was loudly proclaimed.

All this led to an increasing desire for change in the distribution of property. In the 'Social Club of the Friends of Truth', which, founded in October 1790, had many hundreds of members, the Abbé Claude Fauchet preached that every man had a right to the land: that all rights in a well-ordered society should be held in common, that everyone should possess something and no one too much, and that all had a natural right to the necessities of life. To stop 'the three great sources of crime, extreme wealth, extreme poverty and, above all, hatred', he proposed an agrarian law forbidding possession of landed property with a revenue of more than 50,000 *livres* a year; introduction of absolute equality into the inheritance of property, which in no case should exceed an annual value of 50,000 *livres*; and the prohibition of marriages by which husband and wife would have a combined income of more than that amount.

We have reached the point, in fact, at which the problem of private ownership, no longer merely a subject for abstract speculation, had entered the sphere of political propaganda.

I V

We must beware of attaching too great an importance to these early signs of what was later to become a widespread phenomenon. During the first half of 1791 the republicans were still few in number, and their propaganda was of little account. The ancient monarchy, under which the nation had passed through so many centuries of glorious history, and which was endowed by 'divine right' — for so long unquestioned — with a sacred character, was still, although a shadow without substance, a shadow that inspired superstitious awe among the majority of Frenchmen. Robespierre himself, for whom the King was 'a man' like every other and the foremost 'functionary' of the realm, would not risk making an open declaration of republicanism. Brissot, later one of the Girondin leaders, while openly affirming that to his mind the monarchy was 'a scourge', declared that 'it was one thing to have a metaphysical opinion, but another to reject in actual fact a king accepted by the Constitution'; and protested that he himself was not a republican, but only wanted 'the people's representatives given sufficient power to prevent the Government and monarchy from restoring despotism'. In other words, he wanted 'a popular monarchy, under which the balance should always remain in the people's favour'. Pétion declared that such discussions on questions of form were beside the point, since 'there is often more difference between one monarchy and another, than between certain monarchies and republics'. Even Marat, who heaped insults upon Louis XVI, and considered it 'a mistake to believe that the French Government could only be a monarchical one', had to admit that 'a strictly limited monarchy would today suit the country best', and that 'a federal republic would soon degenerate into an oligarchy'.

As to those who preached economic equality, they were fewer in number even than the republicans. Their socialist propaganda had no effect whatever on the great mass of the people. The city workers were still without any clear class-consciousness, because their own class was not yet completely divided from that of the artisans. They complained of unemployment, high prices and poverty; they demanded bread, work and higher wages, but they did not dream of a new social order in which there would be no necessity for wages at all. The peasants, in face of the citizens and wealthy landowners, had a more developed sense of class than the workers; but wretched as they were, and dispersed in regions remote from urban civilization, they were unable to analyse the social order or to envisage another way of life, and simply reacted against the immediate symptoms of their ills, such as taxation and feudal dues. Once rid of these, they asked for nothing more. The democrats' views as a whole were bounded by the idea of political equality. At the most they agreed with Robespierre that 'private property was a necessary evil'. Marat himself, in inciting the workers and lower middle-class against the King, never considered a new organization of society without private property. To him, the ideal society would have been one composed of small landowners and artisans, without rich or poor, without political privileges or economic inequality: in fact, Rousseau's ideal society.

Another characteristic circumstance should be noted. During the summer of 1789, in some of the Paris working-class districts — the abode of tailors, wig-makers, shoemakers and printers — the artisans began to group themselves into trade associations, not only for mutual aid, but with the aim of obtaining higher wages and eliminating competition. Yet the movement was left entirely to its own resources, and no revolutionary leader came to direct and encourage it. In the spring of 1791 this instinctive tendency to demand higher wages — which is the hallmark of the modern working-class movement — brought about a conflict between building workers and master-builders, in which the class-war took on an unusual aspect.

The workers demanded a wage of thirty-six *sous* a day, instead of thirty. The masters refused, whereupon the workers called a strike. The masters declared any increase in pay impossible owing to current conditions in the industry and because existing contracts had been based on the usual wages; they accused the workers of violating the right to work, and invoked the law of free competition as the only basis for reciprocal relations. They then demanded from the municipal authorities 'effective measures against a source of so much disorder'; in other words, 'prohibition of meetings, the annulment of all resolutions already passed at such meetings, and penal proceedings against those responsible'. The workers appealed to the Assembly. They denounced the contractors' 'obstinacy' in opposing peaceful negotiation whilst accumulating large fortunes at the workers' expense. Denying that they had been guilty of violence, they accused the masters of bad faith in 'making the workers appear in the worst possible light by accusing them of criminal intentions'. It seemed to them that if it were permissible for the masters to make agreements among themselves in order to force wages down, the workers should not be denied a right to combine for the opposite purpose; and they expressed a hope that 'the Assembly, in destroying feudal privileges and trade-guilds, and in proclaiming the Rights of Man, had intended that this Declaration should bring some relief to the most indigent class, which had been for so long a victim of the employers' tyranny'.

The Commune of Paris issued a proclamation on April 26th declaring it to be 'criminal violation of the law' to demand equal wages for all workers, since the citizens 'were equal in their rights but would never be equal in their abilities'. On May 4th it prohibited all workers' organizations. On June 14th, 1791, the Assembly passed a law placing all trade associations, whether of masters or workmen, on the same basis as the former guilds of artisans, and prohibiting 'citizens of the same trade or profession, contractors, shopkeepers, workers or craftsmen' from uniting with the aim of 'refusing to work except at a wage or for a price determined by themselves'. This was the famous Le Chapelier law (so-called from the name of the deputy who presented it to the Assembly) in virtue of which any form of workers' organization remained illegal in France for seventy-five years.

Yet against a law of this nature, which would today arouse fierce opposition in any civilized country, not only from the working-class but from liberals and even conservatives, not a single democratic deputy — not even Robespierre — raised his voice in the Assembly. Very few of the extreme revolutionaries protested. Marat defended the workers, 'left to the mercies of a handful of scoundrels who grow fat on their labour and rob them of its fruits'. He condemned the Le Chapelier law, not because it forbade economic organization of the working-class, but because it 'isolated the citizens and cut them off from public affairs'. In other words, he regarded it simply as a measure of political reaction and nothing more.

If extremist theories had any appreciable effect during the first half of 1791, it was only to the detriment of the revolutionaries. In fact, they caused a clear division in the Assembly between the Extreme Left and the Left, who until then had rarely been in disagreement. Not that the Left was slackening in its work of destroying the former régime. Indeed, it was actually in the spring of 1791 (April 8th-15th) that the succession laws were passed, promoting a break-up of the large estates. But while they still remained opponents of feudalism, many influential deputies of the Left and certain Jacobin leaders, like Adrien Duport, the two Lameth brothers, and Barnave, began to feel that they were no longer omnipotent, as they had been, among the revolutionaries; they became aware of a growing restlessness among the Jacobin rank and file, and a tendency to favour the ultra-democratic policy of Robespierre; and they asked themselves, in alarm and irritation, how it was all to end. The time had come to build up again, after so much had been destroyed. Were the principles proclaimed sacred and eternal in the early days of revolutionary fervour really so sacred and eternal, after all? Would it not be as well to subject them to a hasty revision restricting their scope? How was the continuance of disorder to be prevented? And how was this revolutionary movement, which, after destroying privileges of birth, was now beginning to threaten the very principle of private ownership, to be checked?

'The Revolution is over!' exclaimed Duport, on May 17th, 1791. When he was elected president of the tribunal in which Robespierre had been chosen as public prosecutor, he refused the office. He had no wish to be the colleague of a man whose political programme was by now diametrically opposed to his own.

In fact, that revulsion of feeling which Mirabeau had predicted as an inevitable result of increased disorder, and which the King, in his view, should exploit in re-imposing his authority, was now becoming apparent. The Court might easily have availed itself of this new disposition on the part of the Left in order to promote agreement between the more moderate elements in the Assembly, and to form a majority in it able to hold both extremists and reactionaries in check.

Instead, the King and Queen were thinking only of making their escape from Paris. Far from welcoming the recent demeanour of the Left they were distressed by it, for it was not desirable — so wrote Comte de Fersen, who was in their confidence — that 'the rebels should be enabled to draw up the constitutional charter in such a way as to make it tolerable, and so to consolidate the Revolution'. The ferment must not be allowed to abate, lest things should settle down into a state which 'would still be to the King's disadvantage, but which the country would end by accepting, since all would find it preferable to the convulsion of civil war'.

Furthermore, the *emigrés*, although repudiated on every hand, were still proclaiming their intention of saving the King at all costs. Marie-Antoinette, fearing they might succeed, saw this possibility as yet another reason for hastening on with preparations for flight, so that the King might be in time to put himself at the head of the crusade, and thus wrest the exclusive glory of victory from the *emigrés*.

To facilitate the royal family's escape, suspicion had to be lulled by a pretence of final and unconditional approval of the new order. The King, therefore, was profuse in its praise, declaring himself more than happy to govern under laws emanating from the Assembly, and protesting that the idea of his being a prisoner in the midst of his faithful subjects was an 'atrocious calumny'. But he explained in confidence to other rulers that his actions were without validity, since he was not free: and that all his public declarations were to be interpreted as meaning precisely the reverse of what the words conveyed.

It is difficult to credit such blind folly. No less extraordinary was the total absence of ideas as to what should be done once the escape was safely accomplished. Apart from rejecting the wild schemes of the *emigrés* on the one hand, and, on the other, from refusing to follow Mirabeau's advice loyally to accept the Constituent Assembly's reforms, the King and Queen had nothing in their minds but a medley of vague and contradictory hopes and projects; from which none could tell what positive action might arise, should the day for action ever come.

The Queen herself was forced to recognize that there was no one fitted to take over control of their affairs, although the Baron de Breteuil, with a presumption common among the Court officials, had put himself forward as the only person with a right to function as prime minister. The King did not want to leave the national property as security for the *assignats*, because his religious scruples would not allow him to accept spoliation of the Church; yet he dared not think of restoring it to the clergy, since it was obvious that collapse of the *assignats* would produce an appalling social crisis, and a renewed wave of revolution. As to the question of reforming the Government, it was decided, after lengthy consideration, to return to the unfortunate declaration of June 23rd, 1789, which in its time had served merely to demonstrate the absolute im'potence of the King. The only definite idea emerging from all these futile deliberations was that, after victory, those who returned to their allegiance should be treated indulgently, but that no mercy was to be shown towards the revolutionary leaders of Paris. Lafayette, for example, was designated for the firing-squad.

No less confused were their ideas concerning the *emigrés*, and the King's relations with foreign powers. Neither Louis XVI nor Marie-Antoinette desired real armed intervention by the Emperor Leopold and the Kings of Spain, Sardinia and Prussia. It seemed to them humiliating and dangerous to re-impose their authority with the help of foreign armies. The Queen's favourite plan was that the Emperor should lend a sum of 15 millions towards the initial expenses of the campaign against the Assembly, and at the same time summon a Congress of all the Powers to discuss help for the King of France, while concentrating troops along the French frontier. Louis, having by then placed himself at the head of Bouillé's loyal regiments, would thereupon gather his faithful adherents round him, and proceed to act as mediator between an armed Europe about to invade France, and his own misguided subjects. With his prestige increased by having saved his country from a disastrous war, or — should the worst come to the worst — with the Imperial troops acting as auxiliaries to those of Bouillé, he would forthwith impose respect for his authority upon the National Assembly and the rebellious people of Paris.

Unfortunately, the Emperor was disinclined to make even so slight an effort as that demanded by the Queen. He promised support for the royal family after their departure from Paris; but he still insisted that he could undertake nothing without agreement between himself and the Kings of Spain and Sardinia, and the Princes of the Empire; in particular, without the approval of the

King of Prussia and the English Government. Meanwhile, he refused to lend the 15 million *livres*.

In any event, the Queen was counting too easily on surrender by the French people. Four million citizens, already armed and organized in the National Guard, and in control of the country's communal and departmental administration, could not be expected to submit again to the nobility, clergy and old centralized bureaucracy without putting up stubborn resistance.

These citizens seemed, as a whole, almost totally uninterested in public affairs. The traders, industrialists, shopkeepers, artisans, small peasant proprietors, and labourers — lovers, as they all were, of a quiet life — had played a part in the revolutionary crisis of 1789 from sheer necessity and desperation; but they had their daily bread to earn, or their own affairs to think of. Large numbers of them had voted, during the spring of 1790, in the various departmental, municipal, judicial and military elections. But as the elections became multiplied, an increasing number of citizens abstained from any share in them, and left the burden of active political work to those who, by reason of their character or social position, or for other motives, felt themselves particularly drawn to it. In Paris itself, where a more lively interest was taken in public affairs than elsewhere, the number of abstentions was, nevertheless, very great. In the communal elections of August 1791, hardly 14,000 out of 80,000 electors recorded their votes. Bailly was elected *maire* with 12,550 votes. His successor was elected with 2332 out of a poll of 6084 votes. Even among those citizens who went to the polls the majority contented themselves merely with exercising their electoral rights, and took no further share in political affairs.

Very few were those who maintained a serious interest in politics: who went to public meetings, kept a watch on the work of public officials, took a share in organizing elections, or who wrote for the newspapers. Half a dozen, perhaps, in the villages, according to Taine; from fifteen to twenty in the country towns; about fifty in the smaller provincial cities, and some hundreds in the larger ones; a few thousands in Paris. A great number of these were lawyers; but there were also men of letters, doctors, journalists, school-teachers, artisans, and such city workers as were more educated and mentally active than the rest: persons belonging, in fact, almost all of them, to a rank of society inferior to that of the well-to-do middle-class, and superior to the workers. The aristocracy — military, ecclesiastical and bureaucratic — stood aside, owing to the universal hostility with which they were regarded; while the industrial *bourgeoisie* were absorbed in their own affairs, and the mass of peasants and workers had no aptitude for public life. Among this crowd of political zealots were many gifted men, eloquent speakers, and sincere believers in the new ideas: such men as are apt to be termed fanatical by their opponents. But the really fanatical were not lacking either, attracted to politics as moths to a candle; and naturally, there were adventurers, ne'er-do-wells and knaves in plenty.

These men naturally felt the necessity for discussion and for planning common action. Numerous literary, scientific, recreative and masonic societies had become centres of agitation against the Government under the old régime, and these now transformed themselves openly into genuine political clubs. New associations sprang up on every hand, the history of which little by little became merged in that of the Revolution itself.

The most powerful and influential of these societies was that of the Paris Jacobins.

The first nucleus of this club had consisted of the Breton deputies, both commons and clergy, who came to attend the States-General, and who met together in a café at Versailles to discuss their policy from day to day. To these meetings, which acquired the name of the 'Breton Club', deputies from other parts of France were soon admitted at their own request. It was here that the decisions of June 17th, resistance to the King's orders at the sitting of June 25th, and presentation of the Duc d'Aiguillon's motion on the night of August 4th, were all discussed beforehand. When the Assembly moved to Paris after the October rising, the Breton Club was dissolved. But the deputies still felt a need for concerted action; and for this reason some of them rented a room in the monastery of the Dominican monks (nicknamed in France the Jacobins) and founded, between December 1789 and January 1790, the 'Society of Friends of the Constitution with premises at the Paris Jacobins'. This new club was derisively referred to by the royalists as the 'Jacobin Club', but its own members took pride in the title. At first, only deputies belonged to it, but later private citizens too were admitted. In December 1790 the Society had 1100 members. On great occasions its meetings were attended by as many as a thousand members and two thousand spectators. But for a long time the Society kept a predominantly parliamentary character; according to its statute only discussions relating to the Assembly's affairs were allowed, the general public was excluded from its meetings, 'passive' citizens were not admitted as members, and candidates for membership had to be proposed by ten and approved by all members of the club.

'What is to be expected', wrote Marat, in July 1790, 'of this assembly of imbeciles, who dream of equality, boast of behaving as brothers, and exclude the poor, whom they nevertheless declare to be free men?'

More militant and democratic in character was the 'Society of Friends of the Rights of Man and of the Citizen', set up in the summer of 1790, and known as the Cordeliers Club, since it held its meetings in a monastery of Franciscan friars, or *cordeliers*. Danton, Camille Desmoulins, Marat, Hébert, and Anacharsis Clootz were leading members, but Robespierre preferred the more grave and solemn atmosphere of the Jacobins. Meetings at the Cordeliers Club were open to the public without distinction between active and passive citizens. Frequent protests were made against the electoral law and, in particular, against the law of the *marc d'argent*; anti-democratic decisions by the Constituent Assembly and Paris Municipal Council were loudly condemned, and the Jacobin Club was not seldom an object for attack.

Around these two clubs, which were the most important, a host of lesser organizations arose, many of them destined for an early death, such as the Fraternal Society of Both Sexes, the Society of the Poor, the Society of Liberty, the Society of the Enemies of Despotism, the Society of Lovers of Law, the Society of Friends of Truth, and so on. The promoters of these clubs were almost all affiliated to the Cordeliers; they made propaganda amongst the workers, explained the Declaration of Rights to them, read and commented upon the newspapers, and criticized laws passed by the Assembly. All these organizations were effective in drawing the working-classes of Paris closer to the revolutionary parties.

Similar societies arose, towards the end of 1789 and during the first half of 1790, in other important cities of France. In the second half of this year, patriots from the smaller provincial cities, returning home from the Fête of Federation, began to set up clubs in imitation of those in Paris.

These local societies, following the tradition which, under the former régime, had made of the capital city a centre of political and administrative life, affiliated themselves to the Jacobin Club of Paris; they adopted its statutes, asked for its protection, and adhered to its decisions. In August 1790 there were 152 of them affiliated to the Jacobins; in March 1791 they numbered 227; in the summer of 1791, 406; and they continued to increase until, at the fall of the monarchy, there were more than a thousand. Around each one of these affiliated societies gathered yet smaller ones from neighbouring villages and country towns. They existed in large numbers in southern France and in the provinces along the eastern and northern frontiers.

It was a spontaneous organization, developing side by side with the administrative institutions called into being by the new laws. It was indeed the only real political organization existing in France after the absolute monarchy had collapsed; when the National Assembly, in its distrust of the central government, had succeeded in cutting all communication between Paris and the provinces, destroying effective co-ordination amongst the communes and transforming the old centralized France into a conglomeration of forty thousand independent municipalities. No other way existed, for the time being, in which the idea of national unity and the need for common action in face of a threatened counter-revolution could manifest itself: that same urge which found sentimental expression in the fêtes of federation and the taking of oaths to the constitution.

It was in this way that the Jacobin minority ended by becoming a dominant influence in the country. Not only was it active and organized amidst the mass of the people, the majority of whom only wanted a quiet life, but it was itself an integral part of this majority. The people were ready to let the Jacobins indulge in their own whims so long as they prevented a return of the privileged classes and consolidated the new order; they voted for Jacobin candidates, or at least did not oppose them; and they willingly delegated their own powers to this organized minority, though they were to turn to other parties when they found themselves ill-served or injured. But until the time when a deep and irremediable cleavage between the political clubs and the citizens as a whole finally revealed itself, all the hostility of the King and the Court, and every onslaught by the nobles and clergy, only served to close the ranks of the revolutionary army, to intensify hatred and bitterness, and to strengthen the hands of the most aggressive and fanatical leaders of this combatant minority.

v

During the night of June 20th, while the Comte de Provence was taking his own departure for Brussels, the King and Queen with their two children, the King's sister and the children's governess, emerged separately and in disguise from the Tuileries, and, accompanied by three of the Royal Bodyguard, all hastened to meet Count Fersen, who was waiting for them on the box of a hired carriage.

Their aim was to reach the stronghold of Montmédy, on the borders of Champagne, by way of the Châlons-Clermont-Varennes road. Bouillé had posted troops here and there along the route, on the pretext that a large consignment of bullion was being convoyed from Paris for paying the army. He himself was waiting just beyond Varennes, between Stenay and Dun.

On their way to the meeting-place the Queen and her escort were passed by Lafayette with his retinue, without being recognized; they took the wrong turning, retraced their steps, and finally rejoined the others after considerable delay. When at length they started, Fersen, instead of driving directly to the Saint Martin barrier where the travelling-coach was waiting, called at the stables to make sure that it had left punctually, and thus lost yet more precious time.

The travelling-coach into which the fugitives, already two hours late, transferred themselves on leaving Paris at about half-past two in the morning, was a large, cumbrous *berline*, specially built for the occasion and unlikely to escape notice. Even more conspicuous were the three men of the Royal Bodyguard, wearing the bright yellow uniform of couriers; one went ahead to see that relays of post-horses were ready, another cantered beside the coach and the third was on the box.

At Bondy, Fersen took farewell of the royal family and rode off towards Belgium. At Claye another chaise was waiting with two serving-women for the Queen. In changing horses at Vieux-Maisons and at Chaintrix the fugitives, who took little care to conceal themselves, were recognized. Between Chaintrix and Châlons the horses fell twice and a halt had to be made to repair damage. They were now more than three hours late.

At Pont-de-Somme-Vesle a first contingent of Hussars, forty strong, under command of the Duc de Choiseul, should have awaited them. But no one was there. Choiseul, not knowing how to account for the delay in their arrival, and alarmed, not only by the threatening attitude of the peasants (who suspected that the presence of troops denoted plans for armed requisitioning of their goods), but also at news that the King's flight was already known at the post-house, concluded that the royal family must have stopped at Châlons. He therefore made his way across country to Varennes, leaving no one behind at the meeting-place. His only precaution was to send a carriage with Léonard, the Royal hairdresser — another indispensable member of the Queen's retinue! — to warn detachments of troops further along the route not to expect the convoy of treasure that night.

On these instructions the officer commanding the dragoons who were waiting at Sainte-Ménehould ordered his men to unsaddle. When, towards sunset, the Royal coach arrived, there was no one to meet it. While the horses were being changed the King and Queen rashly showed themselves and were recognized by the *maître-de-poste*. By the time the travellers had left the village the news had flown from house to house, and an armed throng of citizens joined the National Guard in preventing the dragoons from accompanying the coach. Drouet, the posting-master, and a companion were immediately dispatched by the municipal authorities with orders to ride at full speed across country to Varennes.

At Clermont, too, a detachment of a hundred and forty dragoons who were awaiting the convoy, had, on receiving Léonard's message, been allowed by their commanding officer to unsaddle.

He called them up again when the coach had passed through the town, but here too the population refused to allow the troops to follow the fugitives.

At Varennes Bouillé's son and the Comte de Raigecourt, having waited for hours with a relay of fresh horses on the town's outskirts, and discouraged by Léonard's news that the enterprise had failed, had towards eleven o'clock retired for the night, shortly before the coach's arrival. The latter was forced to stop while a search was made for the horses. Meanwhile, Drouet arrived, warned the *procureur* of the commune, and with the help of volunteers, barricaded the bridge between the lower and upper parts of the little town.

When the coach moved on again without fresh horses, and came to the archway, the travellers, finding themselves surrounded by armed men and seeing the way before them blocked, were forced to obey a summons to alight and show their passports. Meanwhile the *tocsin* was rung and the National Guard called out by the roll of drums.

If the troops, posted along the route in conformity with Bouillé's orders, had followed the coach, the fugitives might easily have forced their way through. But even the sixty hussars at Varennes were already dispersed about the village, drinking with the patriots; the three men of the King's *garde du corps* who accompanied the royal family had been disarmed; and de Bouillé and de Raigecourt had hurriedly left to inform the General of what was happening. When Choiseul arrived from Pont-de-Somme-Vesle after midnight (in traversing a wood he had been held up by an accident to one of his hussars) a crowd seven or eight hundred strong was already on guard at the grocery shop to which the fugitives had been taken.

The villagers, however, were ill-armed. A desperate attempt to force a way through might have been made with help from the hussars. But Louis XVI was not the man to resolve on such a step; his first thought on alighting at the shop had been to ask for food. Not wishing to expose his family to the hazards of such a skirmish, he preferred to wait for Bouillé.

Bouillé, for his part, was waiting beyond Dun, hidden by the roadside. Towards four in the morning, on hearing of the King's arrest, he sent at once to Stenay to call up the Royal German

Regiment, which had been ordered to stand by with horses ready saddled. Every man was in bed. It took three-quarters of an hour to get them ready for the road, and when Bouillé and his men, riding at full speed, came within sight of Varennes towards nine on the morning of June 22nd, the royal family had already left for Paris.

The coach was escorted by National Guards and a crowd of peasants. At every town and village newcomers joined the throng and further insults were hurled at the royal family. At Chouilly the King was spat upon; his sister and the Queen wept, but Louis remained impassive. The blazing heat, the dust of the high road and the travellers' distress made their journey one long torture for three days.

At Paris, news of the King's disappearance had spread during the early hours of June 21st. The citizens closed their shops and crowded into the streets in their anxiety; or, seizing arms, hastened to the headquarters of the Sections and National Guards. In the King's absence, all regular government seemed in abeyance. But the Parisians' mocking humour soon asserted itself. On the door of the Tuileries appeared a notice with the words: 'Premises to Let'. 'Gone away without leaving an address', commented the passers-by; 'Lost, a King and Queen; anyone not finding them again will be rewarded'.

In the void created by the monarchy's disappearance the republicans were not slow to extend their own influence and activities. The Théâtre Français Section proclaimed universal suffrage, on its own initiative. The Cordeliers Club published an address in which all the members declared themselves 'tyrannicides', and, on Robert's proposal, approved a petition to the National Assembly calling for the institution of a republic in France.

But — such was the influence of a centuries-old monarchical tradition — the majority of the people remained indifferent to these moves. Neither Robespierre nor Pétion, nor any other prominent democrat seemed able resolutely to take the initiative in the Assembly. All idea of a republic was quickly dropped owing to the energetic demeanour of the Left and Centre, under Barnave's leadership.

Having dispatched couriers in all directions with orders to close the frontiers, the Assembly declared itself in permanent session and informed the Ministers that decrees of the legislative body were to be put into execution without royal sanction. Having reaffirmed its trust in Lafayette — who was accused by the democrats of complicity in the King's flight — it expunged Louis' name from the Roll of the Civic Oath, informed foreign powers of its own pacific intentions, assumed conduct of diplomatic affairs, and, in fact, took over all the King's functions. But it was careful not to commit itself over premature accusations; and apart from issuing a strongly-worded statement in answer to the proclamation which the King had left behind him condemning all that the revolutionaries had achieved and disavowing the constitutional oath which he had so lately taken, it made a show of believing that he had not fled of his own free will, and resorted to a legal fiction presuming him to have been 'carried off' against his wishes.

The Jacobins' Club took a similar line. At a meeting on June 21st, a majority of the members, still guided by Barnave — despite Robespierre's accusations of counter-revolutionary activities by the Assembly, and Danton's invective against Lafayette — passed a vote of confidence in the National Assembly and invited all patriots to unite in defence of the Constitution, an integral part of which was still the monarchy. Next evening a resolution having been proposed by Robert on behalf of the Cordeliers, demanding the adoption of a republican policy, four-fifths of those present rose in protest against such 'unworthy' behaviour, and proceeded, without more ado, to the work in hand.

The extreme revolutionaries, therefore, were still, even at this moment, isolated and impotent. And when, in the evening, news spread that the King had been arrested at Varennes and was returning to Paris, the city remained perfectly calm. The conservative majority in the Assembly was able to assure itself that nothing had been changed in France and to hope that Louis XVI might have learnt, from so terrible a lesson, the necessity of accepting the *fait accompli*. It could even feel a certain complacence at the King's stupendous blunder and at a situation which must now force him to rely on the moderates in the Assembly, if he wanted to avoid final catastrophe for himself and his family.

Barnave of the Left, Pétion of the Extreme Left, and a deputy from the Centre were sent, as representatives of the Assembly, to meet the royal family and accompany them on their journey back to Paris. Pétion was stiff and ill at ease: for some reason he suspected that the King's sister had fallen a victim to his charms and hoped to win him over to the royalist cause. Barnave, whose loyalty to the constitution had been plainly demonstrated by his demeanour on June 21st, was reserved but considerate, and quickly gained the trust of Marie-Antoinette. Indeed, this was the beginning of a secret relationship in which Barnave took the place, left empty by Mirabeau, of adviser to the Court; displaying greater personal integrity in his actions but meeting with no better success than his predecessor.

Their return to the Tuileries took place on the afternoon of June 25th. The heat was suffocating. In the heavy coach the prisoners, covered with dust, were spent with fatigue and humiliation. Unending, silent crowds thronged the route. The National Guards carried their muskets reversed, in sign of mourning. There were no demonstrations of any kind. The *mot d'ordre* had been passed from mouth to mouth that applause would be punished by a beating, and insults by death.

On this same day, the Assembly decreed that the royal family were 'provisionally' to be given a guard, which — though it was not admitted to constitute imprisonment — was to be held responsible for anything irregular that might occur. All those who had taken part in the flight from Paris were arrested and brought to trial. The decrees enacted on June 21st, giving the ministers power to dispense with the royal sanction, were also 'provisionally' confirmed. Subsequently, on July 15th and 16th, it was decided that the King, who under the Constitution was inviolable, should be regarded as *hors de cause* (exonerated), since his ministers or — if he acted without their knowledge — his secret advisers must always be held responsible for his actions. This last provision was aimed at de Bouillé, who had now sought safety beyond the frontier. But the decree of June 25th, which implicitly provided for the Royal family's imprisonment and the King's suspension from office, still remained in force, it being the Assembly's intention finally to revise the laws of the Constitution and to present them for acceptance to the King before reinstating him in his former functions. If Louis refused to accept the completed Constitution, he was to be regarded as having abdicated.

These were equivocal and far from courageous decisions. It was natural that the royalists should protest against them, deploring this 'republican *interim*' and the fact that the 'very semblance of monarchy no longer existed'. The republicans intensified their propaganda, and gained support from various political associations, particularly in eastern France. At the Cordeliers Club, and in others of a popular kind, the democrats, as yet uncertain in their republicanism, demanded that the 'criminal and imbecile' King, as Danton described him, should be deposed, and his functions entrusted to an elective council until the Dauphin should come of age: and that in any case the national will should be consulted by holding elections for a 'Convention', which should be empowered to decide on the King's personal responsibility with regard to his attempted flight.

But the majority of deputies felt that abolition of the monarchy, now demanded merely by a few extreme revolutionaries, would lead to increasing violence by the royalists and Catholics, and would undermine that conservative policy — both anti-feudal and anti-revolutionary — which they hoped to pursue. 'Any change,' said Barnave, 'would at this moment be lamentable, any prolongation of the revolution disastrous. Do we intend to set a term to the revolution, or do we mean to start it all over again? If you lose faith in the Constitution, where will you stop? Where will your successors stop? This revolutionary movement has destroyed all that it set out to destroy, and has now brought us to the point where it is necessary to call a halt. If the revolution takes one step forward, it will do so at inevitable risk, because, if it goes further towards liberty, its first act must be to overthrow the monarchy: and if towards equality its first act must be to abolish private ownership of property.'

Furthermore, the majority feared that the King's dethronement would lead to a declaration of war against France by the Emperor. 'We must abstain,' wrote *La correspondance nationale* (a journal of the moderate liberals) on June 25th, 1791, 'from giving foreign powers hostile to our Constitution any pretext for attacking us. If we depose Louis XVI they will arm all Europe against us, on the score of avenging the monarchy. Let us respect Louis XVI, although he is guilty of infamous treachery towards the French nation. Let us respect him and his family, not for his sake, but for ours.'

Nevertheless, no constitutional fiction could wipe out so notorious a fact as the attempted flight. Even those least inclined to support republican ideas were indignant at such indisputable proof that the Court had, indeed, been plotting with the *emigrés*, that all the King's 'civic oaths' were insincere, and that could he have had his way he would not have hesitated to restore the old régime — with all its oppression and injustice, and, moreover, with an inevitable collapse of the *assignats*. Even the American, Morris, who had no love for the revolutionaries and was on friendly terms with the Court, wrote of Louis: 'It would not be surprising if such a dolt were to lose his crown.' The fact that a republic was not immediately proclaimed is very significant, for it shows how strong a reformed monarchy would have been had the King known how to adapt himself to the new order. The royalists claimed that the National Assembly should at once restore the previous state of affairs. But at a moment when, from Flanders to the Pyrenees, invasion, civil war, and counter-revolution were daily expected, and it was only too clear where the King's sympathies lay, it was impossible for the Assembly to proceed as though nothing had occurred to change the situation. In politics, blunders of such magnitude as that of the flight to Varennes cannot be committed without widespread and serious after-effects.

It would have been a different matter had the Assembly been able to depose the King and put another in his place. But the heir was a child, the King's brothers were *emigrés*, and his cousin, the Duke of Orleans, was held in universal contempt. Were an executive council to be set up at the side of a King deprived of power, it would in fact be a republic — disguised, insecure, and necessarily provisional — but a republic all the same. No way remained but that of half-measures: to keep the monarchy so that a total revolutionary landslide might be avoided, and to suspend the King from his functions, in deference not only to the general indignation but in a forlorn hope that he might come to his senses.

The country as a whole approved these decisions. It was only in Paris that there were any hostile demonstrations when they became known on the evening of July 15th. A few theatres had to close down. The Jacobins, yielding to clamour from a crowd instigated, it would seem, by agents of the Duke of Orleans, decided to lay a petition for signature on the Altar of the Country in the Champ de Mars, calling on the Assembly to depose Louis XVI 'by constitutional means', and stating that the signatories 'would never recognize him as their King unless such should be the will of a majority of the nation'. Next day, the Assembly's supporters in the Jacobin Club resigned, not wishing to be dragged at the republicans' heels. For their part, the republicans protested against 'constitutional means' that eliminated the King while preserving the monarchy. The executive committee of the Jacobins, therefore, decided on the morning of July 17th not to proceed with the collection of signatures.

But already, early on the morning of Sunday 17th, a crowd had begun to gather on the Champ de Mars to sign the petition. As they waited, two men were discovered hiding, for some unknown reason, beneath the altar. Arrested, and accused by the excited mob of having intended to blow it up, they were immediately lynched.

Towards midday, the Jacobin decision was announced. The republican group thereupon decided to continue on its own account and improvised another petition inviting the Assembly to consider 'the crime of Louis XVI as proved', and since, by reason of his flight, he had himself abdicated the throne, 'to accept his abdication, and to convene a new constituent body that in a truly national manner might proceed to try the criminal; above all, to replace him and to set up a new executive power'. Constitutional means were not mentioned this time, nor was a republic openly demanded; the weak person of the King was to be directly attacked, whilst indirect steps were taken to overthrow the monarchy.

What better proof could there be of the republicans' weakness and isolation, and of the fact that almost all the revolutionaries, though deeply angered against the King, still shunned such a leap in the dark as would be represented by setting up a republic?

Meanwhile the version of the Champ de Mars lynching which reached the Assembly led to a belief that two National Guards had been murdered. The majority of deputies, perturbed at the news, and exasperated by the campaign of abuse which the democrats had launched against them, decided to put an end to the agitation, and invited the Paris municipality to take all necessary measures for restoring order.

Towards evening, the people who were signing the republican petition on the Champ de Mars found themselves surrounded by troops and National Guards. There were hostile shouts. The National Guards responded with a murderous volley against the mob.

The number of casualties is uncertain. A somewhat vague statement was issued by the municipal authorities to the effect that eleven or twelve persons had been killed and from ten to twelve wounded: it was to their interest to keep the numbers as low as possible. The democrats spoke of six hundred victims, while those most carried away by emotion had seen as many as two thousand. The German Oelsner, in Paris at the time, and usually a calm and well-informed witness, estimated the number of deaths as sixty or seventy: a figure that probably most nearly approaches the truth. But apart from some doubt on this point, the incidents of July 17th have great importance, for they mark the break between liberal-conservatives and democrats. They were the first episodes in the long, bitter and often sanguinary struggle that now began within the revolutionary movement.

VI

Dismayed by the energy of the constitutional party, and discouraged at the country's hostile indifference, the democrats, after the slaughter of July 17th, feared for a moment that all was lost. Robespierre changed his lodgings, thinking he might be arrested by night, and Marat moved his editorial office to a secret hiding-place, intimating that he did not intend to be taken alive. Danton fled to England. The two Robert brothers, Desmoulins and Fréron, all went into hiding to escape arrest. If the constitutional party had been ready to press home their advantage and crush the democratic movement, dissolving the political societies and restricting freedom of the press, it is probable that they would have met little resistance in Paris. 'Let us break up the Clubs!' said the constitutional deputy André to his friends. 'The moment has come!'

Unfortunately for the constitutional party, it not only had to combat extremists among the democrats, but it was also forced to defend itself from the royalist deputies of the Right. The latter — 299 in number — instead of supporting the conservative policy of the constitutionalists, imagined that everything was to be gained from their defeat, and therefore decided to abstain from all voting in the Assembly after the flight to Varennes. Delighted at the apparently irreparable split in the revolutionary forces, they intensified their reactionary propaganda, and continued to demand full restoration of the former régime. 'These people force us to seek protection from their vengeance by turning to the people,' Thouret remarked in irritation, unwittingly echoing what Mirabeau had said of the *emigrés*: 'Their threats of counter-revolution will drive us into a republic!'

In such circumstances it was impossible for the majority in the Assembly to destroy the political societies, which constituted a solid revolutionary force in defence of the new order, and in which, after all, the extremists had no dominating influence. Political ideas and programmes cannot be laid aside like so many garments, at a change of season. Having fought so long for freedom, and having relied so often upon the clubs in combating the royalists, men like Duport and Barnave could not suddenly disavow their whole past, and, as André had advised, ruthlessly suppress all right of association. It seemed wiser to let the clubs alone, but to try and bring their influence to bear in favour of the constitutional party. Those deputies, therefore, who had resigned from the Jacobins on July 16th, founded a new club with premises in the former monastery of the Feuillants. The Feuillants, too, called themselves 'Friends of the Constitution'.

In this crisis, which threatened to undermine their whole organization, the Jacobins, led by Robespierre, Pétion, Grégoire, Buzot and a few other left-wing deputies, began to play for safety. They entreated the Feuillants to unite with them, proclaimed their loyalty to the Assembly and the Constitution, and explained their policy to their affiliated societies as a strictly legal one. Robespierre, in a 'manifesto to the French', protested against accusations of republicanism, and maintained that he had never opposed 'either the existence or the heritage of the monarchy', because 'the words *republic* and *monarchy* are only vague and insignificant terms, not indicative of any special kind of govern-ment', and 'every free state, in which the nation counts for some-thing, is a republic'. What he had always demanded, he explained, was equality of rights and the people's sovereignty.

Any plausible justification for secession by the Feuillants was thus removed, and the Jacobins assumed the rôle of peacemakers at the moment when, in consequence of the royal family's inter-cepted flight, war was expected from one day to the next, and it was obvious that union within the revolutionary movement was more than ever necessary.

In fact, not only was secession towards the new society soon checked, but many members returned to that of the Jacobins. The greater part of the provincial clubs remained faithful to their old traditions. Two political organizations, therefore, now confronted one another: both monarchical, but one of them more extreme in its democratic tendencies and distrustful of the King, while the other was conservative and anxious to strengthen the monarchy. The Jacobins were careful for the time being not to stress this divergence of aims. But it is revealed in a characteristic circumstance: for while the Feuillants continued to exclude 'passive' citizens from membership of their society, as the Jacobins had formerly done, the latter from now onwards admitted them to their ranks.

Notwithstanding the failure of their attempt to destroy Jacobin influence, the Feuillants, in August 1791, still dominated the Assembly. Discussion on the constitutional laws was over. Before dissolving the Assembly all the work of the preceding two years had to be co-ordinated and presented as an organic whole. It was natural that the most influential party should profit from this circumstance to revise the Constitution in a conservative sense.

The electoral system, notwithstanding the difference between 'active' and 'passive' citizens, gave wide scope, as has been already pointed out, to free expression of the people's will. Restriction of the tax-qualification for second-grade electors to the equivalent of ten days' wages, and of candidates for election to the Assembly to the *marc d'argent*, had been no brake on the progress of the demo-cratic party; since in the petty *bourgeois* society that formed the second-grade electorate there were plenty of men with democratic ideas for the four million primary electors, if they so wished, to nominate as their representatives; and it was these who, in their turn, chose the deputies and departmental authorities. If, however, to appease the democrats, the qualification of the *marc d'argent*, against which they had protested so vehemently, were abolished, and, on the other hand, the tax-qualification of those eligible as second-grade electors were considerably raised, the political influence of the journalists, men of letters, lawyers and professional men, who paid little in taxation and were the leaders of the democratic party, would be destroyed; and the result would be a new electoral system which, though apparently fulfilling democratic aims in abolishing the *marc d'argent*, was really conservative and anti-democratic. This proposal was made by Thouret on behalf of the Constitutional Committee, at the Assembly's debate on August 5th.

Immediately, the democrats of the Extreme Left rallied to defend the Constitution, instead of advocating its reform, as they had done hitherto. While still upholding the necessity for universal suffrage they insisted that the existing state of affairs, at least, should be maintained. But the majority needed some defence, as Barnave frankly admitted, against the 'pamphleteers' and 'journalists', with their clamorous demands for more social and political change. The new law was passed on August 27th, 1791. It excluded from assemblies of second-grade electors, in all cities of over 6000 inhabitants, such citizens as did not own landed property on which taxation equalled at least 200 days' wages, or who paid in rent a sum taxed at not less than 150 days' wages; and in the country, those who had an income taxed at less than 150 days' wages or who were tenants or *métayers* of land bearing a tax that was at least the equivalent of 400 days' wages. All 'active' citizens, whatever their degree of wealth, were made eligible as deputies.

This decree did not affect elections for the Legislative Assembly, which had already begun according to the former system; nor, in fact, was it ever put into force, because, a year later, the revolution of August 10th, 1792, resulted in the institution of universal suffrage. But it is a characteristic symptom of the state of mind of the *bourgeoisie* and of the restrictive political tendencies that began to make headway after the ingenuous hopes and illusions of 1789 had faded.

With the aim of still further consolidating the new order, it was decreed that the Constitution could not be altered for ten years, and that the votes of three consecutive legislatures were necessary before a fourth could proceed to any revision.

It may well be asked why, once the Left had been induced, out of fear of the extremists, to proclaim the monarchy necessary for social conservation, no advantage was taken of this revision of the constitutional laws to restore the King's administrative powers. Barnave was not averse to the idea. Since the return from Varennes he had become counsellor to the Court, and was convinced that the King and Queen now intended to adhere explicitly to the new order. Having opposed the monarchy when it served the ends of the privileged classes, he now wanted it restored in the hope of seeing it used to favour the *tiers état*. But the deputies as a whole were ignorant of the secret reasons for Barnave's attitude. They felt far from sure of the King. 'He will accept, he will promise, and he will not keep his word,' said Grégoire. And another Feuillant deputy, Le Chapelier, asked: 'How can we restore effective authority to the King when we cannot but fear he will use it against us?'

Barnave and his friends could only count on carrying a part of the Left with them. To obtain the majority they required, the 299 royalist deputies of the Right would have to lend them their support. But the Right, in blind hatred of the revolutionaries, refused to treat with those who 'after being incendiaries, offer to act as firemen', and still refused to attend the Assembly debates. 'Things are not yet going badly enough,' they explained. 'Order can only be born out of extreme disorder; the important thing is not to allow the constitutional party to consolidate itself, since its origins are odious, and it is preventing the crisis from being resolved.'

Thus any idea of a reformed monarchy was dropped. Indeed, on August 27th, in revising the articles embodying the right of veto, the Constituent Assembly withdrew all financial laws concerning taxation from the sovereign's sanction and thus dealt a further blow to the King's authority.

Having finished drawing up the Constitution, the Assembly decided to present it to the King, so that he might make known his decision either to accept or to abdicate. In the meantime, his guards were withdrawn, and he was left free to retire from Paris to whatever place he wished, so that his reply might be framed in full freedom. The King stated that he preferred to remain in Paris. On September 13th he declared that he would 'accept the Constitution, maintain it at home, defend it against all attack from abroad, and put it into force with all the means at his disposal'. On September 24th he went to the hall of the Assembly to take the oath.

The seat assigned to him on the President's left was without any special sign of distinction: it was a chair like all the rest. Nervous and embarrassed, he had risen, bare-headed, and was beginning to take the oath, when he perceived that the deputies had all remained seated: they were the sovereign people, and he the nation's delegate. He turned pale. The abyss of humiliation into which he, the successor of Louis XIV, had fallen, had never before been so clearly revealed to his confused and torpid mind as in this revolution in ceremonial. He, too, sat down, and finished the oath. When he returned to the Court, spent with shame and grief, he broke down utterly, exclaiming, between his sobs, 'All is lost!'

During its final weeks of activity, the Constituent Assembly approved the new code of penal procedure and the new penal code. It also decided to annex Avignon and the Comtat Venaissin.

Trial by jury, accepted in principle since the end of 1789, was so regulated that the system later served as a model to all other countries. Traditional barbaric punishments, such as mutilation, flogging and branding — torture had already been suppressed by the edicts of 1788 — were abolished; while confiscation of property and penalization of the criminal's family were done away with. These principles, too, have since been accepted by all civilized peoples. Every penalty was carefully proportioned to the crime. In reacting against the former arbitrary system, advantageous to the powerful and oppressive to the weak, all possibility was denied the judge of choosing between a maximum or minimum sentence or of taking circumstances, extenuating or the reverse, into account: the penalty was a fixed one. The right of reprieve was suppressed, from dislike of the former capricious way in which it had been exercised by the kings. In compensation, and in view of possible rehabilitation of a criminal, life sentences were eliminated: condemnation to hard labour being restricted to a maximum of twenty-four years. The next grade was the death sentence. This tendency to exaggerated rigidity in the code was due to a desire once for all to root out the former arbitrary powers, and has been in part removed by progress in legal science. But the great principle that the individual's responsibility for the wrong he has committed must be the same for all, whatever the social condition of the accused, was a lasting victory for the modern moral and juridical conscience.

As to the problem of Avignon, the conflict with the Holy See and the non-juring priests over the Civil Constitution made a solution imperative. Nevertheless, the Assembly hesitated a long time before violating the principle that forbade aggressive action to France. As late as its sitting on May 4th, 1791, two months after the Pope had publicly condemned the revolutionaries' actions, a proposal for the annexation of Avignon had been rejected by a majority of 171 votes; but next day it was stated that the matter should not be regarded as closed. On May 24th a resolution in favour of annexation was again rejected, but only by six votes. On May 25th it was decided to send mediators to make peace between Avignon and Carpentras, 'before reaching a final decision on the rights of France over these places'.

When the flight to Varennes had eliminated the King from this, as from all other questions, the problem was again examined on September 12th. The mediators who had been sent to Avignon reported that peace could not be established without occupation by the French. The Assembly decided on annexation, but declared itself ready to negotiate with the Holy See over an indemnity, as was already being done with the dispossessed princes of Alsace.

Here again, then, the revolutionaries succeeded where the kings, their predecessors, had failed. But the former monarchical programme was brought to completion in the name of a new sovereign: that of the nation. This new fact, as Sorel observes, gave particular importance to the decision of the Constituent Assembly, and made it a definite threat of war against the old Europe. Henceforth a people had only to rise against its legitimate sovereign and demand union with France, for the French rulers to hold themselves authorized by 'the natural and imprescriptible rights of man' to intervene, with the aim, not of making a conquest — for they had renounced conquest — but of defending the people's will. That in so doing they extended the frontiers of France was no disadvantage in the eyes of the French revolutionaries.

CHAPTER VII

ORIGINS OF THE WAR

THE influence of the royalists — nobles, non-juring clerics and their supporters — on the elections for the Legislative Assembly was negligible. Many of them had left the country. The majority refused to take the civic oath before recording their votes; and in many *départements* intimidation by the revolutionaries had reduced them to impotence. The republicans, who were few in number and without popular backing, suffered a similar eclipse. It was the Feuillants and Jacobins who stood in the forefront, contending for victory.

The former were weakened by the fact that on May 17th, 1791, the Constituent Assembly had decided to exclude its members from candidature at the forthcoming elections. This self-denying ordinance had been proposed by Robespierre, ostensibly out of disinterestedness. It was favoured by the Court and the royalists in order to keep Barnave and his friends out of active politics, and was not opposed by the latter, to avoid any imputation of personal ambition. Most of the deputies, weary after the long and stormy struggles of the last two years, accepted it without demur. In effect, it forced the Feuillant party to substitute the outgoing constitutional deputies with new men, and thus prevented them from offering a large number of experienced candidates, who enjoyed the people's trust, for re-election.

It is true that the Feuillants were favoured by the constitutional clergy, by the greater part of the departmental and communal administration, and in general by the land-owning, industrial, commercial and financial middle-classes, who wanted to see order restored and, above all, an efficient, liberal government established in France. But this very desire for a quiet life brought the constitutionalists more loss than gain; for the great mass of peace-loving citizens, though hoping for a Feuillant victory, were tired of being dragged from their own affairs now for one election and now for another. Anxious to keep out of the way of trouble, they stayed at home and neglected to record their votes.

Thus the Feuillants only succeeded in gaining 264 seats out of 745.

The Jacobins, who, though a small minority in the country, were strengthened by the fanatical discipline of their clubs, obtained seats in the Assembly for 136 members of their Paris organization.

Victory, in fact, went to neither Feuillants nor Jacobins, but to the crowd of 345 'Independents' who formed an unreliable central body of neutral opinion. They reflected the general bewilderment and uncertainty of mind caused by the flight to Varennes, which, in a country traditionally monarchical, had deprived the King of all prestige at the very moment when the *bourgeoisie* were demanding an end to revolutionary disorder; and had undermined the position of the conservatives at a time when conditions for a normal rise to power on the part of the democrats did not exist.

With these independent deputies rested the new Assembly's political future. It was not likely to remain long uncertain. Either the Feuillants would succeed in making the King accept the new Constitution, in which case the independents would join them and a gradual reform of the Constitution on more conservative and monarchical lines — as Barnave and his friends desired — would be facilitated; or fresh dissension between the King and Assembly would defeat Feuillant aims and throw the parliamentary majority on to the side of the Jacobins: causing a rout of the conservatives and in all probability the fall of the monarchy itself.

The deputies of the Left dedicated all their energies — in the Assembly, in their clubs and in the press — to bringing about such dissension, in order to compromise the King and involve the conservative Right in difficulties. Among them the most combative group and more effective speakers — Vergniaud of the flowery Ciceronian periods, Gensonné, grave and severe, and Guadet with his biting sarcasm — came from the *département* of the Gironde; from whence arose the designation of the whole group as 'Girondins' in place of their official title of 'Jacobin patriots'. Another leading orator was the impetuous Marseillais, Isnard, always quick to produce some telling phrase to justify acts of violence, however criminal. These leaders of the Left found inspiration in the seductive Manon Phlipon, wife of the elderly and well-to-do Roland: a woman of fine feeling but possessed by a fervent desire for glory (from the time when, in her girlhood, she had devoured Plutarch's *Lives* while helping her father in his work as an engraver) but, like many women, influenced in her opinions and actions solely by her own personal feelings or prejudices. Secret adviser to the party was the Abbé Siéyès, imbued with a bitter hatred for the Court and the Feuillants, who had dispensed with his services: his mind full of ambitious political strategy, he was a tireless fabricator of obscure and empty *formulae*. The most active parliamentary leader was Jacques Pierre Brissot. The son of a pastrycook in Chartres, and an attorney by profession, Brissot had been forced to emigrate for having published seditious matter; but he had returned to France in 1789, and had founded the *Patriote français*, a newspaper widely read in the capital. After a bitter struggle he had been elected a deputy for Paris. Skilled in intrigue, facile and impulsive, he was possessed of a wide, if rather confused, political culture, picked up during his wanderings in the shady world of exiles, pamphleteers and spies.

By what ideas these men were guided and towards what political and social ends they thought they were striving, it is impossible to determine; nor did they know with any certainty themselves. Young, as most of them were, and born into that professional and intellectual *petite bourgeoisie* which at the time formed the general staff of the Jacobin organization, they were possessed of little worldly wealth, but were rich in intellectual gifts and in self-confidence. Their enthusiasm for the Revolution was prompted not so much by the significance of what was being destroyed or changed, as by the fever for destruction and change in the abstract; above all, by the possibility of personal advancement in a world where the old, rigid social categories were being broken up. They never doubted that they were the stuff of which ministers, legislators, diplomatists or warriors are made, and could not envisage the Revolution ending without their personal ascendancy over French affairs: conceiving of their own success as a triumph for true merit over the privileges of wealth and noble birth. Endowed with the imagination of artists and adventurers, and easily intoxicated by their own words, they regarded their efforts to win a more prominent place in the world as a glorious conflict on the part of all oppressed peoples to end inequality and to create a new civilization that would bring justice and liberty to all mankind.

But the people's Revolution now seemed threatened by a new oligarchy of 'big landowners, rich traders, proud and moneyed men', who, argued Isnard, 'comfortably seated in the forefront of the social scene, would not give up their places'. The Feuillants, he pointed out, had now excluded from the second-grade franchise — that is to say from any effective political influence — all but a small minority belonging to the propertied classes; and were constantly repeating Duport's statement that 'the revolution was over'. Were the King to lend them his support this 'aristocracy of bankers' would consolidate itself and soon make common cause with the old privileged classes. Indeed, were not those members of the privileged classes who had accepted the new order already being chosen by the *bourgeoisie* for important offices, in preference to sincere patriots? A new and salutary wave of revolution, like that which had engulfed France after the fall of the Bastille, was therefore necessary to sweep away the conservative interests and fears now paralysing the nation's 'generous impulses'.

In reality, these generous impulses too often took the form of brutal murder. At Avignon, on October 16th, a month after the Constituent Assembly had decreed reunion of that district with France, the patriots were attacked by aristocrats, who brutally killed and mutilated the communal secretary. The revolutionaries, led by a ferocious muleteer named Jourdan, known as the 'executioner', thereupon massacred sixty-one helpless prisoners, including old people, children and pregnant women, and threw their bodies into a pit; while another hundred victims were murdered in the streets and flung into the river.

But (so argued the Girondist lawyers and pamphleteers) just as, to save the living organism, all gangrenous parts must be cut away, so liberty demands extermination of its enemies. Since the law — again according to Isnard — too often let the guilty go unpunished, the People, 'whose wrath is as the wrath of God', must take the law into its own hands, and kill.

Thus the Girondins unloosed the mob — exalting it as endowed with every virtue — against the Feuillants, priests and royalists, to dispense due justice. But having killed, what then? What could they hope to gain, these *sansculottes*, when they had opened a way to the dominion of their friends? Would they be any less wretched or enslaved? Would they find fulfilment, under Girondist government, of those revolutionary ideals which the Feuillants had failed to achieve? This was a question that no Girondin ever asked himself. Not one of them perceived that the time for revolutionary violence was past, and that so far as the political and social needs of the *bourgeoisie* were concerned, any further change was bound to be dangerous.

For the moment, the Girondins were making use of the *sansculottes* for their own ends. They wished to enter the Government, to make fine speeches and win imperishable fame — these petty lawyers who, but for the Revolution, would have lived and died in provincial obscurity. Later on, when they had tasted power, and had let the crowd have what it wanted — out of a love of popularity and the desire to keep up revolutionary enthusiasm — they were to reach a point where concessions were no longer possible; only to find that the sovereign people, still not satisfied, was beginning to threaten them. In their bewilderment they accused the mob — no longer the 'faultless' people — of ignorance and baseness; and in the same reckless manner as that in which they had first armed it with pikes and false hopes, they tried to thwart and oppose it. Then this force which had raised them up and which, in their vanity, they had thought they could master, hurled them into the abyss. But, in victory or defeat, in power or in prison, the Girondins were always the same: artists who had lost their way in politics, lovers of fine words and noble gestures, seekers after glory rather than truth; half play-actors and half heroes.

II

Brissot and his friends hoped that, by intensifying the campaign against the *emigrés*, they might stimulate enthusiasm in the revolutionary party and spur it on to greater achievements.

After the flight to Varennes the *emigrés* had become more

arrogant and irresponsible than ever. The Comte de Provence,
on reaching Brussels, had proclaimed himself Regent of France,
in place of the prisoner King. His agents, abetted by the non-
juring clergy, went about France urging provincial nobles and
army officers, in the name of honour and loyalty to the Crown,
to leave the country and place themselves under the orders of the
only free and legitimate representative of the 'true France'. The
'true France' had not merely found a ruler but also possessed a
court, with Calonne as chief administrator of the affairs — or
rather debts — of the Comte de Provence, and with the Prince of
Condé as commander of its future army. At Coblentz, where this
court was set up, the Regent nominated ambassadors to foreign
powers and distributed offices and decorations, whilst his courtiers
gambled at the hostelry of the Three Crowns. The troops were
encamped at Worms: by the end of October they numbered
about ten thousand men, drilling with staves instead of muskets,
grumbling at their leaders' futility and jeering at the King, whom
they nicknamed 'King Log'. All were eager to give orders but
not to obey them; all proclaimed the impossibility of any agreement with the revolutionaries, and expected — as they had, for
the last two years — an immediate world-wide anti-revolutionary
crusade: of which there were no signs whatever.

In attacking the *emigrés*, Brissot could count on support from
the country as a whole. Not even among the most moderate and
peace-loving of Feuillants were there any who would have dared
defend their insensate provocation. It would be easy, too, to
extend the campaign into one against the German petty princes
who tolerated them within their borders. External war, therefore, would transform the Revolution's enemies into enemies
of the country. Once the dreary sequence of hopes and fears,
of defiance and timidity, in which the work begun by the last
National Assembly had seemed doomed to frustration, were
thus interrupted, and the country forced to choose, no longer
between Jacobins and Feuillants, but between political liberty
and the re-establishment of the feudal régime through foreign
intervention, the people's energies would be revived by the danger.
It would then be easy for the more daring spirits to displace the
timid by arraigning their lack of revolutionary ardour as complicity with the enemy and treachery towards their own country.

The first move was made by Brissot with a speech on October 20th, 1791, in which he demanded the death sentence *in contumacia* against the *emigrés*. On October 31st the Legislative Assembly decreed that the Comte de Provence should lose all right to the regency if within two months he had not returned to France. On November 9th it designated French nationals assembled beyond the frontiers as 'suspect of conspiring against the nation'. Army officers absent from their posts were proclaimed deserters, and all prominent persons and officials abroad who did not return home before January 1st, 1792, were to be held guilty of threatening the safety of the State and Constitution. On November 29th the Legislative Assembly invited the King to request those neighbouring princes who harboured Frenchmen engaged in intrigues against their own country to disperse them forthwith. In every debate Brissot, Isnard, Vergniaud, Gensonné and their followers, weakly opposed by the Right and supported by noisy applause from their hired partisans in the public galleries, hurled insults at the German princes, accusing them of complicity with the *emigrés*, and threatening war against all who did not immediately comply with the demands of France.

The Girondins took advantage of the general tension to begin an assault upon the refractory clergy. On November 29th they won the Assembly's approval for another decree, by virtue of which every priest who within the ensuing eight days should refuse to make his oath to the Constitution would be deprived of his stipend, regarded as suspect of rebellion against the State, and as such, subject to special surveillance by the authorities. Furthermore, such non-juring priests as were still to be found in the communes were to be removed by order of the departmental authorities, and those who resisted, condemned to a year's imprisonment. Priests held guilty of instigating disorder were liable to two years' imprisonment.

Step by step with the nationalist and anti-clerical campaign went the struggle against the Feuillants in the communal administration of Paris. On November 16th, 1791, the Girondins succeeded in electing Pétion *maire* of Paris in the place of Bailly. On December 9th, Danton, President of the Cordeliers, was appointed Deputy Procurator-general of the Commune. By occupying every official post, one by one, they became masters of the whole municipality in the spring of 1792. In this vital conquest they were assisted by the electors' abstentionism: at Pétion's election, for instance, the votes numbered 6728 for the winning candidate and 3126 for Lafayette, out of an electorate of 81,000 registered voters. The stupidity of the Royalists also contributed to Pétion's victory, for on Court advice they voted for Pétion, out of hatred for Lafayette; and thus opened the way to their own defeat.

At the same time the Girondins, in agreement with the extremists among the Jacobins, began to arm the Parisian workers with pikes. While this new democratic force was coming into being, the *bourgeois* and constitutional National Guard was beginning to disintegrate, since the Constituent Assembly, on September 12th, 1791, had suppressed its General Staff and had replaced Lafayette by six legionary leaders who were to command it in turn. In December, Lafayette went to take over one of the armies on the frontier. The Paris National Guard was left without either unity or continuity of command.

Barnave and the more prudent of the Feuillants knew at what the Girondins were aiming and realized the dangers involved. 'The war,' wrote Barnave, 'will be a terrible one, and waged in a most ferocious way. The hotheads and fanatics will prevail over public opinion. The King, forced to fight his own brother-in-law, will be subject to a thousand doubts and fears; in order not to increase them he will have to act against his better judgment, and exaggerate his own intentions; if he urges moderation or prudence he will be thought in league with the foreigner and will be accused of treachery both by his enemies and by such honest people as are easily misled. The Emperor's aid will encourage the *emigrés* in their obduracy. There will be no place for men of moderate views in this struggle between two extreme parties. Civilized principles, together with the nation's real interests, will be forgotten.'

For these reasons Barnave, in giving secret advice to the Court, insisted, as Mirabeau had done, that military escapades must at all costs be avoided, and everything possible done to consolidate the constitutional monarchy. It was imperative, he pointed out, to restore order and restrain the Jacobins, to collect taxes once more and to impose discipline in the army. The new administrative authorities should be strengthened and subordinated to the central authority. In other words, once for all, a strong and properly constituted government must be set up.

The Queen accepted Barnave's pacific *memoranda*, expressed her approval and forwarded them to the Emperor and Comte de Mercy by means of trusted members of the Feuillants. At the same time she sent other *memoranda* through different channels repudiating all that she had written or agreed upon with Barnave and making frantic appeals to her brother for help. Neither she nor the King, she explained, intended to subject themselves to the 'monstrous' Constitution set up by the Feuillants. The King had taken the oath simply because 'he had no power to do anything but gain time', while waiting for the situation to improve. And if, having taken the oath, he was now to all appearances observing it, this was only to bring out its defects in the light of experience, and at the same time to win the people's trust by giving proof of his good will.

'Rest assured,' wrote Marie-Antoinette to Fersen, in explaining her relations with the Feuillants, 'I shall never give in to these madmen; if I treat with them, it is only to serve my own ends. They fill me with so much loathing that I could never give them my confidence. I have to use them, to avoid even greater evils; but as to doing any good, I know that they are incapable of it.'

She still wished the Emperor to convoke a Congress of Powers, which, backed by formidable armies, and with the *emigrés* relegated to the background, should use such firm language as to strike fear into the revolutionaries' hearts, and thus encourage all good citizens who were favourable to the monarchy. The nation, she was sure, would gather round the King to avoid war and ruin, and the King, with full authority restored to him, would be enabled to make peace and re-impose order in the country.

Leopold, however, was reluctant to make any decided move. He had promised to help his sister if she should escape from Paris, and after the ill-fated attempt that ended at Varennes he had issued a circular (on July 16th) from Padua to all reigning sovereigns inviting them to agree upon measures to 'vindicate the freedom and honour of the King and his family and restrain the excesses of the Revolution'. But the associated Powers were merely asked to publish a joint declaration on the necessity of preserving the freedom and inviolability of the King and his family; and the Emperor stressed that, in calling upon the revolutionary leaders to exercise restraint, the way should not be closed to 'an honest recognition of their errors', nor should they be prevented from spontaneously making their peace with the King.

The invitation had, naturally, been warmly received by Catherine II, who was always ready to join in urging others to take action, and by Gustavus III, who posed as the Chief of Staff of monarchical Europe. But the English Government had replied that they intended to maintain absolute neutrality, and the Prussian ministers, though theoretically in favour, wanted, before committing themselves, to know what practical advantage their royal master might hope to gain from joining in the noble enterprise.

Repulsed by England and uncertain of Prussia, anxious to look after his own affairs and to keep an eye on Russia's moves in Turkey and Poland, Leopold was careful not to press the matter further, and the situation remained as before.

Towards the end of August, in the course of a meeting at Pillnitz between Leopold and Frederick William, a number of French *emigrés* led by the Comte d'Artois and the Prince of Condé presented themselves in the hope of concluding a definite treaty against the revolutionaries. In order not to send them away empty-handed, Leopold and the King of Prussia agreed to publish a declaration which, whilst giving evidence of a desire to see order restored in France, pledged the two sovereigns to nothing whatever, and in fact clearly showed that there was no hope of intervention on their part. The Comte d'Artois appealed in vain against the lukewarmness and ambiguity of this famous 'Declaration of Pillnitz' (August 27th, 1791), though he afterwards passed it off as the official proclamation of a European alliance against France. In it the Emperor and the King of Prussia again expressed a hope that there should be consultation between the Powers regarding the position of Louis XVI. They also declared themselves ready, when agreement among them had been reached (an agreement which the neutrality of England made impossible of achievement), to 'employ efficacious means for enabling the King of France full freedom to set up a monarchical government in conformity with his rights and the welfare of the nation'.

When, later, Louis XVI officially communicated the fact that he had sanctioned the Constitution, Leopold expressed hearty approval: 'since the King had given his sanction, there was nothing more to be done'. On October 22nd, he ordered the *emigrés* assembled in Belgium to disperse. Of the two series of secret messages that reached him from Paris, he reserved those inspired by Barnave for warm commendation and paid no heed to the Queen's personal views. Finally, that the *emigrés* should have no excuse for deceiving themselves nor any pretext for stirring up further trouble, he sent out a new circular to the Powers on November 2nd in which he stated that a Congress no longer appeared urgently necessary, since recent events gave good hope for the future. 'The Emperor is deceiving you,' wrote Fersen to the Queen, 'he will do nothing for you.'

Bitterly disappointed at the failure of her plans and exasperated by the difficulties that beset her, Marie-Antoinette in desperation gave her own support to the war championed by the Girondins.

The instrument for this new policy presented itself in the Comte de Narbonne, a *grand seigneur* of the old régime who, out of vanity and a desire to appear in the fashion, had posed as a liberal. Disliked at Court for his opinions, he belonged, with Talleyrand and Lafayette, to a group of constitutionalists who regarded war as a useful way of saving the Constitution and the King. The *emigrés* mustered in the Electorate of Trèves were to serve, according to Narbonne and his friends, as a pretext for the French Government to start a brief and easy campaign against the Elector. During the war, discipline could be tightened up in the army, which, braced by victory, might then be used by the King to reinforce the Feuillants and suppress the revolutionary clubs. The Emperor was to remain neutral while this harmless little enterprise was being carried out: in the unlikely event of his opposition, the Governments of Prussia and England could be brought in as allies or at least as friends by the offer of generous territorial concessions.

This was not precisely the same programme as Marie-Antoinette's. Her desire was to assail the reluctant sovereigns in their own territories and force them to join in crushing both Feuillants and Jacobins. But after all, she thought, Narbonne and his friends could start the adventure well enough, and it would be convenient to make use of them; the rest of the project could be thought out little by little. One thing would lead to another.

Dismissing, therefore, the Ministers for War, Foreign Affairs, and the Marine, the King promoted the Feuillant de Lessart from Home to Foreign Affairs and appointed another Feuillant, Cahier de Gerville, as Minister of the Interior on November 29th. On December 7th he entrusted the Ministry of War to Narbonne and informed the Legislative Assembly, on December 14th, that he had requested the Elector of Trèves and other German princelings to expel the *emigrés* from their territories before January 15th, 1792.

At the same time he sanctioned the decree of October 31st against the Comte de Provence, but placed his veto on the decrees of November 9th and 29th against the other *emigrés* and the clergy. On December 3rd he resumed his secret appeals for help to the King of Prussia and, on December 10th, to the King of Sweden; while Marie-Antoinette followed suit, in writing to Catherine II on December 3rd. On December 16th the Queen sent a last despairing cry for help to her faithful Mercy: 'This is the moment to come to our aid; if the Emperor misses it, all is lost.'

'What joy it would be,' she wrote to Fersen, 'if one day I were strong enough again to show all these scoundrels that I am not their puppet.' And on December 7th and 9th, 'The imbeciles do not perceive that they are furthering our plans, because, once war is started, all the Powers will in the end have to intervene to protect their rights. But they must fully understand that we, here, can only carry out the will of others, and that the best way of serving our interests is to fall upon us with the full weight of their armed forces.'

All those, therefore, who in this uncertain autumn of 1791 were united in their desire for war, wanted it on their own terms and hoped to exploit it as an instrument of internal policy. For the Queen it was to be a make-believe war, to startle the other reigning princes out of their inertia and force the Powers to intervene in French affairs. For the *emigrés* it was to be a fight to the death, to re-establish their feudal dominion over the serfs and over the King himself. Narbonne intended it to be a war limited in scope, but one which, through victory, would restore order in the army and strengthen the constitutional party's position. For Brissot it was to be a daring and auspicious campaign to destroy the *emigrés* and establish political supremacy for the Girondins. To everyone, war was the unknown, attracting them with the fascination of a great abyss. And all, more or less, were wrong in their calculations: for war, in a brief space of time, was to wipe out the constitutional party, overthrow the monarchy, disperse the *emigrés* and bring the Girondins to ruin.

In fact, as the Girondins increased their war propaganda, they became aware of a danger in their rear, which they had not as yet taken into consideration.

Rather than wage an external war, wrote Marat in the *Ami du Peuple* on November 12th, the inevitable civil war should be prepared for: 'Only after exterminating our internal enemies can we move effectively against foes beyond our frontiers.' He thereupon started a ferocious campaign against Brissot and the 'Brissotins', denouncing them as traitors and hirelings of the Court who, in league with the aristocrats, were distracting their patriotic countrymen from internal affairs by leading them into a foolhardy and unnecessary war.

Desmoulins and Robespierre were in agreement with Marat.

'To whom will you entrust the direction of this war?' inquired Robespierre. 'To the agents of the Government? You will give supreme power to those who want your ruin. War, therefore, is what we should most fear. In our present circumstances it is the greatest scourge that can threaten liberty. If we consider the real motives for war, if we penetrate our enemies' true intentions, we must see that our only course is that of waiting' (December 12th, 1791). 'War, cunningly provoked and directed by a treacherous government, has always been the rock upon which free peoples have foundered ... The Court is setting a trap for you by proposing war ... Let us first subdue our internal enemies and then march against our external ones, if they still exist' (December 18th). 'The victories of our generals would be more disastrous to us than our defeats' (January 11th, 1792).

Discussion in the clubs and the press was continuous and extremely animated. At the Jacobins' Club, Robespierre pontificated on the stupidity of Brissot's policy. In these wordy duels feelings grew bitter, accusations of bad faith and of connivance with the Court flew back and forth, and the friends of yesterday began to turn into the enemies of tomorrow.

In this way the Girondins, on the one hand, saw their programme filched from them by Narbonne, and on the other, found themselves regarded with deep suspicion by Robespierre. If victory were achieved, it would redound to the credit of Narbonne; if defeat came, it would be Robespierre's triumph.

Feeling themselves trapped, but unwilling to give in, the Girondins endeavoured to outdo Narbonne in patriotism and Robespierre in revolutionary ardour. They threw themselves into the campaign against the Court and accused the King of complicity with the *emigrés* and priests in refusing to sanction the decrees of November 9th and 29th; they listened without protest in the Assembly to demands for the death of all tyrants, acquiescing in noisy disturbances that silenced the speakers of the Right; and they increased the distribution of pikes to the Paris *sansculottes*, approved amnesties for mutinous soldiers, and went so far as to pardon Jourdan and the other brutal murderers of Avignon. Moreover, they cultivated the fashion of wearing the red cap as an emblem of the *sansculottes*, and allowed the Assembly's premises to become a scene of republican demonstrations. They even applauded Anacharsis Clootz, who proposed universal war and the division of Europe into *départements*, beginning with Savoy, Belgium, Holland 'and so on, as far as the Arctic Ocean'; and joined in attacks, not only on the *emigrés* and the princes who gave them asylum, but on the Emperor himself.

A war against the House of Austria, in Brissot's opinion, would mean abandonment of that foreign policy which had alienated France from her traditional friendship with Prussia. The new alliance had subordinated French interests ever since the Seven Years' War to those of Austria, and had led to the defeat of Rossbach and the loss of valuable colonies. The marriage of Louis XVI and Marie-Antoinette had set the seal upon this 'Austrian system': and in truth, so long as her mother was alive, all Marie-Antoinette's political influence over her husband — when not prompted merely by a desire to satisfy some personal caprice — had been exerted in accordance with advice and pressure emanating from her country of origin. To advocate war against Austria would ensure support from many diplomatists who had remained faithful to the former tradition — indeed, from a majority of officials in the Foreign Ministry and Embassies. Furthermore, this wider war would mean giving an outlet to the accumulated hatred against Marie-Antoinette, 'the Austrian'. Above all, it would bring the King to the cross-roads, and force him to decide, once for all, either on open conflict with the nobility and clergy, as well as with Austria — thus cutting himself off, for ever, from the past: or on letting himself be overwhelmed by the rising tide of angry national feeling.

It mattered little to the Girondins if Louis were to continue his treachery even in face of the enemy, and so drag his country with him to the brink of ruin. In such a case it would be easy to arraign him before the people; and once the traitor king had been suppressed, France, casting off the trammels of the past, would triumph over her enemies from without and free herself from all those ills which threatened to overwhelm her at home.

'Either we shall conquer the *emigrés* and priests,' predicted Brissot, 'and establish the country's credit and prosperity upon a solid basis, or we shall be betrayed and defeated, the traitors will be unmasked at last and punished, and we shall then sweep away everything that stands in the way of the nation's greatness. I have, I confess, but one fear, and that is that no one will betray us. We have need of treachery on a grand scale; our salvation lies that way, for strong doses of poison still remain in the body of France, and strong measures are necessary to expel them. The body is sound and will not succumb.'

Not one among the Girondins felt doubtful of victory. They all had unbounded faith in the strength of France, and attributed untold efficacy to the lure of liberty. 'We shall create what has never existed before!' asserted Brissot with supreme self-confidence. 'The French people,' proclaimed Isnard, 'have become the greatest in the world; their conduct should correspond with their new destiny. Enslaved, they were courageous and undefeated; shall they be weak and cowardly when they are free? Under Louis XIV, most proud of despots, the people fought with success against the greater part of Europe; now that they are freed from their chains, shall they fear all Europe together? The standard of freedom is that of victory. When the light of philosophy flashes upon the enemy armies, the peoples will defy their tyrants and embrace one another, in a land restored to peace beneath the propitious heavens.'

In depicting the glory that awaited their country through this 'propaganda war' — which was to consolidate liberty within her frontiers and spread it throughout Europe — and in exalting the people's natural generosity, the Girondins did not fail to refer to France's 'natural frontiers' of the Alps and the Rhine. In so doing, they added to the growing ferment of nationalism and lust for conquest. They alarmed the French people by depicting a formidable conspiracy of foreign tyrants, and seduced them by affirming that nothing would be more easy than to overcome it, provided that they would fight promptly and well. They mixed invective against their external enemies with threats against their internal ones; and in the irritation thus engendered among the nobles and priests they found new arguments for demanding war with the foreigner, who was the natural ally of both nobles and priests. And in all their speeches they took care to insinuate — vaguely indicating the King — that there was fear of treachery, and to threaten reprisals against whoever might be guilty of it: 'To us, the word responsibility,' shouted Isnard, 'means death.'

III

News of the French ultimatum alarmed the little Electorate of Trèves. The Prince-Bishop, as a member of the Holy Roman Empire, at once claimed assistance from the Emperor Leopold. But for a long time, as Voltaire once ironically pointed out, the Holy Roman Empire had been neither holy nor Roman, nor even an empire. Leopold, who owed nothing to Charlemagne, invited the Bishop to comply with France's demands and wrote to the French Ambassador, on December 21st, informing him that the Bishop had expelled the *emigrés* from his territories. At the same time, added the Austrian note, the Emperor had ordered his troops to defend the Bishop in case of attack, since 'current events gave little proof of stability or moderation in the conduct of French affairs, or of adequate control over the provinces and municipalities'. In such conditions an attack by French troops was not impossible, even against the will of the central government and the King. At all events the Emperor manifested a lively desire that nothing of the kind should occur, and that 'the inevitable consequences, affecting not only the Emperor and Imperial States, but also the other sovereigns united in the defence of peace and for the safety and honour of their reigning houses, might be avoided'. Union among these sovereigns had never been less evident than at that moment, and the Emperor referred to it only because Marie-Antoinette had repeatedly assured him that the mere mention of such an understanding would check the revolutionaries and strengthen the monarchy in France.

All this played into the Girondins' hands. Now that the Elector of Trèves had complied with French demands and the original pretext for war was lacking, they took advantage of Leopold's references to the union of Princes and his commendation of 'moderation' in French affairs— in other words of the Feuillants — to intensify the anti-Austrian campaign. Henceforth the existence of an 'Austrian committee' was regarded by the democratic press as indisputable; its members were believed to consist not only of the Queen and the Royalist agents but also of the Feuillant leaders. The latter, to whom the Emperor's approbation came as a death-blow, were embarrassed by charges of treachery and divided by disagreement between those who supported Barnave in his opposition to the war and those who, following Narbonne, were in favour of it. They were thus rendered completely helpless.

Masters by now of the Assembly, the Girondins obtained an act of indictment on January 1st, 1792, against the Counts of Provence and Artois, and against Condé and Calonne. At the sitting of January 5th, Isnard, stating that France was on the brink of a war 'which, although indispensable for completing the Revolution might well set all Europe ablaze', denounced the Austrian alliance as source of all the country's ills. He accused the Government of having failed to secure allies for France, since all nations were now ranged against her, and demanded from the Minister for Foreign Affairs a statement on the precise relations existing between France and other European governments. The motion was approved. On January 14th Gensonné, on behalf of the diplomatic committee, read a long indictment of Austria, and declared that the Congress summoned by the Emperor would be 'a final step towards the shame and humiliation of the French People and the French King'. He, therefore, proposed that the Emperor should be requested to explain his intentions before February 10th, and asserted that 'war was necessary, since public opinion demanded it and the public interest required it'. While Gensonné was reading the report, Guadet, who was presiding over the sitting, left his place and with one of those theatrical gestures so frequent at the time, rushed to the speakers' tribune, and moved a resolution that 'whosoever should take part in a congress having as its aim a modification of the French constitution or any mediation between France and the rebels conspiring against her should be declared a traitor to his country'.

'The mask is off at last!' cried Brissot at the sitting of January 17th, unmindful of the fact that on October 20th he had declared that the Emperor wanted and had need of peace. 'Your true enemy now is known: it is the Emperor. The Electoral Princes were his men of straw and the *emigrés* instruments in his hands. Upon him alone must you turn, to him alone must you give battle. You must either oblige him to dissolve the league he has made against you, or conquer him.'

It was in vain that a few courageous Feuillants, facing a hostile Assembly and organized disorder in the public galleries, attempted to restore a more reasonable view of the situation. De Lessart, the Foreign Minister, who, like Barnave, was opposed to war, made every effort to prevent open rupture between the Assembly and the Emperor. In the Government itself, Narbonne was supporting Brissot's manœuvres under the illusion that the war might be limited in its extent; not perceiving that it had already gone beyond even the programme of the Girondins.

On January 25th the Legislative Assembly decreed that the Emperor should be invited to declare, before March 1st, 'whether or not he would renounce every treaty and convention directed against the sovereignty, independence and safety of the French nation'. A few days later, on February 9th, the property of the *emigrés* was ordered to be sequestrated.

The decree of January 25th was a genuine ultimatum, which placed Leopold II in considerable embarrassment. He himself had no doubt of victory. But Catherine II, having made peace with the Turks by signing the Treaty of Jassy, on January 9th, 1792, was at this very moment assembling troops upon the Polish frontiers. Frederick William of Prussia, on whose support Leopold had hoped to rely both in restraining the Tzarina and in subduing France, was ready to make a treaty of alliance (finally concluded on February 7th, 1792), but was not in agreement as to the territorial conquests that were to result from the war. He wished to leave the disagreeable business of annexing any French provinces to Leopold and demanded for himself, in return, a good slice of Poland. Leopold wanted to keep what remained of Poland intact, and, uncertain what course to pursue, sought to gain time in order to secure his rear against Russia and to come to terms with Berlin. He endeavoured, therefore, even after the ultimatum of January 25th, to keep the path open for further negotiations; and in a conciliatory note on February 17th, while not undertaking to comply with French demands, he reiterated his desire for peace and accused the Girondins themselves of deliberately fomenting war. He also expressed a hope that the saner elements in the country would find in themselves sufficient energy to restore order and call the extremists to heel.

The Girondins did not disarm. Indeed, they believed the moment had come to drive the Feuillants from the Government, seize power themselves and start the war without more ado. They therefore launched a new and violent campaign not only against the Emperor but against de Lessart, the Foreign Minister, whom they accused of treachery in not having replied with sufficient energy to the Austrian note. Narbonne, in order to rid himself of de Lessart and other ministers who were opposed to war, most improperly supported the Girondins; while the King, obliged to dismiss either his Foreign Minister or Minister for War, parted with Narbonne, who was the more insolent of the two. This was a signal for further outbursts by the Girondins, the fury of which was increased by the news, which reached Paris on the very day of Narbonne's dismissal (March 9th), that Leopold II had suddenly died on March 1st.

The sitting of the Assembly on March 10th was extremely stormy. The statement that Narbonne's services had been dispensed with was received with loud protests, and a vote of confidence was passed in the fallen minister. Then Brissot, in the name of the Diplomatic Committee, made a report on the policy of de Lessart. No act, he declared, of this weak and mediocre, though honest man, justified an accusation of treachery. But there was no reason to be influenced by the threats of Robespierre and Marat and their followers: war must be precipitated. The death of Leopold was a disaster for the Feuillants; this was the moment to force the King to form a government of men faithful to the Gironde. Brissot's report was, in fact, a terrible indictment of de Lessart. Where arguments failed him, he had recourse to sophistry and when his sophistry appeared inadequate the howls of those present intervened to drown his words. Other deputies, in order to be allowed to speak, were careful to point out that they did not intend to defend the accused. The famous 'Austrian Committee', too, came in for its full share of invective. Vergniaud openly accused the Queen, and amidst clamorous applause threatened her with the full vengeance of the law. By a large majority the Assembly decided to impeach de Lessart, and that same evening he was arrested.

To gain time while waiting for war to set him free, the King accepted the resignation of the remaining moderates in the Government, and on Brissot's advice appointed General Dumouriez as Foreign Minister, Roland as Minister of the Interior, Clavière as Minister of Finance and other lesser Girondins to the remaining posts in the Government.

Among the new ministers, Dumouriez was the most authoritative. Born in 1739 of poor parents, he had fought bravely in the Seven Years' War. He hated Austria and had an unbounded admiration for Frederick of Prussia. When peace came he had left the army wounded, with the rank of captain and a pension of 600 francs a year; and had wandered about, as soldier, mercenary or spy, in Corsica, Spain, Portugal and Poland. He was imprisoned in the Bastille for having incurred the displeasure of Louis XV while acting as his secret political agent; but having been pardoned on the occasion of the marriage of Louis XVI, he again took up his military career. When the Revolution broke out he was Commandant at Cherbourg; dissatisfied and deeply in debt, he was obsessed by the desire to make his fortune, at an age when most men would have been thinking of settling down after half a century of adventurous life.

In his heart of hearts he was a lover of order and discipline, and had a cordial contempt for the *canaille*. Nevertheless, he hoped to find his way to power and fame through the Revolution. He had been a friend of both Mirabeau and Lafayette. Later he had become intimate with the Girondin leaders, having been prompted to approach them by his hatred for Austria and by a hope of furthering his own career in the expected war. At the same time he secretly offered his services to the King, ready to attach himself to one side or the other, as occasion offered.

Having entered the Government under the aegis of Brissot, he had perforce to play the democrat. As soon as he was nominated Minister he went, on March 19th, to the Jacobin Club, donned the Phrygian cap of liberty, addressed the members as friends and brothers, and promised a secure peace or a decisive war: asking blandly for the benefit of Jacobin advice through the medium of their press. Robespierre remarked that he awaited deeds not words, and pointed out that in the Club all members were equal, whether simple citizens or ministers. Dumouriez embraced him warmly, to the great delight of the onlookers, who thought they had at last found a genuine Jacobin minister.

Although in public he appeared as a trusted associate of Brissot, Dumouriez was aspiring, in private, to win the King's confidence. Like Narbonne, he hoped that the monarchy might be saved through a victorious war which would consolidate the army, restore the King's prestige and enable the Government once more to subdue the *canaille*. But Dumouriez held that the war could not be kept within such bounds as Narbonne had proposed to set. Just as it had already gone far beyond the *emigrés* and the Elector of Trèves, to whom no one any longer paid the slightest attention, so it could not be confined merely to Austria, but must become a war in which all countries would be involved. To seize the advantage, France must abandon defensive tactics, which would merely give the other sovereigns time to agree among themselves and to launch an attack, and which in any case would be difficult to sustain for long owing to her uncertain financial situation and the difficulty of protecting a frontier hardly fifty leagues from Paris. She must start an audacious offensive campaign by attacking Savoy, in order to seize the Alpine defences and ensure the safety of Southern France; then, secure on this flank, she must invade Liège and Belgium, where there was general hatred for the Bishop's rule and for the House of Austria, and where conquest would be easy with the people's help. The 'natural frontiers' of France, the line of the Alps and the Rhine, having thus been attained, her victorious armies should then move against Holland and the lands of the neighbouring German princes. Once occupied, these could be used as a bait to tempt the King of Prussia, who might thus be detached from Austria and turned against the 'hereditary enemy' of France.

IV

On March 27th, Dumouriez requested the new Emperor to give a categorical and final reply to French demands. While awaiting a pretext for launching an attack on Savoy, he sent General Montesquiou to Lyons to make the necessary preparations.

Francis II, who had succeeded Leopold II, was a young man of twenty-four, unintelligent and obstinate, wholly under the domination of the absolutist and militarist party, and without his father's prudence. The appeals of Louis XVI and Marie-Antoinette now combined with the anti-French ardour of Frederick of Prussia in urging him to make war. On February 28th Frederick had obtained assurances from Catherine II regarding the acquisition of territory in Poland if Austria were involved in war with France, and, his last doubts set at rest, he now readily joined the Russian empress in her war-mongering. Gustavus III of Sweden had been mortally wounded by one of his nobles during a masked ball at Stockholm on the night of March 16th, and had died within two weeks; but this loss made no difference to the forces of the anti-revolutionary crusade.

In agreement between Vienna and Berlin, war was decided upon early in April. On the 7th, the Austrian cabinet, in replying to the French ultimatum of March 27th, requested the French Government to restore the rights of the Alsatian princes who had suffered from the anti-feudal laws, to indemnify the Pope for the illegal occupation of Avignon, and to impose such order in the internal administration of France as should reassure her neighbours against a possible breach of the peace.

At the morning session of the Assembly on April 20th, Louis XVI made his appearance, surrounded by his ministers. He asked

Dumouriez to report on relations between his Government and that of the Emperor. In an effort to make himself heard above the commotion, he proposed a declaration of war against Austria. The Assembly, full to overflowing and seething with excitement, adjourned until five in the afternoon for further debate. In the evening, the crowd outside the hall clamoured incessantly for war. Within, any speaker who attempted to utter a word in favour of caution, was shouted down; even the Feuillants seemed dazed and carried away by the general delirium, and only seven deputies had the courage to record contrary votes. The motion approving a declaration of war was accompanied by a statement of the principles by which it was ostensibly prompted: 'In accordance with the sacred principles of the Constitution, which do not permit France to take part in a war of conquest or to use her forces against the liberties of other peoples, the French nation is taking up arms solely in defence of its own independence: it is fighting, not in a war between nation and nation, but in rightful defence of a free people against the unjust aggression of a King.'

Noble words, expressing all the best that eighteenth-century humanitarian philosophy had produced in the field of international law. In stating that wars of defence alone were justified and that force must be guided by moral principles, they indicate the ideal towards which, despite every set-back, the political development of civilized peoples is always striving. But were these words really in conformity with the political actions of the revolutionaries? Is it not clear that in the long series of wars started by this decree of April 20th, 1792, the French revolutionaries themselves were always the real aggressors? Was it consistent on their part, in addressing Europe, to repudiate all idea of conquest, and at the same time to speak to France of her 'natural frontiers', to be won by marching to the Alps and the Rhine?

Nevertheless, the language of the revolutionaries was, in fact, much more in accordance with the facts than would seem at first sight, and more so than they themselves realized. France, as Albert Sorel observes at this point in his great work *L'Europe et la Révolution Française*, had brought about radical changes within her own frontiers in the condition of her people and her territories. She had suppressed feudalism, proclaimed not only civil and political liberty but equality between her citizens, and had founded all her national institutions upon the people's will. The rest of Europe, on the other hand, still preserved those institutions which had been destroyed in France. The principles of liberty and equality, in virtue of which the French middle-classes had made their revolution, were too dangerous to be disregarded by the old Europe: for they might well be taken over and imitated in every country where there was oppression to shake off, injustice to resist or serfdom to be abolished. The influence of the French Revolution was spreading irresistibly among neighbouring countries, and undermining the security of their rulers. The latter had not at first clearly perceived the danger in which they stood, nor the necessity of uniting to suppress it. Nevertheless, the co-existence of two forms of society governed by such diverse principles must ultimately prove impossible. In the end, feudal Europe would be forced either to reform its institutions in imitation of the French, or to attack France with the aim of restoring the old régime. This was the true basis of the conflict, whatever its immediate causes might be. The latter, in the spring of 1792, comprised the machinations of the Court and the *emigrés*, the clamour of the Girondins, the diplomacy of Catherine II and the King of Prussia, the intrigues of this party, the greed of that, and the delusions under which one and all laboured. But these, as Sorel rightly observes, were only external symptoms, the pretext and occasion of the conflict, not the conflict itself. Although the French revolutionaries deliberately provoked war they were not wholly wrong in feeling themselves threatened. This is why their contemporaries, as well as popular tradition, threw responsibility for the war upon Austria and not upon France.

This war appeared to them as different in character from any that had occurred in the past. It was not a conflict between two monarchs, whose armies obediently killed one another in the course of some territorial dispute. It was the struggle of a whole people against the armies of several kings, not in defence of a city or frontier province, but to safeguard their own independence; a struggle which they urged the opposing peoples to join, affirming that France had taken up arms not against them but against their rulers; offering to help them in gaining their own freedom, and opening the doors of their country to those who deserted the flag of despotism and rallied to the side of freedom. A war on kings, but peace between the peoples! And if the peoples, giving ear to the voice of freedom, were to shake off the yoke of servitude and unite with France, could this be looked upon as conquest, in the same sense as that of the conquests of former times? According to the revolutionaries, 'what is given spontaneously is acquired justly: what is added to France is added to the realm of freedom. The greatness of France is bound up with the happiness of mankind'. Naturally, the countries with which France sought solidarity and union were her nearest neighbours: the future of other peoples could remain in obscurity.

Yet this war, apparently so novel, suddenly revealed a surprising similarity of purpose with the wars of former French kings. If, in fact, we suppress the superstructure of revolutionary ideas and sentiments that accompanied it, and suppose, for a moment, that of all these events from 1788 onwards which we have been narrating we know only the one fact of the declaration of war on April 20th; and that, of what happened later, history has recorded no more than the conquest of the Alps and the Rhine: in what way would the aims and objects of this campaign appear to differ from those of the wars waged by Francis I, Richelieu and Louis XIV? What, after all, were the revolutionaries doing, if not carrying on, with new catch-words and greater promptitude of execution, the same international policy as that of the kings they had displaced: just as they had already followed the programme of the monarchy in their anti-feudal, anti-clerical and totalitarian internal policy?

While all believed and proclaimed that a new phase of history was opening, the nation's perennial history continued in the Revolution. Democratic France was merely preparing to subject other European peoples, in the name of liberty, to that domination which her former rulers had always tried to acquire over other sovereigns by right of conquest.

If Louis XVI had not been endowed by nature with an incurable inability to think, and if Marie-Antoinette had possessed a grain of the political genius which was so remarkable in Catherine de'Medici, they might have realized how much power and glory awaited the heir of Henri IV were he only loyally to support this final triumph of France's age-old monarchical policy. But instead, the hapless couple, drifting steadily towards disaster, awaited their own salvation from an Austrian victory. In a secret message of March 26th, Marie-Antoinette, endeavouring to hasten the march of the Imperial armies upon Paris, revealed Dumouriez's plans and the approximate date of the French attack to Mercy: adding, 'It is well that you should know of this project, so that you can hold yourself in readiness and take the necessary measures.' In internal politics they sought safety in illusions; in external, they had recourse to treachery. In both spheres they were themselves chief authors of their ruin.

v

As soon as the Assembly's decision of April 20th was known in Berlin, the Prussian army, in accordance with the pact of alliance with Austria, made ready for active service. Victor Amadeus of Savoy, for his part, had already withdrawn the French envoy's passports on April 19th.

The French army appeared in no condition to put up any serious resistance. Such fortresses as were designed for frontier defence had been dismantled and were useless. The three generals who should have directed the war were in disagreement between themselves and with the Government. Lafayette, conceited, and determined to take the lead, made no secret of his contempt for Dumouriez, and thought more of promoting Feuillant interests in Paris than of securing the frontiers against attack. Rochambeau was regarded with suspicion by all the revolutionaries as a general of the old régime, and Luckner, a selfish and incompetent old mercenary, cared only for the safety of his post, his pay and his skin. The commissariat functioned well; it had been much improved during the last sixty years and was in the hands of officials drawn from the middle-classes and favourable to the Revolution. The cavalry was good, though crippled by recent desertions, and the artillery excellent: admirably organized by Gribeauval, a worthy follower of the Vauban tradition, it had suffered little from defection by the royalists, since specialist officers were not forced to prove the usual four grades of nobility, and the majority of them, therefore, did not belong to the families of reactionary nobles. But the infantry was in complete disorder. According to the military provisions of the Constituent Assembly, it should have consisted of 150,000 men. In reality it was only possible to mobilize 82,000, since part of its forces had to be withheld for garrison duties, and disease, death and above all the number of desertions prompted by royalist agents had wrought havoc in the remaining units. Of the officers, 6000 out of 9000 had joined the *emigrés*. Under a decree of June 21st, 1791, the Constituent Assembly, alarmed by the flight to Varennes, had added 169 battalions of volunteers theoretically numbering 101,000 men, to the regular forces. These volunteers had to be drawn from members of the National Guard, and were allowed to choose their own officers by ballot. But their units were slow in forming and lacked uniforms and firearms, while the men were undisciplined and badly trained.

The war began inauspiciously. A column of about four thousand men which had entered Belgium during the night of April 28th–29th retired upon Lille in complete disorder at sight of the Austrians, cursing their leaders for traitors. General Dillon was dragged through the streets and put to death by the fugitives. The following night at Boussu two regiments of dragoons were dispersed. On April 30th, 10,000 men under the command of General Biron fled from Quiévrain to Valenciennes without even having made contact with the enemy. On May 9th, a regiment of hussars deserted *en masse*, and three other regiments from the north, corrupted by royalist agents, soon followed their example. General Montesquiou reported from the borders of Savoy that a rupture of relations with the King of Sardinia must be postponed, if the French forces were not to be caught unprepared. De Grave, now Minister of War, had completely lost his head and was signing official documents as *maire* of Paris. Feeling unable to deal with the situation he resigned, and the Ministry for War thus changed hands three times in six months.

Lafayette made secret contact with the former Austrian ambassador to France, who had retired to Brussels, and proposed that hostilities should be suspended until he could march on Paris with his troops, disperse the Jacobins, dissolve the National Guard and recall the *emigrés*. And in fact, from May 18th onwards, the generals, in agreement among themselves, ordered a complete cessation of military operations.

If the Austro-Prussian-Piedmontese League had taken swift

and energetic military action, the French revolutionaries would have found themselves in a bad way. But instead, for four months, the Allies remained completely inert.

In Poland, Catherine II, her hands freed now that Austria and Prussia were involved with France, was encouraging the pro-Russian nobles to rise against the King and the patriotic party, whose influence was predominant in the Diet. Insurrection broke out at Targowitz on May 14th. Ninety-six thousand Russian troops immediately invaded the country. Despite Kosciusko's heroism the small patriotic forces were overwhelmed, and by the second half of July the Russians were masters of all Poland.

These events paralysed the Austro-Prussian offensive against France. During the Russian campaign in Poland messengers continually hurried to and fro between the courts of Vienna, Berlin and Petersburg with proposals and counter-proposals. In the long series of intrigues that ensued the French question became inextricably entangled with the Polish, and bad faith, mutual suspicion and conflicting interests made any agreement impossible.

Catherine maintained that the Polish patriots, who were seeking to do away with feudal anarchy by strengthening the power of the King, belonged to the same dangerous category as the French Jacobins who were destroying the monarchy: were not they, one and all, attempting to overthrow the ancient political constitution of their country? And was not this a most pernicious example for other countries? While the Prussians and Austrians, therefore, were engaged in combating the Revolution to the west, she would do her duty in the east. Naturally, all good work deserves some recompense. Poland, occupied by her troops, was her reward: let the Emperor and the King of Prussia go forth and earn their prizes in France, where the unfortunate Louis XVI was so much in need of help, and in Germany, where there were so many small, independent states incapable of maintaining themselves unaided; easy to take and well worth keeping.

Frederick William was not of the same opinion, and watched Russian progress in Poland with envious eyes. His advisers regarded the Austrian alliance as only a temporary phase of Prussian politics. They proposed, for the future, an anti-Austrian pact with France; and they therefore gave out that Prussia was not interested in the Rhine, but anxious only to strengthen her position on the Baltic. At all events, they were careful not to move the Prussian armies too precipitately against France, but kept them at hand in case Catherine should fail to go 'fair shares' in the division of Poland.

The Austrian Government would have much preferred to maintain the integrity of Poland, which it regarded as a most useful bulwark against Russian expansion. But Polish independence had been ended by the Russian victories. It would be impossible to prevent partition of the country if Russia and Prussia were agreed upon it; in which case Austria did not intend to remain empty-handed. But she had no great desire for new acquisitions in Poland itself, and therefore revived a proposal that the Bavarian reigning house should be transferred to Belgium. In exchange for Belgium, Austria would then occupy Bavaria; while by obtaining cession from Prussia of the principalities of Anspach and Bayreuth, she would be enabled to round off her own territories most satisfactorily. The trouble was that the King of Prussia firmly refused to give up an inch of his territories. Another project was then put forward: the extension of Austrian possessions in Belgium by taking over Flanders, Hainaut, Artois and all the frontier fortresses from Thionville to Dunkirk, from France. That such a programme might easily be put into effect, no one doubted. But in so doing, it was pointed out that 'restitution of order in France must no longer be considered the principal aim of military operations'. Indeed, a continuance of disorder and civil war would be favourable to the Austrian cause, and once the revolutionaries were overthrown, a government should be set up in France that would be 'reasonably good, but such as to keep the country in a continual state of flux and ferment, weak internally and of no account in foreign affairs'. To reach this goal, however, Austria would have to undertake serious military operations against France, leaving Catherine and Frederick William a free hand in Poland: but meanwhile neither the one nor the other showed any intention of coming to a clear understanding beforehand as to division of the spoils. Until agreement on this issue was reached, therefore, it was impossible for the Austrian army to move.

In the end, Catherine, in her anxiety to urge the two monarchs in Vienna and Berlin to begin their assault upon France, decided to clear matters up on her side, and did so in characteristic style.

She concluded a secret treaty of alliance with the Emperor (on June 14th) in which she guaranteed Polish integrity; and made another treaty of alliance, also secret, with the King of Prussia, on August 7th, based on an implicit promise of territorial concessions in Poland. Nothing, therefore, remained for the Emperor and the King of Prussia to do — now that each had, on his own account, secured himself against Russia — but to throw themselves upon France, re-establish order and win those rewards which Catherine had so insidiously held out to them. And in fact, on August 19th the first Prussian troops crossed the French border. The real war thus began four months after it had been officially declared.

This delay was one of the most potent causes of France's salvation. While the allies hesitated to begin the attack, the French army had had time to reorganize and, in gaining experience from frontier skirmishes, to prepare for a decisive encounter. The emigration of royalist officers, although at first a shattering blow to the whole military hierarchy, turned out to be a useful mode of selection in favour of those who were well-disposed towards the new order of things: since for every superior who deserted there was a subordinate who rose in rank and, in occupying the former's post, had an interest in preventing his return. It was owing to this process that, on September 11th, 1791, Napoleon Bonaparte was prematurely promoted to be captain. The mass of the regular army was whole-heartedly for the Revolution, which had swept away all barriers between the nobles and lower classes, removed restrictions on promotion, increased the pay of the rank and file and abolished degrading punishments. Moreover it promised pensions, decorations and honours to all those who served worthily under the new Government. The royalist officers had been a constant cause of suspicion and insubordination among the troops; but with the purging of the *cadres* through emigration, confidence was restored between officers and men, and, with confidence, discipline and *esprit de corps* returned. Volunteers were added to the regular troops in two consignments, those of 1791 and 1792. The volunteers of 1792 took no part in military operations that year, as there was no time to train and instruct them. The 1791 battalions were at first turbulent and undisciplined; the law allowed them to elect their officers from among persons who had already served in the regular army or National Guard, and consequently many of those chosen were better at making revolutionary speeches than at directing military operations. But during four months of skirmishing with the enemy in expectation of serious hostilities, those who were unfitted for their posts were readily discovered, while the trustworthy remained: Bourbon, Chabran, Championnet, Davout, Delmas, Hardy, Jourdan, Laharpe, Marceau, Masséna, Moreau and Oudinot — in fact, many of the Revolution's best generals — were officers chosen by the volunteers of 1791. Amidst the healthy hardships of life in the field, the defence of the *patrie* and the Revolution grew to be a single dominating idea; all felt themselves brothers-in-arms in their enthusiasm and love for their native land. The generals took care to assign duties in common to regular troops and volunteers; and from this proximity, despite early, inevitable discord, the volunteers learnt military ways from the troops of the line. Very soon their battalions compared favourably in appearance, discipline, and precision of movement, with the regulars; while the mercenary troops of the old army caught the enthusiasm and spirit of sacrifice of those who felt that they were fighting in a sacred cause.

Thus, when the Austrian and Prussian armies entered France with their mercenaries, brutalized by an iron discipline enforced through savage corporal punishment — with their fat and indolent old generals, lacking in initiative and slavishly attached to out-of-date strategical and tactical methods — they found themselves faced by a young, compact military organization, animated by indomitable courage, and strong in all those moral qualities which in war are the chief requisites for victory.

VI

Behind the army, France seemed a prey to anarchy.

In the provinces — since the communes no longer were subordinated to the *départements*, or the *départements* to the central government — each city was left to fend for itself more or less as an independent republic, with its municipal administration at the mercy of whatever political faction happened to be dominant. In February 1792, from three to four thousand Jacobins from Marseilles marched on Aix-en-Provence, drove out the troops, deposed the Feuillant administration and set up another to their own liking. A month later, 4500 strong, they entered Arles, imposed a tax of 1,400,000 *livres* on the landowners, demolished the fortifications, replaced the Feuillant municipality by Jacobins, and sacked houses belonging to the moderates.

The nobles, thirsting for vengeance, were leaving the country in their thousands and joining the *emigré* army. In rural districts of western France, particularly in the Vendée, the peasants gathered together to defend their old faith and, armed with muskets and scythes, drove the priests who had taken the Constitutional oath from the churches and villages. Similar persecution was the fate of non-juring priests and their supporters in the east and south, where, particularly in Burgundy and the Lyonnais, the constitutionalists were in a majority.

Food-prices had risen steadily, although the grain harvest of 1791, unlike those of the two previous years, was good. The abundance of *assignats* contributed to high living-costs.

The 600 million *assignats* issued under the decree of June 1791 had all been spent by December: 472 millions in payment of debt, 128 millions for current expenditure. The 1792 estimates allowed for a deficit of 244 millions. With additional expenses due to the war, the discrepancy between income and expenditure increased month by month in 1792, until in September alone it reached 145 millions, whilst between January and September it amounted to the colossal sum of 599 millions.

The Legislative Assembly extricated itself from this difficulty just as the Constituent Assembly had done: it issued 300 million *assignats* in December 1791, another 300 million in April 1792, and another 300 million in July.

The nationalized property of the Crown and the Church had been valued at about three milliards. The Constituent and Legislative Assemblies had issued *assignats* to the value of 2700 millions; the decree of February 9th, 1792, sequestrating property belonging to the *emigrés*, which, valued at enormous sums, was to be used for the same purpose as that of the clergy, had greatly increased the number of estates available for sale, and strengthened the backing of the *assignats*. Nevertheless, these were still a fiduciary issue, the value of which depended entirely on the fate of the Revolution: and the fate of the Revolution, owing to its international relations, was beginning to look extremely precarious. Furthermore, so great a number of *assignats* on the market could not fail to be a cause of depreciation. During the first months of this year they lost from 20 to 40 per cent of their value against the French metal coinage, and 50 per cent against foreign currencies.

Prices rose steeply in consequence. The high cost of living produced the usual series of riots. At Paris, in January 1792, grave disturbances broke out over the cost of sugar, which had risen from three *sous* to three *livres* a pound. During the spring, in the *départements* round Paris, where the capitalist system of leasing large estates was widespread and there were many landless peasants, bands of unemployed infested the countryside, levying charges on the price of grain, bread, butter, eggs, wood, iron, on working hours and on rent. In other *départements*, the peasants, in fear of a food shortage, prevented the milling of grain in their communities.

It was impossible to ignore the nature of these outbreaks. They were very different in origin from the disturbances of July and October 1789, for they were directed not against the old régime, but against the shortcomings of the new. It was no longer a question of conflict between middle-classes and privileged, but of one between the proletariat and owners of property.

Naturally the royalists protested indignantly against these new assaults upon private property, and published pamphlets demonstrating to all landowners the necessity of rallying round both throne and altar, to defend them from the un-propertied classes.

The Feuillants, too, were anxious. They would have preferred to substitute the word 'property' for 'fraternity' in the triple watchword of the Revolution. They perceived that they were drifting steadily into the position of having to admit that the royalists had reason on their side. The Girondins, who represented provinces affected less acutely than Paris by the high cost of living, and who wavered between Rousseau's theories and those of the Physiocrats — or rather, who were followers of Rousseau in the political struggle against the royalists and Feuillants, but Physiocrats in their social and economic ideas — admitted that the poor were justified in complaining of high prices and poverty. But they felt themselves powerless to improve matters: 'To control food-prices would conflict with the principles of the Constitution and violate the rights of property.' They hoped that the crisis would prove a passing one. In their view, free play of economic forces and a natural increase in wealth due to the new political system should put an end to want. Robespierre and other Jacobins of the Extreme Left, who had broken with the Girondins over the question of war, attacked their rivals also on that of living costs. They did not deny the fundamental principle of private ownership of property, indeed they defended themselves from accusations of wanting a new distribution of the land; but they considered popular discontent fully justified and insisted that the Government should take measures to reduce prices.

'We find,' a delegation from one of the Paris sections to the Assembly declared on January 24th, 1792, in complaining about the high price of sugar, 'that the vile provision-brokers and infamous capitalists tell us that the Constitution has established freedom of commerce. Can a law exist in conflict with that fundamental law which is expressed in Article 4 of the Declaration of Rights: "Liberty consists in being free to do all that is not harmful to others", and in Article 6: "The law may forbid only actions harmful to others"? Now we ask of you, you who are our legislators and our representatives, is it not injuring others to hold back foodstuffs of prime necessity in order to sell them at prohibitive prices?' On January 26th the spokesman of a deputation from the suburb of Saint-Antoine declared: 'We hereby denounce all provision-brokers of every kind. Even the most necessary foodstuffs are in the hands of these murderers. They talk of private property; but is not their property a crime against the nation? Does not the tale of so much misery arouse your indignation against these devouring beasts?'

Thus the polemics between Girondins and Jacobins increased both in scope and bitterness. The revolutionaries found themselves in disagreement upon every problem of importance. Their lack of unity seemed likely to lead them to speedy and inevitable defeat.

'The *bourgeoisie*', wrote Pétion, himself a Girondin, in a letter published on February 6th, 1792, 'believe that the nobility no longer exists and the people are the sole object of its distrust. In its turn, the people become angry with the *bourgeoisie*, taxing them with ingratitude and reminding them of the services rendered the common cause by the populace, when all were brothers in the glorious days of liberty. The privileged classes, by underhand means, are fomenting this struggle, which, little by little, will bring about our ruin. The *bourgeoisie* and working-classes made the Revolution together. Only unity between them can preserve it.'

But it was precisely this unity that was lacking. In March 1792, during a food riot, the *maire* of Étampes was killed by the mob, who believed him to have profiteered in foodstuffs. The Legislative Assembly — Feuillants and Girondins in perfect accord — decreed (on May 12th) that a monument should be raised to him, as a martyr who had died in defending the law. Robespierre protested at the Jacobin Club and demanded a reprieve for those accused of the murder.

Nevertheless, the revolutionary parties still possessed immense reserves of energy, especially in country districts, thanks to the destruction of the feudal régime and the sale of Church property.

Rural feudalism, as we have seen, had been consolidated rather than abolished by the Constituent Assembly, and agrarian revolt continued to be directed against the new laws as it had against the old. But when war appeared inevitable, the Girondins and Jacobins thought they saw an opportunity of finding favour in the eyes of the peasants.

On February 29th, 1792, Couthon, Robespierre's future colleague, referred in the Assembly to the Constituent's decrees as 'a golden dream' that had left the peasants with nothing but grievances. He declared that speeches would not suffice to 'bind the people to the Revolution': they must become attached to it through 'just and beneficent laws, the ever-present memory of which must make them value their rights and duties as citizens'. He proposed that feudal charges which the landowners could not establish as legitimate by production of the original title-deeds should be abolished. Whereas the Constituent Assembly had put the onus upon the peasants of proving illegitimate imposition of these rights, Couthon made the landowners responsible for proving legitimacy. Since nearly all the ancient title-deeds were now lost or destroyed Couthon was inciting the peasants to contest every feudal right with almost certain success.

The Feuillants opposed this, maintaining that feudal rights

were a form of private property like any other: once violated in this sphere, once 'this predatory idea, which seems to herald the anarchical system of collective ownership — an alarming one for every landowner and subversive of every social system', was accepted, where would the greed of the unpropertied classes come to an end?

The Girondins took a middle course. Those feudal dues which the Constituent Assembly had not abolished but had declared commutable were divided into annual and casual: the former were imposed at fixed dates by the landowners, the latter when a property changed hands, or when the peasant cultivating the land died. On June 18th, 1792, the Girondins established that, so far as this latter category of charges was concerned, proof of legitimacy, if called into question, must be furnished not by the peasant but by the owner, on production of the original title-deeds.

The annual dues remained. The Constituent Assembly had decreed that a peasant cultivator who wanted to rid himself of any charge upon his land must at the same time claim redemption from all the rest; and that if several peasants were involved in discharging an annual due, one alone could not commute his obligation, but all must commute theirs together. Such obstacles had been skilfully imposed to discourage the peasants from seeking redemption.

When the monarchy fell on August 10th, the Girondins threw caution to the winds. On August 16th they suspended all legal proceedings concerned with redemption of feudal dues; on August 20th they removed every impediment to the right of redemption; and on August 25th they declared that all feudal dues, casual as well as annual, the legitimacy of which was not clearly proved by the original title-deeds, were abolished. A year later, on July 17th, 1793, the Convention administered a final blow, and abolished forthwith all feudal charges except payment for leaseholds legalized by an original concession of land: thereby recognizing explicitly the great anti-feudal, economic revolution which the Constituent had tried to prevent, and the Legislative Assembly had indirectly legalized. But already, from August 1792 onwards, all feudal charges had, in fact, been abolished.

Furthermore, on August 14th, the Legislative Assembly, in its effort to preserve the peasants' goodwill, decreed the distribution

of communal property, the sale in small lots of property sequestrated from the *emigrés*, and, on August 28th, restoration to the
municipalities of land seized *ab antiquo* by the feudal lords.

At the same time, the sale of Church property in the cities and
country districts was creating a vast net-work of interests that
were inextricably bound up with those of the revolutionary
parties.

The Constituent Assembly had decreed that the sale of this
property should take place by auction: the land was to be divided
up into lots, and payment made by instalments in such a way as to
make it possible even for the poor to have a share in acquiring it.
Sales of land had begun early in 1791, and by November 1st, 1791,
had amounted to 1526 millions. Those unable to pay the requisite
first instalment were not accepted as purchasers. It was a heaven-
sent opportunity for the property-owning classes. The prices fixed
by those charged with valuing the land were often as much as
50 per cent below its real worth. In many places rings were
formed among would-be buyers in order to keep prices down,
and the land acquired was shared out later for ludicrously low
sums. Municipal and departmental administrators secured a
considerable increase of property. But the purchasers were chiefly
army contractors, bankers, merchants, lawyers, shopkeepers and
country landowners. Speculation was so profitable that even the
nobles and clergy indulged in it.

Near the great urban centres, wealthy *bourgeois* buyers pre-
ponderated over competitors from the country. Round Paris
almost all the property was bought by Parisians, while in the
Toulouse district the local *bourgeoisie* laid hands on 86 per cent
of the land put up for auction. In districts surrounding small provincial cities it went in about equal proportions to citizens and
country-dwellers: at Sens, for instance, nearly all the buildings
and five-ninths of the land went to townspeople, and four-ninths
of the land to those who lived in the nearby countryside. Only in
the most remote small towns were the country people masters of
the situation. Altogether, it may be calculated that four-fifths of
the booty went to city property-owners and one-fifth to rural proprietors. No new rural democracy had arisen and no change in
the economic régime had taken place, as was believed before a
systematic study of the records of sale had been made. The

middle-classes who since the eleventh century had been fighting their way towards conquest of the land and of political power reached their goal in these years of revolution.

But while the city capitalists bought land on a large scale, the small country landowners and artisans laid hands on it little by little. At Sens, the five-ninths of the land bought by the *bourgeoisie* were swallowed up by only 76 buyers; the four-ninths that went to the country people were divided among 1461 buyers. In the region of Laon, 171 townspeople secured 18,000 *arpents* of land; 4787 countrymen divided 23,700 between them.

The fall in value of the *assignats*, which had raised living costs and weighed heavily upon consumers in the towns, had no ill effects on rural landowners, either new or old. They lived on their own produce, sold their surplus products at a high price, and paid in *assignats* for their national property.

When the Prussians entered Lorraine in the summer of 1792, they were amazed to see the land well-cultivated and the peasants' houses newly done-up. When asked the reason for their comparative prosperity, the peasants replied that such luxuries were not to be had 'in the days of despotic rule', because their money was wrung from them, to the last farthing, by the Court, nobility and clergy.

Each one of these peasant landowners was, in his own neighbourhood, an outpost against the nobles and non-juring priests. It was this class that, during the war, produced those obscure but tenacious fighting-men to whom defence of the revolutionary régime and of national independence meant also defence of their own ancient holdings and their newly-acquired property against a return of the feudal landlords and the restoration of the clergy to their former power.

The condition of the artisan classes, too, was on the whole satisfactory. The sale of Church property and the abolition of feudal dues had produced a great demand for work, especially in the building-trades. Every purchaser of land, every peasant who had at last freed himself from taxation and exploitation by his feudal lord, demonstrated his new independence by restoring old buildings, improving his crops, and breaking up uncultivated land.

The very depreciation of the *assignats* at first favoured production, for foreign buyers in their dealings with the French preferred to receive payment in goods, the value of which was real and safe; while they found it convenient to pay in *assignats* for what they bought, thereby gaining on the exchange. Thus there was much exportation of raw materials and industrial products from France to other countries. In the first six months of 1792 the export trade increased by 600 millions. On the other hand, imports were limited, since the poor credit attaching to the *assignats* was an obstacle to French purchases abroad, and French factories profited from this lack of competition.

It is true that in such a maelstrom of economic forces much was precarious and uncertain. When the peasants had laid out their savings in the first enthusiasm for agricultural renewal, they found themselves in considerable difficulties. Industry, which had flourished unexpectedly, was destined soon to decline, because the increase in exports had depended not on improved production but on exceptional monetary conditions. A continual flight of capital from the country resulted. In the end, prices rose to such a point that it was no longer advantageous for foreign markets to seek supplies from France; and France was then to find herself short of capital, with low stocks of her own products, and inundated with useless paper money. But for the moment, although the first symptoms of a crisis were already to be discerned, her general economic condition appeared relatively good, and France faced Europe as a nation that, far from being weak and exhausted, was vigorous and rich in resources.

CHAPTER VIII

THE FALL OF THE MONARCHY

I. June 20th. — II. The Feuillants, the Girondins and the Court after June 20th. — III. August 10th. — IV. The Paris Commune and the National Assembly after August 10th. — V. Preparations for the September slaughter. — VI. The massacre of the prisoners. — VII. Valmy.

I

THE disastrous opening stages of the war in April and early May afforded some justification for Robespierre's ridicule of the Brissotins, who had seemed convinced that even cannon-balls would give way before the Declaration of Rights. Experience had brought swift proof to the contrary. What else could be expected, asked Robespierre, from a war directed by the Court and supported by revolutionary deserters in league with the Court?

Infuriated by such sarcasm, the Girondins endeavoured to vie with the extremists in accusing the King, aristocrats and clergy of treachery. It was on their initiative that the Assembly decided, on May 5th, to equip forty-five more battalions of volunteers. Next day the formation of fifty-four companies of foreigners who had taken refuge in France was ordered. On May 23rd Brissot and Gensonné renewed their accusations against the 'Austrian Committee', aiming, this time, directly at the ex-minister Montmorin. On May 27th, the Legislative Assembly authorized the Directors of the *départements* to deport non-juring priests without trial, on a simple denunciation by twenty 'active' citizens. On May 28th the Assembly declared itself in permanent session. On the 29th the King's Constitutional Guard, suspect of subservience to the reactionary party, was dissolved, and its commandant, the Duc de Brissac, sent to the High Court of Orleans. On June 8th it was decided that on the occasion of the national Fête of Federation (July 14th) twenty thousand volunteers should meet in Paris to form a permanent garrison in defence of the capital. On June 14th the Assembly dealt a shattering blow, as we have seen in the preceding chapter, to the feudal system. On June 19th it decreed that all genealogical cartularies should be burnt.

The decree summoning twenty thousand volunteers to Paris had been proposed in the Assembly by Servan, now Minister for War and a creature of the Girondins, without informing the King or Dumouriez. Dumouriez upbraided his colleague in such forceful terms that the two men nearly came to blows in the King's presence. The Feuillants opposed the assembling of so large a body of armed men which, though too far from the frontier to be of use against the enemy, would constitute a powerful weapon in Girondin hands. There were immediate protests from the Paris National Guard, who considered this parade of newly equipped volunteers an affront to their own organization. As to Robespierre and Marat, they and their followers would have nothing whatever to do with the '*fédérés*', not only because it was their policy always to oppose the Girondins but because they suspected a hidden threat to themselves in this force at the Government's disposal. The King, for his part, supposed that the Girondins intended to use the twenty thousand *fédérés* for removing himself and his family into southern France, so soon as the Austro-Prussian forces approached Paris. As to the decree against the non-juring priests, Louis XVI intended to refuse it his sanction even at the cost of his own life. Realizing, however, that serious consequences might attend an open refusal, he hoped to gain as much time as possible without making any compromising official declaration.

The Girondins, however, had no intention of tolerating delay. On June 10th Roland, Minister of the Interior, intimated to the King, in a rude and threatening letter, that he must immediately sanction the two decrees of May 27th and June 8th, and loyally accept the Constitution, if he did not wish to see the Monarchy overthrown. Disgusted at such arrogance, the King dismissed Servan, Clavière and Roland from the Government, and nominated Dumouriez Minister for War.

Dumouriez thought that Louis might be persuaded to sanction the decrees in order to deprive the revolutionaries of a pretext for violence. He hoped in this way to gain a respite of some weeks, and trusted that, once the first victory of the war had been won, the Government, with increased popularity and backed by the army, would easily bring the revolutionaries to heel.

But Louis XVI still refused his sanction. Dumouriez, feeling that he had been tricked and realizing that a great political crisis was near, but resolved to do all in his power to secure the high destiny that now seemed slipping from his grasp, resigned on June 16th, after having been in office for three days.

As was to be expected, these incidents greatly increased the tension in political circles. Things became still more serious when a threatening letter written from camp by Lafayette reached the Assembly on June 18th, bitterly attacking Girondins, Jacobins and Dumouriez together, and insisting, on behalf of the army in the field, that the Assembly should re-establish respect for the King, and suppress the corruption, arrogance and subversive fanaticism of the revolutionary parties.

Finally, Louis, on June 19th, informed the Assembly of his veto against the two decrees relating to the gathering of the *fédérés* and to the non-juring priests. This produced an explosion of wrath. If the King intended openly to oppose the Assembly's wishes, it must mean that he was against the Revolution, and therefore against France! He must be compelled to take the right road, as he had been compelled in July and October '89: he must withdraw his veto and recall to power the ministers who had been dismissed.

A few days previously, on June 16th, a group of citizens from the working-class suburbs of Saint-Antoine and Saint-Marcel, led by the beer-seller Santerre (commander of a battalion of National Guards, and popular owing to his enormous bulk and to the beer which he issued free of charge to all and sundry at the Duke of Orleans' expense), had asked the General Council of the Paris Commune for permission to celebrate the anniversary of the Tennis Court oath by a grand armed demonstration. This was to be accompanied by a presentation of 'suitable petitions' to the Assembly and King, and the planting of a tree of Liberty in the Assembly precincts. Armed demonstrations were expressly forbidden by law, and the Council refused its permission. But the applicants protested, and declared their intention of holding the demonstration all the same. The Girondins, eager to renew their hold upon the Government, were surreptitiously fomenting rebellion and inciting the mob to demand a 'recall of the good ministers'. The Duke of Orleans' agents, who on every occasion mixed with the crowd, joined in fanning the flames of revolt. Robespierre, on the other hand, advised his supporters not to take part in this move: he had no wish to see the Girondin ministers back, and would have nothing to do with 'partial insurrection' when a decisive, general insurrection was now, in his view, necessary. Brissot refused to become involved in the matter at all. Pétion, whose business it was, as *maire*, to maintain order, felt reluctant to jeopardize his own popularity by resorting to repressive measures recalling those of the Champ de Mars, and, giving contradictory orders, allowed things to take their course. This lack of agreement between the different revolutionary cliques explains the disconnected character of the events which took place in Paris on June 20th.

Early that morning, the first groups of *sansculottes* armed with pikes, swords and sticks, accompanied by artillerymen with cannon, Jacobin members of the National Guard, women, old people, and youths, had begun to gather in the suburbs of Saint-Antoine and Saint-Marcel. Officers of the National Guard who were loyal to the Feuillant party, confused by the lack of clear orders, found themselves disobeyed when they ordered their men out against the illegal assemblies. Although most of the Paris *bourgeois* who formed the National Guard were afraid of mob-violence, according to Roederer (a member for the *département* and a reliable witness of these occurrences), 'they feared treachery by the King even more, and would have liked to confine popular outbreaks to just such limits as might conduce to greater sincerity and loyalty on the part of the Court'.

Towards twelve o'clock, Santerre assumed command of the demonstrators, and a mass of about eight thousand people moved off towards the Assembly. Singing and dancing, they urged one another on with shouts of 'Long live the patriotic ministers and down with the Veto!' Santerre sent a letter to the Assembly requesting that the citizens, gathered together to celebrate June 20th, might be admitted to present their homage and to confute accusations that they wished to break the law. The spectators in the tribunes, recruited for the occasion by the Girondin ringleaders, applauded wildly. The Feuillants opposed the demand. Vergniaud and Guadet supported it. Finally the Assembly agreed that a deputation from the demonstrators should be admitted to present their petition. But the building was already invaded. In the name of the people, or rather, in that of the mob that thronged the vicinity, a customs clerk named Huguenin read a lengthy speech protesting against dismissal of the patriotic ministers, and threatening terrible vengeance by the people, who, he declared 'were ready to plunge their hands in the conspirators' blood'. He complained, furthermore, that the French army was not fighting, and demanded that the Legislative Assembly should discover the cause of this inaction: if it were due to the Government, then the Government should be got rid of, since 'patriotic blood must not flow to satisfy the pride and ambition of the Tuileries'.

'The will of twenty-five million men must not be subject to that of one man alone; if we are so considerate as to keep him in his place, it is on the understanding that he occupies it in a constitutional manner. If he departs from the Constitution, he no longer has any claim upon the French people.' And again, 'We hope that this last appeal of ours will reach your hearts; the people are here, silently awaiting a reply worthy of their sovereignty.'

After listening to this harangue, the Assembly agreed to let the crowd parade through the Chamber. At the head of the procession came Santerre, and after him a motley throng of people, in diverse costumes and with the oddest assortment of weapons. They passed before the deputies, singing *Ça ira*, and stopping every now and again to dance; warmly greeting their friends of the Left, and shouting threats and gibes at the Right. Many were drunk. A pair of torn trousers carried on a stick served as the standard of the *sansculottes*, while a calf's heart, stuck on a pike, bore the inscription 'The heart of the aristocrat'.

Towards four in the afternoon, the crowd, weary after demonstrating for ten hours on end under a blazing sun, reached the Tuileries and was about to disperse, when the ringleaders started a demand for the people to go and see the King. What they were to see him for, no one knew; but the majority interpreted the proposal as meaning simply that they should see him at close quarters and make him understand that it was time to come to a decision. 'We mean no harm to the King,' they declared, 'but after all, the right of petition is sacred.' The leaders, however, hoped to intimidate the King into recalling the Girondin ministers and accepting the two decrees.

When the crowd pressed forward to the outer entrance of the palace, making ready to force the door, they found it unbolted. How this came about has never been discovered. The internal doors were then broken down without resistance from the National Guards on duty in the palace, and the mob, carrying a cannon with them to the first floor, surged up the stairs and into the great hall known as the *Œil de Bœuf*.

Here they came upon the King, standing on a bench in the embrasure of a window, a few faithful friends at his side. The uproar continued. 'Down with monsieur Veto! To the devil with the Veto! Recall the patriotic ministers! We shall not go away unless you sign the decrees!' 'Monsieur!' shouted the butcher Legendre, 'Yes, monsieur,' he repeated, seeing the King's amazement at not being addressed as Sire, 'listen to us, it is your business to do so. You are a traitor; you have always deceived us, and you are still deceiving us. But beware! Your time is coming. The people are tired of being your dupes.' With that he pulled a petition from his pocket and read it aloud, in the name, as usual, of the people. For two hours the mob thronged the hall, shouting, jeering, swaying back and forth as those behind pressed onward, and exasperated by the noise and heat. Louis XVI, impassive, betraying neither weakness nor anger, repeated that he would do what the Constitution demanded of him, and reminded the citizens that they owed respect to the law.

Apart from the ringleaders, the crowd had no evil nor even clearly-defined intentions. In the end, they were conquered by the King's heroic composure. Poor man, they said, after all he is not bad: it is the aristocrats, the priests, his wife, who are leading him to his ruin. A woman presented him with a sword decked with flowers and a tricolour cockade; he took it, brandished it and cried, *Vive la nation!* Others handed him a red cap, on the end of a stick: he put it on his head. He was offered wine, for all were consumed with thirst in the great heat, and he accepted it, saying: 'People of Paris, I drink to your health and that of the French nation.' There was loud applause. 'Long live the King, long live the nation, long live liberty!'

Finally Vergniaud, Isnard and Pétion arrived to play the part of rescuers. 'Citizens,' said Isnard, 'if what you demand were granted you at this moment, it would not be done in the cause of liberty. Go away, therefore, in the name of the law and the Assembly.' But a big, fair-haired man shouted to the King: 'If you do not sanction the decrees, if you do not recall the patriotic ministers, if you do not support the Constitution, we will dethrone you! The reign of tyranny is over and done with. We will have your sanction for the decrees or your death.' The King reminded him that the law must be observed.

Other deputies now came on the scene. The crowd was becoming exhausted. Pétion, too, invited them to retire, taking care to point out that the King 'would not refuse the clearly expressed wish of the people'. When told that Louis invited the citizens to visit the rest of the palace, they drifted away out of curiosity. The King, surrounded by his friends and the deputies, was able to leave his corner and disappear through a secret door.

The Queen, on hearing of the invasion, had rushed to share her husband's danger. Prevented by her intimates, who knew how her presence would infuriate the mob, she had taken refuge with her son and a few friends behind a table in the Council Room. Penned in here, they were forced to remain as the crowd issuing from the *Œil de Bœuf* passed before them. At half-past eight in the evening, she too was freed from her ordeal.

The agitators had hoped to frighten the King into submission, but he had had the courage not to yield to their threats. It was the Assembly that sustained a moral defeat on June 20th. Armed invasion of its premises undermined the respect that until then had surrounded the nation's representatives. It tore the veil from their material weakness, and was the first example of those *coups de main* by means of which the Paris mob, and later, the military caste, were to hold the legislative assemblies of revolutionary France in subjection.

II

The mob-violence on June 20th aroused much indignation, and widespread sympathy was expressed for the King. Protests flowed in from every hand. Almost all departmental directories, a number of municipalities and many groups of citizens of every class, sent addresses to the Assembly demanding punishment for those responsible. In Paris, one of these petitions quickly collected no fewer than 247 pages of signatures. The General Council of the Commune itself passed a vote of censure on Pétion for his lack of energy. The Council of the *Département* ordered a judicial inquiry.

Lafayette, thinking the moment for action had come, left his headquarters and appeared in the Assembly on June 28th to protest in his own name and that of the army against the outrage of June 20th. The Left, highly incensed, proposed that he should be reprimanded for having abandoned the armed forces in the field. The motion was rejected by 339 votes to 234.

Now was the moment— so Lafayette urged— for the King to accept his help and rally the constitutionalists and royalists in a last attempt to subdue the revolutionaries. He was convinced that the Centre in the Assembly, once it were no longer intimidated by clamour in the tribunes and threats from the democratic clubs, would unite with the Feuillant Right against the Girondins. By pushing on vigorously with military operations the Government might then turn the general patriotic fervour in the country to its own advantage.

The King and Queen, whose hopes were still fixed exclusively upon the Prussians and Austrians, would have nothing whatever to do with such a course of action. 'We would rather die than be indebted to Lafayette and the constitutionalists for our salvation,' declared Marie-Antoinette. 'Our position is frightful,' she wrote, on July 3rd, to Fersen, 'but do not be alarmed; I am not afraid, and something within me tells me we shall be saved.' 'Towards midnight,' one of the Queen's serving-women recounted later, 'gazing at the moon, which lit up her room, she said to me that before another month was out she would be able to look at the moon in freedom from her chains.'

Lafayette wished to take advantage of a review of the National Guard, fixed for June 29th, in order to muster the forces of the royalists and Feuillants, carry out an assault on the Jacobin Club and close it by force. The Queen advised Pétion to put off the review. Hardly one hundred persons attended a meeting to which Lafayette summoned friendly members of the National Guard. He thereupon postponed it till the following day, but this time only thirty appeared.

Convinced that nothing was to be done in Paris, Lafayette returned to camp on June 30th. In agreement with Luckner, he then proposed that the King should retire to Compiègne, protected by troops which the two generals would move up for his defence. This offer, too, was rejected at the wish of Marie-Antoinette.

Thus the revulsion of feeling caused by the rising of June 20th led to nothing. The Feuillants lost heart, perceiving that they could count on no support. The way lay open everywhere to the revolutionaries, who, with renewed confidence, were now preparing for their next onslaught.

From the provinces, the boldest set out for Paris, proclaiming that with or without the King's approval they intended to form the camp of volunteers decreed by the Assembly. In some places the municipalities themselves organized their departure: the commune of Marseilles, for instance, sent five hundred men off to Paris 'well provided with patriotism, strength, courage, arms, provisions and munitions'. At the same time, addresses began to rain in upon the Assembly from Jacobin municipalities and associations demanding the King's removal or suspension, revision of the Civil List, recall of the ministers, abolition of the veto, and the arrest and trial of Lafayette. The Communal General Council of Marseilles demanded outright that the monarchy, which was 'the heritage of a line of perjured kings', should be abrogated, and protested that 'it was absurd and unreasonable to claim inviolability for a King who had once been so cowardly as to flee from his post, and did not cease, by means of the Civil List, to foster an inexhaustible source of treachery and abuse; whilst with the Suspensive Veto he caused the will of one man alone to prevail over that of all'.

Bad progress at the front favoured the campaign against the Court. The French troops, having penetrated into Belgium and occupied Courtrai on June 18th, were soon forced to withdraw behind their own frontiers. Luckner warned the Assembly that he could not guarantee that the Austrians would not reach Paris within the next six weeks. The royalist newspapers exaggerated the strength of the Allies and *emigrés*, in an attempt to dissuade the citizens from volunteering to fight against hopeless odds.

In the Assembly, Vergniaud, Brissot and Guadet repeated accusations of treachery against the Court which were the refrain of every article in the democratic press and every discussion in the Clubs.

'It is in the King's name,' declared Vergniaud in a famous speech on July 3rd, 'that the French princes have tried to rouse every court in Europe against the French nation. It is to vindicate the King's dignity that the Treaty of Pillnitz and the monstrous alliance between the courts of Vienna and Berlin has been concluded. It is for the King's defence that former companies of the Royal bodyguard are now in Germany, raising the flag of rebellion. It is to come to his aid that the *emigrés* obtain posts in the Austrian armies, and prepare to stab their country in the back. It is to join these valiant gentlemen that other heroes, full of honour and delicacy, desert their posts in face of the enemy, break their oath of loyalty, plunder the military chests, try to corrupt their men, and glory in cowardice, perjury, insubordination, theft and murder! It is to overcome the French nation and the National Assembly and to maintain the splendour of the throne that the Emperor makes war on us and the King of Prussia marches towards our frontiers. It is in the King's name that our freedom is threatened: when they have succeeded in overthrowing it, the realm will soon be dismembered to pay the Powers for their trouble. In other words, all the evils that beset us, and all those we have yet to fear, are brought about in the name of the King. If we can raise units of only ten or twenty thousand men against a hundred thousand Austrians and a hundred thousand Prussians; if the measures needed to repel an imminent invasion of our country are too tardy; if the precautions taken to check the enemy at home have had no backing; if one of the generals in charge of the defence [Lafayette] is suspect, and the other [Luckner] is not allowed to win; if, finally, France is plunged in bloodshed and subjected to foreign rule, if the Constitution is overthrown and counter-revolution overwhelms us all, the King may well say, in his own justification: "It is true that the enemies of France maintain that they only wish to restore my authority, which they believe destroyed, to vindicate my dignity, which they think offended, to give me back the royal rights which they suppose me to have lost; but have I not shown that I am not their accomplice? By setting the armies in motion have I not obeyed the Constitution, which requires me to oppose the assault of foreign powers? It is true that these armies were not strong enough: but the Constitution does not lay down the degree of strength that I should have given them. It is true that I have assembled them too late: but the Constitution does not indicate how long I should take over mobilization. It is true that they might have been supported by reserves: but the Constitution does not oblige me to set up camps of reserve troops. It is true that when the generals advanced victoriously into enemy territory I gave the order that they should be stopped: but the Constitution does not compel me to win victories, indeed it forbids me to make foreign conquests. It is true that my ministers have continually deceived the Assembly as to the number, position, and provisioning of the troops: but the Constitution entrusts the nomination of ministers to me alone, and in no article does it oblige me to put my trust in patriots, or to have nothing to do with counter-revolutionaries. It is true that the Assembly has passed a certain number of useful decrees, and that I have refused to sanction them: but I am fully within my rights in so doing. Finally, it is true that despotism will soon restore to me the iron sceptre with which I shall crush you, and that when you are at my feet I shall punish you for your insolence in desiring freedom: but I have carried out everything that the Constitution demands of me, and have committed no act that it condemns. Therefore, it is not permissible to doubt my loyalty to it or my zeal in its defence . . ." O King, you who have doubtless believed like the tyrant Lysander that Truth is of no more account than falsehood, and that men can be put off with promises, as children with playthings; who have made a show of upholding the Law only in order to keep the power necessary to defy it; of approving the Constitution only because, to destroy it, it was advisable for you to remain on that throne which it preserved for you; and of loving the nation only in order to win its trust and to ensure success for your perfidy; do you believe that you can still deceive us with hypocritical protestations? . . . No, no, O man unmoved by the generosity of the French people, O man conscious only of a love for despotism, you have not fulfilled that which the Constitution enjoined upon you. You are nothing now to this Constitution which you have so unworthily betrayed, and to this people that you have so vilely deceived.'

To add weight to their threats and to prevent any impression that another ineffectual June 20th might be impending, the Girondins — abetted by their partisans in the tribunes, who

287

shouted down speeches by the Feuillants — insulted the President, came to blows with other deputies at the entrance of the hall, and proceeded to extort from the Assembly, one by one, a series of decrees that reinforced the revolutionary party and undermined the monarchy's remaining defences. On July 1st it was decided to dissolve the general staff of the National Guard in Paris and other cities of more than fifty thousand inhabitants: so that, the armed force of the *bourgeoisie* having thus been finally disrupted, the constitutional party was left with no means of defending itself. On July 2nd, a decree was passed authorizing free board and lodging to all citizens from the provinces attending the Fête of Federation on July 14th, and arranging for their subsequent transfer to the camp at Soissons. The decree of June 8th was thus renewed in another form, and the forces for a possible rising mustered beforehand. By a decree passed on July 11th, and not submitted for the King's sanction, a state of emergency was proclaimed. In consequence, the executive bodies of all the *départements*, districts and communes were summoned to continuous session, citizens trained to arms were ordered to supply themselves with weapons, volunteers were enrolled in every district, everyone was ordered to wear the national cockade, and the whole of France was aroused and called upon to look to her own safety, since hope could no longer be placed in the King. Pétion, owing to his inaction on June 20th, had been suspended from his functions as *maire* by a decree of the Paris *département*, sanctioned by the King. On July 13th the Assembly annulled his suspension; at this blow to their prestige and authority, the departmental administration promptly resigned, and the capital remained in the power of Pétion. By a decree passed on July 15th, all regular troops stationed in Paris, except a battalion of Swiss, were removed from the capital. On July 27th a decree was passed declaring the *emigrés* 'traitors to their country', and their property, already sequestrated, was ordered to be sold in the same way as that of the clergy. Every message from the King was received in the Assembly with jeers, or in contemptuous silence.

Such measures led inevitably to the insurrection of August 10th and to proclamation of the Republic. But it would be wrong to conclude that from this moment — as they later boasted — the Girondins directed all their energies towards this end. They only wished the King to recall the three ministers, entrust the Dauphin's education to someone of their choosing, dismiss Lafayette, and give up the right of veto. Once the government was in their hands they had no doubts as to their own capacity for saving the country and holding the extremists in check. If the King refused to give way, the Assembly would dethrone him and seize the reins of government. But they did not expect to be driven thus far; they believed that a mere threat of serious violence would be enough to force the King's hand. Proof of their attitude is to be found in the fact that while in public they attacked the King they were making him peace proposals in secret. They intended to rid themselves of Robespierre by bringing him to trial on skilfully prepared charges.

At one moment they believed themselves so near victory that on July 26th Guadet again declared in the Assembly that the King 'might still save his country and his crown', and ended a report on the petitions demanding his deposition by moving that further discussion should be postponed. Brissot, despite howls of wrath from the gallery, supported the suspensive veto, bitterly attacking 'the regicide party, who aim at establishing a republic on the ruins of the Constitution'. Louis XVI repudiated this clandestine zeal on his behalf. But for that matter it was now too late.

III

Some of the provincial revolutionaries who had come to Paris for the Fête of Federation had afterwards set up a 'Central Committee of *Fédérés*', with the Jacobin Club as its headquarters. In a manifesto addressed to the nation on July 20th this Committee declared that it did not intend to leave Paris before gaining mastery over the 'treacherous Court and the coalition of insolent patricians'. In the Jacobin Club the extremists, led by Robespierre and Danton, were now predominant, and, disowning the Girondins, took an independent line. Most of the *fédérés* left punctually for Soissons, in accordance with the decree of July 2nd; but a couple of thousand refused to do so, and gathered round the Central Committee. To reinforce this first nucleus came three hundred Bretons on July 24th and the company of Marseillais on the 29th. In these men from the provinces, the left-wing Jacobins now had a bodyguard of their own.

At the same time, forty-seven out of the forty-eight Paris Sections set up a 'Central Office of Co-ordination'. By a decree of July 25th the Legislative Assembly declared the meetings of the Paris Sections in permanent session: with the result that, since all citizens who had to attend to their own affairs were absent from these day and night sittings, the Sections, dominated by the more extreme elements, were wholly given over to politics, and became centres of intense revolutionary activity. On July 27th the Office of Co-ordination obtained permission from Pétion to hold its meetings in the Hôtel de Ville, and at once put itself in touch with the Central Committee of the *Fédérés*.

Under Robespierre's influence, these two organizations accepted a single programme: the deposition of Louis XVI and convocation of a new national assembly elected by universal suffrage, to decide on the new form of government. This programme, which had first made its appearance after the flight to Varennes and had been dropped after the 'massacre' of the Champ de Mars, now reappeared and triumphed. It had the advantage of temporarily eliminating disagreement on the question of monarchy and republic, and of concentrating all forces against the King.

When all was ready for the explosion, it was the Duke of Brunswick, Commander-in-Chief of the Austro-Prussian forces, who finally set it off. In a proclamation issued from Coblentz, on July 25th, he stated that the monarchs of Austria and Prussia were intervening in France to suppress anarchy, restore the King's lawful authority, and protect those who were loyal to him; that National Guards found with arms in their hands would be punished as rebels; that cities defending themselves would be destroyed; that the lives of the deputies and Paris administrators would be held forfeit for whatever might occur; and that their Majesties of Austria and Prussia swore on their faith and royal word to extract memorable and eternal vengeance for the 'least violence', the 'slightest outrage' inflicted on the royal family by giving Paris over to 'complete military subjection and martial law'.

This proclamation, as the American Morris pointed out, was, in effect, simply a call to the French revolutionaries to resist to the death, since they had nothing to hope from their conquerors. A year later, the Duke of Brunswick was to say: 'I would give ten years of my life not to have put my name to that manifesto.'

The text of this 'death warrant by the French princes against the King and royal family' was known in Paris on August 1st. On the 3rd, Pétion went to the Legislative Assembly in the name of the Co-ordinating Office of the Paris Sections to demand the King's deposition. He declared that Louis XVI was the 'first link in the counter-revolutionary chain; that his interests were no longer those of the nation; that far from putting himself in formal opposition to the enemies from within and without, he continually defied the Constitution; and that so long as France had such a King, it would be impossible to make liberty secure'. He proposed that the executive power might be provisionally entrusted to ministers elected by public vote in the Assembly, and that a national Convention should in due time pronounce on the will of the people.

On the same day, the *fédérés* presented a final ultimatum to the Assembly: 'We demand a categorical answer: can you save us, yes or no?'

On August 4th, the 'Quinze-Vingts' Section resolved that if the legislative body had not agreed to the people's demands by eleven o'clock on the evening of August 9th, the populace was to rise at the sound of the tocsin. This date was chosen because on August 8th the Assembly had to discuss a proposal for Lafayette's arrest and trial, and on the 9th, the King's deposition.

Hardly knowing where to turn, between the Jacobin onslaught and Feuillant efforts at resistance — in fear not only of the revolutionary organizations but of Lafayette's army — the majority of independent deputies, aghast at the storm of passions now threatening to overwhelm the Assembly itself, made a last effort, and threw their weight towards the Right: on August 8th, by 406 votes to 224 they rejected the proposal for Lafayette's trial. As they left the Assembly, they were insulted and roughly handled by an angry mob.

What would happen next? The majority who had voted in favour of Lafayette would certainly not vote for the King's deposition. It seemed that the revolt about to be unloosed against the Court must surely now involve the Assembly too.

The Girondins, having reached the brink of the abyss, were daunted by the situation which they themselves had brought about. Defeat of the Assembly by mob violence would bring them back to the government, but only as slaves of their own extremists. On August 9th, in a last effort to put off the conflict, the Assembly accepted Condorcet's proposal to suspend all discussion on deposing the King. Pétion sent an urgent circular to the Sections advising them to keep quiet for the time being.

At the decisive moment, the hearts of the revolutionaries themselves all but failed them. When the Assembly's decision was made known, only five or six out of the forty-eight Sections immediately nominated delegates with full powers to direct a revolt, notwithstanding their recent agreements in the rebel councils of war. But little by little the boldest brought over the rest. About midnight, the Cordeliers' bell gave the first signal. Here and there others replied. The more resolute agitators hurried to those Sections where enthusiasm was lacking, urged on the doubtful, assaulted opposition supporters, and thus succeeded in obtaining the nomination of representatives from another twenty Sections. Between one and two o'clock in the morning the first of these Sectional representatives, escorted by workers armed with pikes, entered the Hôtel de Ville, where they established themselves in the People's name. At three, when nineteen Sections were more or less formally represented, the chair was taken by Huguenin, who had played so prominent a part in the June rising. The legal Municipal Council, presided over by the philosopher Cousin, was meeting in another room when a group of rebels pushed their way in. All decisions of the Sectional representatives were then transmitted to the Municipal Council, which proceeded to legalize them, amidst the shouts and threats of the crowd. In this way, Mandat, commandant of the National Guard, was summoned from the Tuileries, guards were withdrawn from various posts, and the whole defence of the Palace was thrown into jeopardy.

Towards half-past six, Mandat arrived, believing he had been sent for by the Municipal Council. He was brought before Huguenin, subjected to a show of interrogation and then dismissed from his post, which was taken over by Santerre. On being ordered to arrange for withdrawal of the troops from the Tuileries, Mandat resolutely refused.

Towards eight in the morning, by which time twenty-eight Sections were more or less well represented, Huguenin and his companions took possession of the old Council room and, in the name of the People, suspended the twenty councillors who until then had been passive instruments of their will. Having usurped their seats, they proceeded to confirm Pétion in his office of *maire*; but at his own wish sent 600 men to sequestrate him in his house, not only for his protection, but to exonerate him from all responsibility. Orders were given to remove Mandat to the Abbaye prison. No sooner had he left the door of the Hôtel de Ville than he was killed by a pistol shot in the head.

While these events were taking place at the Hôtel de Ville, a crowd of Jacobin National Guards and *sansculottes* from the suburbs, joined by the *fédérés*, Bretons, and Marseillais, assembled and set out for the Tuileries. At seven, the first contingent reached the Palace, which was defended by 950 Swiss Guards, a couple of hundred nobles who had hurried there at the approach of danger, and sixteen battalions of National Guards. The ill-armed but elegantly attired aristocrats joked about the fight that was to take place and gave themselves such lordly airs that the humble *bourgeois* members of the National Guard soon lost any inclination to kill or be killed in their defence.

When the King, depressed and apathetic, came to review his defenders, and spoke a few disconnected words calculated to dispel rather than to inspire courage, there were few National Guards who cried *Vive le roi*. The majority received him in hostile silence, and a number shouted: *à bas le veto, vive la nation!* 'All is lost!' exclaimed the Queen, when her husband returned to her, 'the review has done more harm than good.' Yet, since most of the National Guards were posted outside the Palace, and unreliable companies could be removed or disarmed if necessary, it was thought that an attempt at defence should be made, and that victory might well be obtained over the undisciplined mob.

But even at this critical moment Louis XVI was unable to shake off his mortal lethargy. After the review he retired to his room with his confessor. No doubt he came to the conclusion that bloodshed was useless in view of the imminent arrival of the Austro-Prussian forces at Paris. When the insurgents were battering at the doors of the Tuileries, the Queen urged that a last desperate stand should be made: 'Better let ourselves be nailed to the walls of the Palace than leave it.' The King, however, was persuaded to take refuge with his family within the precincts of the Assembly. On arriving there at eight in the morning, escorted through a hostile crowd by Swiss and National Guards, he said: 'I have come to prevent a great crime, and I believe that nowhere am I safer than among you.' At this a young artillery officer who had attended the royal refugees on their passage from the Palace to the Assembly, exclaimed in Italian *'Che coglione!'* ('What a confounded fool!') It was Napoleon Bonaparte.

At the Tuileries, the King's departure was a signal for almost all the defenders to disperse. Many National Guards went over to the insurgents. The doors were thrown open and the mob rushed into the entrance hall and vestibule.

The great staircase leading to the first floor was blocked by Swiss Guards. Faithful to their duty, they refused to give way. For three-quarters of an hour they and the insurgents confronted one another: the Swiss declaring that they had no evil intentions towards the people but could not desert their posts, and the mob making efforts to fraternize. A few Guards had already been persuaded to leave their ranks when, at the command of their officers, the rest fired upon the closely-packed throng below them. They then rushed down the stairs and, clearing the vestibule and entrance, seized two pieces of artillery from the *place* outside, and returned. The more courageous of the rebels re-entered the Palace, and firing continued on both sides until nearly ten o'clock.

In the Assembly no one had any clear idea of what was happening. The benches of the Right and Centre were deserted, but the Girondins were in their places, waiting passively for the last battle to be fought to a finish. Shortly before the King's arrival the deputies had been given proof of how little respect remained for their authority. A band of insurgents, led by a woman, Théroigne de Méricourt, had massacred some prisoners who had been found in a nearby guard-house: among these unfortunate people was a journalist of monarchist views who had satirized Théroigne in the press. The woman, who later ended her life in a lunatic asylum, had seized the opportunity to revenge herself upon her enemy.

In all this confusion, the deputies expected the hall to be

invaded at any moment by the loyal Swiss Guards or the victorious mob. Finally, the King sent an order to the Swiss to cease fire and withdraw to their barracks. This was the signal for an appalling scene of butchery. The crowd, which had been under fire at close range in the Palace, was infuriated by its losses. It was now reinforced not only by new waves of insurgents but by the very National Guards who should have defended the Palace and by mounted *gendarmes*, all of whom were united in their hatred for the foreign soldiery. Their revenge was ruthless. A stream of people invaded the Tuileries, killing, sacking, burning, destroying. Many of the Swiss perished in the Palace after a last heroic stand. Others were shot down while retreating to their barracks. Some sought sanctuary in the Assembly and laid down their arms, only to be slaughtered later in the streets, on being removed under arrest to the Hôtel de Ville.

When victory by the mob appeared to be decisive, the Gironde set about legalizing the *faits accomplis*; disguising in pompous verbiage their own impotence before the victors.

'We are here in the name of the people,' declared Huguenin truculently to the deputies, 'to agree with you upon measures necessary for the public welfare. The people have authorized us to inform you that you still have their confidence. But at the same time they declare that they recognize no right to pass judgment on actions occasioned by legitimate resistance to oppression, save that of the French people, who, met together in its own councils, is sovereign over you and us.'

The Legislative Assembly, with only 285 deputies present, still dared not decree the King's deposition. They suspended him from his functions, and declared that he and his family were to remain 'as hostages'. Furthermore, they decided that a National Convention should be elected by universal suffrage, to 'pronounce upon measures for assuring the sovereignty of the people and the reign of liberty and equality', and they dismissed the King's ministers. A provisional Executive Council was thereupon nominated, consisting of six members, with Roland, Clavière, and Servan in their former posts of Home Affairs, Finance and War, and with Danton as Minister of Justice, Monge as Minister of Marine and Le Brun as Minister for Foreign Affairs.

Unlike the rising of June 20th, which had aroused so much

protest, the revolution of August 10th was received by most people with resignation. The French nation as a whole, alarmed and exasperated by the Duke of Brunswick's manifesto and accustomed by long tradition passively to accept orders from the capital, had long been prepared for the King's dethronement. They adapted themselves to the consequences of August 10th as to an unfortunate necessity, forced on them by war and Court intrigues. Secret documents discovered in the Tuileries had shown that the King was not only in contact with leaders of the Feuillants but was using the Civil List to pay for royalist propaganda and to subsidize the *emigrés*.

In the Vendée alone, at the end of August, the first of those royalist insurrections occurred which a year later were to be so widespread and persistent. But this time it lacked support and was immediately suppressed.

No better fortune attended Lafayette's last attempt. At news of what had happened on August 10th, he tried to call out the troops at Sedan in the King's defence, and won the municipality of Sedan and the *département* of the Ardenne to his side. On August 14th he arrested three envoys sent by the Assembly to spread propaganda in the army, and invited the civil and military authorities to agree upon measures for repressing disaffection and for liberating the King. Very few responded. The Assembly struck swiftly. Proclaiming Lafayette a traitor, they dismissed the administrations in league with him and dispatched three new officials to the camp, armed with full powers. The troops, recovering from their first uncertainty and influenced by the Jacobin emissaries, turned a deaf ear to their general's appeals.

On the night of August 19th, Lafayette, with his staff, deserted the army. He had intended to reach Holland and from there England or America, but he fell into the hands of the Austrian army and was declared a prisoner until the King of France should decide his fate. The *emigrés* celebrated this easy capture as a good augury for future victories, declaring that the marquis of liberal sympathies, the aristocratic traitor to his rightful King, had at last been singled out by the 'Finger of God' for due punishment.

Lafayette's post with the army of the north was given to Dumouriez, who, since June 20th, had been serving on the Belgian

frontier. Believing the Revolution of August 10th to have opened
a way for him to restore his own fortunes, he had warmly approved
it. Luckner, mistrusted by the revolutionaries, was removed from
the Army of the Centre under the pretext that he was needed at
Châlons to organize the volunteers, and Kellermann, an unintelligent but courageous veteran, loyal to the Revolution, was
appointed in his place.

IV

After August 10th, the Legislative Assembly and the Commune
confronted one another in Paris. The Girondins were masters of
the Assembly. The Jacobins were encamped in the Commune.

Robespierre had seen at once the immense significance of this
dualism. Fortified by his influence over the Jacobins, he had
joined the new General Council of the Commune on August 11th
as delegate for the Place Vendôme Section. He could safely expect
to dictate the policy of his colleagues as he wished; and he now
set himself to ensure the Commune's supremacy over the Legislative Assembly, and to cultivate the idea that it was the former's
business not only to direct the approaching general election but
to keep a careful watch on the future Convention. With support
from the Paris Commune, a Jacobin majority would have to be
introduced into the Convention, the Girondins crushed, and the
Revolution brought to completion in accordance with the teaching of his master, Jean-Jacques Rousseau. To Robespierre, with
his doctrinaire theories and illusions, the insurgents of August 10th
and the men of the revolutionary Commune personified all the
authority, virtues and perfections of the sovereign people.

The Jacobins and new Communal administrators, exulting
in victory, were only too pleased to be flattered, to hear their own
importance acclaimed, and to believe themselves the sovereign
people in flesh and blood. They tolerated Pétion in the office of
maire on condition that his duties were merely nominal and that he
kept out of their way. As to the Assembly, what right had it to
oppose the will of the people?

In fact, from August 11th onwards, the Commune began to
concentrate all authority in its own hands. It took over every
function of government, and acted as the supreme autonomous

body in the State, invested, by the people's will, with unlimited powers. It organized a Vigilance Committee; closed the city barriers and allowed no one to leave Paris without a special pass; proclaimed all those who had signed protests against the camp of the *fédérés* and the June rising deprived of their electoral rights and of eligibility for public office; and decreed that all 'anti-civic' journalists and printers should be arrested and the tools and type from suppressed printing-presses distributed amongst 'patriotic' ones. It forbade post offices to handle royalist or constitutional newspapers; ordered dismissal of such postal *employés* as were not reliable from the revolutionary point of view and the arrest of thousands of suspects in Paris and the provinces; exercised a postal censorship; searched the carriage and imprisoned the servant of the Venetian ambassador, obliging the latter to appear before the General Council to clear himself; abolished all distinction, in the recruitment of volunteers, between 'active' and 'passive' citizens, and invited all Parisians to organize themselves into armed companies according to their electoral Sections. It also sequestrated arms and ammunition belonging to National Guards suspected of sympathy with the Feuillants, and requisitioned arms and provisions in the neighbouring provinces. Lastly, it decreed that 'all crucifixes, reading-desks, angels, devils, seraphim and cherubim of bronze should be melted down to make cannon', that church railings should be used for pikes, and bells and silver vessels from churches turned into coinage. The Marseillais were not allowed to leave Paris, despite orders and appeals from the Minister for War, who thought it preferable to have them on the frontier.

The Assembly, now without material backing or moral prestige, explicitly approved or let things take their course. Their decisions met with no opposition so long as they coincided with Jacobin policy; but if they conflicted with the views of the dominating group in the Commune they immediately aroused protests, threats and rebellion. On August 11th the Assembly, distrustful of the magistrates elected when the constitutional party had had a majority in the Chamber, transferred all police duties 'connected with crimes against the safety, internal or external, of the State' to the municipalities; at the same time, in order to limit the power of the Paris Commune, it decreed that new members of the Departmental Directory should be elected in place of those who resigned when Pétion was reinstated. Violent protests immediately broke out at the Jacobin Club. There was no need, it was stated, for any Directory to set itself in opposition to the measures of the patriotic municipal body. On August 12th, Robespierre, heading a Commission on behalf of the Commune, presented himself at the Assembly, and addressed the deputies as follows:

'Guided by the same patriotic feelings that have raised the people of Paris and all France to their present greatness, you may, or rather, you *must* listen to the voice of truth, which speaks to you through the mouths of the people's delegates. The people are forced to provide for their own security, and they do this by means of their representatives. It is necessary that these chosen representatives of the people should be endowed with all the authority that befits a sovereign. If you create another power, that overrides or limits the authority of the people's immediate representatives, the latter's strength will be divided. The people will then again resort to arms in freeing themselves, and will take revenge upon this power that is destructive of their authority.'

To disguise its own weakness the Assembly decided not to abolish the Departmental Directory outright, but to confine its duties to the supervision of public works, the administration of national property, the sequestration and sale of the *emigrés'* estates, and to apportioning taxation. The lords of the Commune were still displeased, and tried to prevent constitution of the Directory. Though unsuccessful in this, they at once extracted from the newly-elected members an oath renouncing all authority beyond that of supervising taxation. Virtual abdication of their powers having thus been obtained, Robespierre, on August 22nd, heading a delegation of Communal representatives and accompanied by the members of the Departmental Directory themselves, informed the Assembly of the decision and requested it to 'consecrate this act of brotherhood by decree'. Some of the deputies protested against such high-handed action, and the decree was refused. But, in fact, the Commune had its way.

Besides transferring control of the police to the Communes, the Assembly had decreed on August 11th that a court-martial should be set up to try those Swiss officers who had escaped the massacre of the preceding day. In the revolutionaries' eyes the

Swiss had speedily become transformed from attacked into
attackers: a conspiracy had clearly been hatched at Court to
assassinate the patriots, and the burst of fire from the staircase —
after the crowd had entered the Tuileries so easily — was indisputable proof of a trap laid with diabolical cunning for the unfortunate demonstrators. By instituting a court-martial the Assembly
hoped to appease the revolutionaries and prevent the mob from
resorting to summary vengeance. But in what manner the
Jacobins regarded this tribunal's functions was revealed on the
same day in a manifesto issued by the Commune: 'Sovereign
people, suspend your vengeance: justice, so long in abeyance,
will today again affirm her rights; *the guilty will perish on the scaffold.*'

It was soon clear that a court-martial was not enough to satisfy
those who demanded reprisals; it was intended merely to try the
Swiss officers, but there were many other accomplices in the plot,
neither military nor Swiss. The Assembly thereupon quashed the
court-martial and on August 14th sent all the accused to stand
their trial before the ordinary courts. Even this did not content
the sovereign people. 'Legislators!' proclaimed Robespierre,
addressing the Assembly next day in the Commune's name,
'from August 14th until today the people's vengeance has remained unsatisfied. *I know what the invisible obstacles are.* Your
decree seems to us inadequate. The people is quiescent, but it is
not asleep. It rightly demands punishment for the guilty. You
must not give it laws in conflict with its unanimous wishes. Rid
yourselves and us of the regular judicial authorities, in whom we
have no faith. Suppress the right of appeal, which functions so
slowly that it assures impunity. We demand that the guilty be
judged in sovereign manner, and by commissaries chosen from
each Section.'

The Assembly half yielded; it limited itself to abolishing the
right of appeal against sentences passed for the crimes of August
10th. This was the worst thing it could have done.

'The French people,' proclaimed an emissary of the Commune
to the Assembly on August 17th — not Robespierre this time, for
his tactics were to keep himself aloof from all responsibility when
the explosion that he had prepared was about to take place —
'the French people, having overcome a terrible conspiracy and
defeated the blackest treachery, have as yet exacted no retribu-

tion. This evening at midnight the bells will be rung and the alarm sounded. The people are tired of waiting for vengeance. Beware that they do not take justice into their own hands. I demand that you decree without delay a revolutionary tribunal formed of citizens nominated by each Section. I demand that Louis XVI and Marie-Antoinette, who thirst for the people's blood, may be satiated by that of their infamous satellites.'

Some of the deputies rebelled against such effrontery.

'Liberty is dear to me,' said Thuriot, who later was to join the group headed by Danton in the Convention, 'and so is the Revolution; but if a crime is necessary to make the Revolution secure, I should prefer to plunge a dagger in my breast.'

Yet the Girondins submitted, and sanctioned the revolutionary tribunals demanded by the Commune.

Even this was not enough for Marat. During August 10th, the 'Friend of the People' had remained hidden in his cellar, prepared for defeat. When all was over, he returned to the fray.

'Beware of letting yourselves be carried away by false pity,' he wrote on August 11th. 'Your enemies will not spare you, if they have their way. No one abhors bloodshed more than I do, but if you do not want a veritable sea of blood, you must exact a few drops yourselves. To reconcile the public welfare with the needs of humanity, I propose that you decimate the counter-revolutionary members of the Commune, the magistrature, the *départements* and the National Assembly.'

He still raved about the delay in carrying out vengeance on the Swiss.

'What is the people's duty?' he wrote on August 19th. 'The people have two ways only open to them. The first is to bring the traitors held in the Abbaye prison to judgment, to surround the courts and the Assembly, and, if the accused are absolved, to massacre them without more ado, together with the new tribunal and the scoundrels who passed the fraudulent decree of August 17th. The other way is safer and more wise; it is to go armed to the Abbaye, drag out the traitors, in particular the Swiss officers and their accomplices, and put them to the sword. What madness to bring them to trial! The trial has already taken place! You have seized them with arms in their hands, in the act of fighting against the nation; you have killed the rank and file; why do you spare the officers, who are incomparably more guilty? It was a stupid blunder to listen to those who advised making them prisoners of war. They are traitors, who should have been done away with on the spot.'

Such were the murderous words that gave rise to the September slaughter.

v

On August 17th news had reached Paris of Lafayette's rebellion. On the 19th the Duke of Brunswick's advance-guard passed the frontier at Redange, without meeting resistance. On the 20th the siege of Longwy began. In Paris all were convinced that the Duke's approach would be the signal for a general rising of royalists, constitutionalists and non-juring priests, who, with help from the invading army, would kill the patriots and restore the former régime. The thought of treachery became an obsession. Suspicion and fear intensified hatred for the prisoners.

In such a state of moral anarchy, intensified as it was by news of invasion and the clamour for vengeance raised by the clubs, the idea of a mass murder of prisoners and royalists made headway, and ended by being adopted — it would seem on August 23rd — by the leaders of the revolutionary Commune themselves. Marat would willingly have included the 'putrid and disloyal' deputies of the Gironde.

'These infamous men,' he wrote in the article quoted above, 'are betraying the people and seeking to postpone the trial until the arrival of Lafayette, who is marching on Paris with his army to murder the patriots.'

It was on this very day that Lafayette had left his post with the army and fled. But the 'Friend of the People' was never at a loss for invective. On August 21st he accused Lafayette's 'vile accomplices in the Assembly' of having helped him to escape. As to Robespierre, he was ready to accept a massacre of the prisoners as a means of influencing the elections in favour of the Jacobins; but he left it to others to take the initiative, being careful to assure himself of a way of retreat in the event of failure: choosing and weighing his words with circumspection, saying one thing on one occasion and unsaying it the next.

It would seem that Danton, Minister of Justice, was not ignorant of the plan to kill the prisoners, though the scanty and contradictory information available to us regarding his conduct at this time leaves the matter open to doubt.

Danton, too, came from that frustrated intellectual middle-class that had provided the Girondins and Jacobins with all their leaders. 'The former régime,' he said in 1793, 'made a great mistake; it brought me up free of charge at the College of Plessis, in the company of great lords with whom I lived on familiar terms. When I had finished my studies I was penniless. I sought a post. It was extremely difficult to enter the order of Paris advocates, and I had to make great efforts to be accepted. I could not hope to enter the army, as I was not of noble birth and lacked protection. The Church had nothing to offer me. I could not buy any office, as I had no money, and my old comrades turned their backs on me. So I remained without work. It was only after many long years that I was able to acquire the office of advocate to the King's Council. Then the Revolution took place. I and all those like me hastened to join it, because the former régime had given us a good education without affording us an opening for our abilities.'

Of cyclopean build, Danton had the face of a mastiff, ugly and expressive. Endowed with a powerful voice, he was capable of vigorous and spontaneous eloquence, passing rapidly from the expression of generous impulses to that of incitement to brutal violence. He was the very lord of the *sansculottes*: the Mirabeau of the mob, as Madame de Staël used to call him. Unfitted for assiduous work or a sedentary life, he craved for power and the satisfaction of his appetites; unscrupulous where money was concerned, he had been accused, not without reason, of being in the pay both of the Duke of Orleans and the Court. He had little learning and was no *doctrinaire*, but, possessed of abundant common sense, was an acute observer of the world around him and an able judge of men. Loving his country above all things, and being without either cruelty or bravado, he held the lives of others, as his own, in little account. Danton was in fact an odd mixture of plebeian coarseness and magnanimity. He almost always presided over the meetings at the Cordeliers, and was an influential and outstanding leader of the revolutionary movement.

The Girondins included him, as Minister of Justice, in the

Executive Council of August 10th, since they could not refuse this satisfaction to the victorious revolutionaries.

'It was necessary,' wrote Condorcet, 'to have a man in the Government with sufficient prestige to restrain the contemptible instruments of a useful, necessary and glorious revolution. And it was essential that the eloquence, temper and character of this man should be such as not to degrade the Government and the National Assembly, in having relations with him. Danton was the only man with the requisite qualities.'

Since he took little interest in his duties as Minister, Danton left them to his subordinate officials, and, with restless energy, interfered in all that went on, usurping the functions of his colleagues, finding posts for his friends, and intervening whenever a grave or sudden decision was called for. He was always ready to shoulder responsibility, being both fearless and unscrupulous; yet — shouting, raging, threatening, swearing — he preserved an extraordinary balance of mind in the most complicated and dangerous of situations.

It is not possible, therefore, that his friends in the Commune had left him uninformed or unconsulted before carrying out their plans. Nor is it likely that he raised many objections. It is true that, on being nominated Minister, he recommended mercy for the victims of August 10th, and undertook to 'pledge his life to save the remaining Swiss from the continuing fury of the populace'. He may have thought that the setting-up of a court-martial on August 11th would calm the excitement; and he had maintained, in the Assembly, that 'where the work of justice begins, popular vengeance must cease'. But, unprejudiced and far from sentimental observer that he was, he must have soon perceived the impossibility of restraining that rising tide of hatred. He could not prevent his friends' designs from being carried out, for command of the armed forces lay in the Commune's hands, not those of the Executive Council; and he could hope for no support from the people of Paris — exasperated as they were against the royalists and *emigrés* — in any attempt to save the prisoners' lives. To provoke a civil war between Commune and Government while the enemy was advancing upon Paris — and merely in defence of persons for whom he felt dislike or at least indifference — would have seemed to him quixotic, to say the least.

Furthermore, the fact that the Girondins were showing signs of a desire to leave Paris and thus escape from Jacobin pressure did not escape him. At the end of August, Roland had proposed to the Executive Council that the Assembly and the Government should transfer themselves to Blois, for safety from the Prussians; and he was supported by the rest of the Girondins. Danton alone opposed them vigorously.

'I have brought my seventy-year-old mother to Paris,' he declared, 'and my two children; they arrived yesterday. I wish my family to perish with me before the Prussians enter Paris: I want 20,000 torches to reduce Paris in an instant to a heap of ashes.' Then, turning to Roland, he added in his usual threatening tone, 'Take care, Roland, do not talk of flight; beware of arousing the people's wrath.'

In his opinion every patriot should face the invasion by remaining in the capital at all costs. If the Assembly and the Government were to abandon Paris it would be a triumph for the reactionaries and cause dangerous discouragement among the troops. But in Paris, as in the whole of France, the Jacobins were an 'infinitesimal minority', and to maintain their position they had perforce to strike fear into royalist hearts. 'We are the *canaille*,' he said, 'we have come up from the gutter; we must govern by fear or be thrust back into the mire.'

A massacre of the prisoners, therefore, might be useful in 'placing a river of blood between the people of Paris and the *emigrés*'. It would render any back-sliding on the part of the timid impossible, and give mastery over the capital to those who were not merely disposed but forced to fight to their last breath.

Finally, it seems that he thought he could preserve his own popularity among the Jacobins by not opposing the massacre, and then exploit his prestige to prevent Marat's folly from transcending all bounds and injuring the revolutionaries themselves; and also that he might divert, in some measure, the citizens' fury towards their external rather than their internal enemies. It was Danton, in fact, who during these days of bloodshed defied Marat's venom and saved Adrien Duport from certain death; who frustrated Robespierre's manœuvres against the Girondins; and who directed all his formidable energies into turning the citizens' thoughts towards preparations for war.

As has already been noted, it was probably on August 23rd that the bloodthirsty threats made in the political clubs first took shape as a definite plan in the minds of the Jacobins who controlled the Commune. The General Council had that day appointed Marat as its official journalist. On that day, too, one of the Sections sent to the Commune declaring that it was 'tired and disgusted' at so much delay in condemning the prisoners, and threatening to have them put to death in prison. The policy of making one of the Sections put forward ideas with the object of having them later accepted by the Commune was a method frequently adopted by the leaders of the revolutionary movement. Again, on that day the General Council of the Commune decided to separate the political prisoners from those detained for common crimes or debt: with the obvious intention of isolating the prey for the assassins. Finally, on this same day, the Communal Council demanded that the Assembly should have the political prisoners who were held at Orleans, at the disposition of the High Court of Justice, brought to Paris; and as the Assembly refused, the Commune sent for them next day on its own responsibility. It is reasonable to suppose that they wanted them at hand, so that they might be butchered with the rest.

On August 25th a report reached Paris, to be at first received with incredulity, but soon confirmed, that Longwy, after a siege of three days, had capitulated on the 20th without attempting serious resistance. Amid the universal dismay at such grave news the Communal Council informed the Assembly that several deputies had applied for passports to leave Paris, under false names. It was a general accusation, aimed at no one in particular, but it exposed the Girondins to fatal suspicion. Realizing at whom the blow was aimed, they promptly responded by swearing unanimously not to leave the capital before the new national representative body had met. Furthermore, on August 26th, they decreed that the cowardly city of Longwy, when restored to the nation, should be destroyed; and that whoever, in a besieged city, advocated surrender, should be punished by death. Next day the Assembly decided that a levy of 30,000 men should be raised in Paris and the neighbouring *départements*, and that all non-juring priests must leave their places of residence within eight days and be out of France within fifteen, on pain of deportation to New Guinea. Another decree, on August 28th, gave the municipal officials authority to search houses for arms and ammunition, to discover what horses and vehicles were in the possession of private persons, and to arrest all suspects. From ten in the evening of August 29th until the evening of the 31st, every house was subjected to a most rigorous search; yet instead of finding 80,000 firearms, as had been expected, only 3000 came to light. According to different accounts from 3000 to 8000 arrests were made: so many, at all events, that the Committee of Vigilance could only select a certain number for detention, and released the rest. At the same time, by virtue of the decree of August 27th, all non-juring priests were ordered to give in their names to the Commune. When the lists were complete — although the requisite eight days had not yet gone by — they were imprisoned on August 31st and September 1st, on the pretext that the Commune wished to ensure their departure.

Marat was still not satisfied, and on August 28th he placarded the walls of Paris with a manifesto attacking Brissot, Vergniaud and Condorcet: 'These infamous men have gone so far as to inform the directories of all *départements* that the National Assembly is held in subjection by the rebels of the Paris Commune. They have done this with the aim of having some city rotten with aristocrats chosen as the seat of the Convention.'

He had a reason for making this accusation. The primary assemblies had been summoned to meet on August 26th and the following days to carry out the first-grade elections; and from September 2nd onwards, the second-grade electors would be meeting to nominate deputies for the Convention. By accusing the Girondins of a desire to remove the seat of government from Paris Marat hoped to discredit them in the eyes of the Paris electorate.

To prepare the ground for the second-grade elections, Robespierre, on August 27th, suggested to the Place Vendôme Section that the electors should meet at the premises of the Jacobin Club; that those considered unworthy of the people's trust should be excluded from voting by decision of the majority; and that the remaining electors should vote aloud and in presence of the public. Having obtained the Section's support for these proposals, he had them approved on the following day by the Communal General Council.

The Girondin deputies in the Assembly, though infuriated by these moves, were powerless to oppose them. In the end, an act of overweening presumption directed against themselves forced them to give battle.

A journalist who was a follower of Brissot and editor of the *Patriote Français* accused the Commune of intimidating the electors by their house-to-house searches. The Communal Council ordered him to appear within twenty-four hours to 'explain the imposture which he had printed'; but, ignoring the summons, he appealed to the Assembly to protect the freedom of the press. The Assembly thereupon summoned the municipal authorities before them to report on their illegal action. They had only just taken this step when it was announced that the Commune had issued an order of arrest against the journalist. Moreover, supposing him to be hiding in the Ministry of War, they had blockaded the building for two hours and had refused to allow anyone to leave it, thus paralysing the work of the officials. Such provocation was not to be tolerated.

The Assembly, now extremely angry, accepted a proposal made by the Commission for Extraordinary Affairs (known, from the number of its members, as the Commission of Twenty-one) and ordered dissolution of the Communal Council. It then invited the Sections to set up a new one within twenty-four hours by each nominating two commissioners. Next day it quashed the illegal measures taken against the journalist. Furthermore, the dismissed administrators were ordered to render an account within two days of all the objects removed from the Tuileries and the Paris churches after August 10th and handed over to them for safe-keeping. As these objects, many of which were of great value, had been dispersed, a request for a statement as to their disposal implied direct moral condemnation of the suppressed revolutionary Commune.

Before embarking on open and irrevocable rebellion, the Communal Council, on August 31st, sent emissaries to the Assembly to demand that the decree of dissolution should be revoked. They were accompanied by a threatening group of *sansculottes*. The Assembly refused to consider their demand.

On the evening of September 1st the Council, presided over by Huguenin, debated what action to take. The second-grade electors were meeting next day, and plans to intimidate them with a mass slaughter of the prisoners were ready. It was decided to defy the Assembly. Robespierre, during the discussion, launched an atrocious accusation against the Girondins: 'No one dares name the traitors. Then I will name them, to save the People. I accuse the liberticide Brissot, the whole Girondist faction, and the infamous Commission of Twenty-one. I accuse them of having sold France to the Duke of Brunswick, and of having already received the price of their villainy.'

Open war between the Assembly and the Commune that had seized power on August 10th was about to break out.

But next day the scene suddenly changed. Verdun, the only stronghold barring the enemy's approach to the capital, had been invested on August 30th. News of its imminent fall had reached Paris in the early morning, with that of the royalist rising in the Vendée. Shaken by these disasters the Assembly lacked courage to give the signal for an open conflict with the Commune. On Thuriot's proposal it formally abdicated its own powers by decreeing that the new Communal Council should consist not of two but of six members appointed by each Section, and that all those representatives whom the Sections did not wish to replace should remain in office. Once again the Commune had triumphed.

VI

Meanwhile, the news of Verdun and the Vendée rapidly spread, becoming greatly exaggerated. It was said that Verdun had already fallen, that the foreign soldiery were sacking the city, and that the *emigrés*, following on their heels, were restoring the former authorities, closing revolutionary clubs, and imprisoning the patriots. A fictitious letter from Germany, published on August 31st in the *Gazette Nationale de France* and reproduced on September 1st and 2nd by other journals, stated that the King of Prussia was planning to starve Paris out, to decimate the inhabitants, and to extend pardon, at most, to women and children. On September 1st a carter, who had been put in the pillory as a common criminal, exasperated by the jeers of the passers-by and probably drunk, had begun to shout 'Long live the King, long live the Queen, down with the nation!' Upon this trifling incident a fantastic rumour was founded: the carter was said to have revealed that the prisoners were all armed, and only waiting for the volunteers to leave Paris; and that they were then going to issue *en masse* from the prisons and kill the undefended women and children, with the help of royalists lurking in the city and its neighbourhood. 'Our most ruthless enemies are not at Verdun,' said the people to one another, 'they are in Paris, in the prisons. Our women, our children, left at the mercy of those scoundrels, will be sacrificed.' The tribunal set up on August 17th, which had been expected to deal out exemplary punishment to those guilty of crimes against the nation, was said to have condemned only three of the conspirators to death in five days, and to have released the rest to continue their machinations against the people. 'Very well,' declared the more hot-headed of the volunteers, 'let us strike at our enemies before we leave Paris; we must take the only way of stopping these cut-throats.'

As usual, the Jacobins of the Sections were the first to take action. The Poissonière Section passed a resolution to the effect that all priests and other suspected persons held in the prisons of Paris, Orleans and elsewhere, should be put to death, and that the wives and children of the *emigrés* and all those guilty of anti-patriotic sentiments should be forced to march before the front rank of volunteers to protect the brave *sansculottes* from enemy fire. The Luxembourg Section decreed that 'before the volunteers' departure the prisons should be purged by the blood of the political *détenus* of Paris'. At the same time the four members of the Committee of Vigilance decided, 'in view of the crisis and of important work that must be undertaken', to co-opt three additional members, including Desforges, who was an associate of Danton's, and Marat, the 'Friend of the People'.

At two o'clock on the afternoon of September 1st, while the guns were sounding the alarm and on every hand the peal of church-bells seemed to voice the people's anguish — while the young men flocked to inscribe themselves as volunteers or hastened, their arms in their hands, towards the Champ de Mars — four carriages conveying twenty-two non-juring priests and two suspect laymen, accompanied by an armed escort, set out from the *mairie* for the Abbaye prison. On the way, the guards loudly threatened their prisoners with death. Passing from words to deeds, they were soon raining blows upon them through the windows of the carriages. When they reached the Abbaye, the prisoners were dragged into the courtyard, and most of them killed. From thence the murderers went to the former Carmelite monastery, and shot or put to the sword some 120 priests imprisoned there. On their way back they killed thirty more who were held in another prison. Having returned to the Abbaye, they first carried out an indiscriminate massacre of about fifty Swiss and Royal Guards; then, having been ordered by the Committee of Vigilance 'to try all prisoners without distinction, in the name of the people', they set up a kind of tribunal at the entrance to the building. Maillard, who had led the women's march to Versailles in October 1789, was appointed to preside over this, with twelve others to assist him as judges. In the flickering torchlight the prisoners, one by one, were summoned before them — their names called from the prison registers — and invited briefly to clear themselves. Sentence of death or release, the former more frequent than the latter, followed at random, according to the mood of the moment. Those condemned to death were immediately executed by armed men waiting in the street, who struck down their victims with swords, pikes, clubs or the butt end of muskets so soon as they were thrust from the door of the prison.

The same procedure — if such it can be called — was repeated on the night of September 2nd-3rd at the Châtelet, Conciergerie and Force prisons. On September 3rd further massacres took place at the Tour de Saint Bernard, at Saint-Firmin and Bicêtre. On the 4th it was the turn of the Salpetrière, while at the Force, Saint-Firmin and the Abbaye the slaughter went on without ceasing, and continued until September 6th.

While some 'worked', others rested, drinking at the nation's expense or providing an audience for the executions; becoming every moment more brutalized by wine, bloodshed and fatigue. When a prisoner (his death sentence successfully contested by the tears or entreaties of some dear one, or lucky enough to chance upon a momentary impulse of mercy) was declared free, the judges, guards, executioners and spectators all cheered and embraced him, offered him drink, and made it their duty to see him safely home lest any harm should befall him on the way. Upon those prisoners who had the misfortune to bear a well-known and hated name the most bestial fury was unloosed. The Princesse de Lamballe, an intimate friend of Marie-Antoinette, was killed on the morning of the 3rd at the Force, and her body subjected to abominable abuse. Her head, struck off and fixed upon a pike, was paraded by a howling mob beneath the Queen's window at the Temple.

Thus perished, according to reliable estimates, about 1600 helpless people. Many were in prison for common crimes; at the Bicêtre reformatory forty-three boys, aged from twelve to fourteen and detained at their parents' request, were put to death. 'The poor boys were dispatched with difficulty, for at that age, life is tenacious. Their bodies were heaped in a corner. Next day, when they had to be buried, it was a heart-breaking sight: there was one who looked like a sleeping angel, but the others were horribly mutilated.'

While so many hapless wretches, unable to defend themselves, were thus being butchered by a few hundred bloodthirsty ruffians, the rest of the population, out of hatred for the royalists or panic at the disastrous war news, looked on at their fellow citizens' misdeeds with indifference or ill-concealed approval.

The General Council of the Commune, which met at four on the afternoon of September 2nd, two hours after the slaughter had begun, sent officials to protect all who were imprisoned for debt. This was equivalent to abandoning the rest to their fate. It then informed the Assembly of what was happening, and demanded 'an immediate decree to restrain the citizens': as though experience, for many a long day, had not shown the futility of such decrees. Two other emissaries were dispatched to the Abbaye 'to calm the agitation'. Of these, one, Manuel, confined himself to recommending 'a certain degree of justice', and returned to the Commune to report that the people would not listen to reason, but that in his opinion the prisoners deserved their fate; while the other, Billaud-Varennes, merely urged that the victims should not be robbed, since the murderers would be paid, 'as had been agreed'.

Robespierre, who was present at the meeting of the Council, took no step, made no proposal, and spoke no word to restrain the frenzy of those whom he called the People. But his friends of the Committee of Vigilance, mindful of the accusation he had made the previous evening against the Brissotins, issued orders for the arrest of Brissot, Roland and thirty other Girondist deputies.

Danton had gone to the Assembly at two in the afternoon to make a patriotic speech, recommending 'daring, and again daring, and always daring' in face of the enemy's approach. From the Assembly he proceeded, at the head of a large crowd, to the Champ de Mars to encourage the volunteers who were mustering in defence of their country.

He did not in any way concern himself with what was going on in the prisons. That night, on hearing that Brissot and Roland were threatened with arrest, he hurried to the Commune to have the order rescinded: he had none of Robespierre's personal hatred for Brissot and was possessed of too much good sense not to see what dangers, in the circumstances, would attend a mortal conflict between the Assembly and the Commune. Nevertheless, Brissot's house was ransacked on the morning of the 3rd; while the Ministry of the Interior was invaded by armed men in search of the Minister who were persuaded to leave by Madame Roland with considerable difficulty.

As to the Assembly, from six to eight on the evening of September 2nd, it feigned ignorance of what was taking place. At eight o'clock, after receiving the Commune's message, it sent the usual officials to 'speak to the people and restore calm'. The emissaries returned towards ten, declaring that they 'had been forced to retire', that they had not been able to see what was happening in the dark, and that 'they could not reassure the Assembly as to what might not ensue from this unfortunate occurrence'.

Santerre, commandant of the National Guard, gave no orders and his subordinates asked for none. When evening was already far advanced, Roland wrote to Pétion, asking him to take the necessary measures; Pétion replied that it was too late. The combined efforts of the Minister of the Interior and the *Maire* of Paris amounted merely to this polite exchange of views.

On September 3rd the authorities remained unchanged in their attitude, but the responsibility of each was more clearly brought out. The General Council of the Commune ordered effective protection for the Temple, since it was intended that the Royal family should be held as hostages against the Prussians. They awarded 12,000 *livres*, belonging to the victims, to the Committee of Vigilance for expenses incurred by the murderers; and dispatched an unfortunate journalist accused of anti-civic opinions to the Abbaye, where he was immediately killed. At the same time they decided to issue a proclamation 'to remind the people that they must look to the law to punish the guilty', and sent six commissioners to 'restore calm and impose the observance of right principles upon those who have abandoned them'. The officials, naturally, accomplished nothing. The Committee of Vigilance concerned itself primarily with burying the dead. It ordered that the bodies were to be 'removed from Paris and buried in deep trenches well covered with earth; that all blood-stains were to be washed with water and vinegar, then sprinkled with sand; and that, above all, the work was to be carried out with speed and no trace of blood allowed to remain'.

Provision was then made for an extension of the slaughter to other places. 'The Commune of Paris,' proclaimed a printed circular signed by members of the Committee and bearing Danton's official stamp as Minister of Justice, 'hastens to inform provincial Communes that a number of the ferocious conspirators held in the Paris prisons have been put to death by the People. Without doubt the whole nation will wish to adopt similar measures, so urgently required in the common interest, to the end that all Frenchmen may exclaim like the Parisians: Let us march against the enemy, but let us not leave traitors behind us to kill our wives and children.'

It seems that this circular was the work of Marat, who had it printed with the names of his colleagues appended to his own text; and that Danton's stamp was arbitrarily added by his secretary, Fabre d'Églantine, who had the die in his keeping.

To those who urged him to repress the wave of violence, Danton answered: 'Stay at your post; it had to be.' Roland confined himself to writing another letter—the man did nothing but write letters—to the Assembly, in response to Robespierre's accusations, defending his own patriotism and energy and deploring the fact that the Commune had 'exceeded the legal limits of its authority'. He concluded, 'Yesterday was a day over which a veil must be drawn. I know that the people's vengeance, terrible as it may appear, imposes a kind of justice: it does not claim as its victims all who stand in the way of its fury, but directs its wrath against those whom it believes to have been spared too long by the sword of justice, and who, it is persuaded, must, owing to the present danger, be immolated without delay. But I know that it is easy for some traitors to exploit this state of ferment and that it is necessary to end it. Well-justified anger and irrepressible indignation give rise to these incidents which are directed only towards the guilty, but in which the good man, owing to private passions or error, may also become involved. We still have time, but there is not a moment to lose: let the legislators speak and the people listen; let the reign of law be re-established.'

After composing this masterpiece of ineptitude, he went off to a gala dinner at the Ministry, where 'the day's events formed the subject of conversation', as Madame Roland informs us in her *Mémoires*. To the inquiry as to who was going to pay for the food and drink given the unofficial executioners in the prisons, Roland blandly replied that 'there were no funds at his disposal for such expenditure'.

All that day the Assembly remained inactive. At eleven in the evening it issued a proclamation condemning 'incitement to treachery' and all those who 'foment discord, hatred, or disunity, who instigate civil war or provoke disorders in Paris, or who prompt others to commit crimes'. Furthermore, it ordered the Communal authorities to present themselves at the bar of the House in order to take an oath to fulfil their duty or die in the attempt.

On September 4th Roland was still writing letters to Santerre, and Santerre was still inactive. Officers commanding the National Guard entered the words 'nothing new' in their reports. The Committee of Vigilance continued its efforts to ensure that 'all dead bodies should be carried away, and all bloodstains removed, especially from the courtyards, rooms and staircases of the Abbaye'. The Commune coolly sent to inform the Assembly that 'Paris was calm, that guard was being kept and that according to Santerre's assurances there was nothing to fear that night'. In the Assembly there were denunciations of 'incitement to crime', and of 'agitators whose secret aim is to be elected to the National Convention, and who are more barbarous, criminal and cowardly than the enemies who lay waste our frontiers and murder peaceful citizens with their wives and children'. But these were no more than passing references, made while discussing the resignation of the Committee of Twenty-one, in protest against the calumnies of Robespierre and Marat. No one dared refer openly to the massacre; the resignation of the Twenty-one was rejected but no definite measures were taken to prevent a continuance of acts of violence.

On September 5th the slaughter died down, and next day it ended, not through active intervention by either the Commune or the Assembly, but simply because the murderers were at last weary and satiated with killing.

The truth is, in fact, precisely what writers of revolutionary sympathies always endeavour to contest: that the slaughter was the spontaneous work, not of an uncontrollable mob, but of a few hundred people belonging, for the most part, to the fringes of the criminal world, carried away by temporary homicidal mania and driven on by hate and fear; many of whom in normal circumstances would have remained comparatively harmless all their lives. And it is also true, though the historians of anti-revolutionary opinions seek to deny it, that in Paris the whole body of citizens allowed the murderers five days of full liberty in which to wreak their will. In view of their passive complicity and that of the National Guard, and in view, too, of the murderers' frenzy, it would have been impossible for the Assembly, the Commune, the Executive Council, or for Santerre to have stopped the bloodshed, at least during the first two days. But at the same time it is incontestable that the public authorities made no serious effort at all to check the disorders. Some remained inactive. Others attempted feebly to intervene. Most were content with merely verbal expressions of disapproval, while many excused the crimes, and not a few encouraged and supported them.

In Paris the elections for the Convention turned out as the Jacobins desired. With the Girondin, Feuillant and royalist electors *hors de combat* and terrorized by the slaughter, the first to be elected was Robespierre, followed by Danton, Billaud-Varennes, Desmoulins, Marat, Lavicomterie, Robert, Fréron, Robespierre's younger brother and other acolytes of the revolutionary Commune; lastly, the Duke of Orleans, who had assumed the name of Philippe Égalité and posed as an enthusiastic Jacobin. In the rout of the Gironde even Papa Pétion — as the revolu-

tionaries had affectionately called him only a few months before
— failed to survive. Offended at the ingratitude of the sovereign
people, he at once resigned his office as *maire*.

In the provinces there were few murders in imitation of those
in Paris. Nine prisoners were killed at Rheims on September 3rd;
two more at Rheims, one at Gisors and fourteen at Meaux on the
4th; one at Caen on the 6th; four at Couches and one at Grenoble
on the 8th; ten at Lyons and sixty-six at Versailles on the 9th.
The Paris revolutionaries were directly responsible for the Versailles murders; the victims consisted, in fact — apart from
twenty-two ordinary prisoners — of forty-four out of the fifty-three
political suspects previously held at Orleans, whom the Paris
Commune had sent for on August 24th.

The provincial elections, too, proved almost all favourable to
the Girondins. Quick to profit by the exaltation of the moment,
well-organized in their political clubs, fanatically convinced of
having right on their side, and ready to use violence, the provincial
revolutionaries ignored all differences between the factions of
Brissot and Robespierre. To them — after the Duke of Brunswick's proclamation, Lafayette's desertion and the proofs of the
King's treachery found in the Tuileries — one thing only was clear:
that the royalists and Feuillants must, once for all, be crushed.
In this field victory was certain, because both royalists and Feuillants were divided by recent disagreement, weakened by emigration and without popular support. In the struggle against the
King, August 10th had been a victory for the Paris Commune,
but the Assembly had approved and legalized it; and it had been
the great Girondist orators who had led the parliamentary battles
against the Court. Thus the provincial revolutionary electors,
remote, as they were, from the conflict between the Paris Commune and National Assembly, had no reason for throwing over
outgoing Girondist deputies in favour of Robespierre's adherents.

If anything, they had good cause to do the contrary. Indeed,
the longer political unrest continued, the greater grew the alarm
of property-owners concerning agrarian redistribution, about
which nothing definite, as yet, was known, though all felt it an
abyss beneath their feet. 'The revolution,' wrote the Girondist
Lindet on August 20th, 1792, 'is leading us too far; beware of an
agrarian law!' Some of the more extreme revolutionaries, in their

talk of 'levelling fortunes', and 'putting the poor in the place of the rich', gave substance to these fears and suspicions. Although Robespierre and his followers tried to repudiate such views, they shared, to some extent, in the dislike aroused by those who were too logical in their application of democratic dogma. Brissotin candidates were immune from this kind of accusation, and it was natural that the electors' votes should go to them rather than to Robespierre's party.

On September 20th the Legislative Assembly held its last session. It decided that registration of births, deaths and marriages should be removed from the clergy and handed over everywhere to the Communal authorities; and it also legalized divorce between married persons. On the same day the Convention had a private preliminary meeting, with only 371 out of its 749 deputies present; the rest, owing to difficulties of transport, being still on their way to the capital.

On September 21st, at its first official meeting, the Convention began by proclaiming, on Danton's proposal, that 'no Constitution can exist other than that accepted by the people; security of life and property is guaranteed by the nation'. It then unanimously decreed, after a long and heated discussion, that 'the monarchy be abolished in France'. 'It is impossible to describe to our readers,' wrote a newspaper, 'the impression produced upon all present by this decree. Shouts, cheers, hats in the air, oaths to maintain it against every tyrant in the world, cries of "long live liberty and equality!" — this is but the faintest indication of what we saw; if the beating of every heart be added to it, some feeble impression of such a spectacle may be conveyed.'

The Abbé Grégoire, a forceful speaker who supported abolition of the monarchy, recalls, in his *Mémoires*, that he was almost beside himself with emotion after the proposal had been accepted. 'I confess,' he writes, 'that for several days the excess of my joy deprived me of both sleep and appetite.'

Next morning, the Convention decreed that all official documents should, from September 20th, 1792, bear the date of the first year of the Republic.

On the afternoon of September 2nd, when the slaughter was starting in Paris, Verdun had surrendered.

The Duke of Brunswick had under his personal command 42,000 Prussians and 5600 troops belonging to the Landgrave of Hesse. On his right were 15,000 Austrians, under the orders of Clerfayt, and on his left another 14,000 under the Prince of Hohenlohe-Ingelfingen. The rearguard was made up by 4500 *emigrés* commanded by the Counts of Provence and Artois. Further to the north, 25,000 Austrians under the Duke of Saxony-Teschen and 4000 *emigrés* led by the Duke of Bourbon threatened Lille. To the south, on the upper Rhine, 17,000 Austrians and about 5000 *emigrés* were assembling under command of the Prince de Condé.

France, apart from garrison troops, had 43,000 men in the north, between Dunkirk and Montmédy, with their headquarters at Sedan. In the centre, facing the enemy's main forces, 17,000 men were stationed between Montmédy and Bitche, with their headquarters at Metz. On the Rhine, between Landau and Porrentruy, there were 22,000 men, only 15,000 of whom were fit for active service. The fall of Verdun cut the lines of communication between Sedan and Metz in a most dangerous manner. Lafayette's flight had greatly increased unrest among the troops; while changes made in the General Staff after August 10th held up almost all military operations until the new leaders could become acquainted with the situation and win the trust of their subordinates.

Had the Duke of Brunswick, in these circumstances, thrown a body of even 10,000 men against Sedan, the whole army of the north, so Dumouriez declares in his *Mémoires*, would have been dispersed without difficulty.

Happily for France, the Duke was not the man to take advantage of so favourable a situation. Of a philosophic turn of mind, he was by nature cautious and irresolute; better suited to discuss and to criticize than to take rapid practical decisions. Although he would pay great attention to detail and always showed calm on the field of battle, he was without the energy and resolution needed to win victory in the field. Moreover, he was doubtful of his own forces and expected obstinate resistance from the French.

Austria, he argued, had been bled white by her recent wars, and her internal administration was reduced to a state of chaos by the rapid succession of three emperors who had all governed according to widely different principles. She had thus been able to put only 71,000 men in the field out of the 106,000 promised. The *emigrés* were of little or no assistance. A medley of young and old, weak and strong, continually quarrelling among themselves, they were ill-armed and without funds: Chateaubriand had a musket with a trigger that did not work, and a marquis was to be seen marching barefoot, his shoes slung on his bayonet to save wear. The invading army, having suffered much from the heat during the first half of August and having drunk from the infected waters of the Moselle, had been overtaken, on entering France, by a spell of almost wintry cold, with incessant rain. In consequence, dysentery was already rife among the men. The supply services functioned badly and rations were always in arrears. As the army advanced, strong detachments had to be left behind to guard lines of communication, and the number of fighting troops was thus reduced.

The royalists had boasted that they had only to appear, with a white handkerchief on a stick, and the King's flag would be run up once more on every church tower; the Jacobin rabble would scatter, they maintained, at the first shot. But instead the peasants fired on the foreign troops, abandoned their villages *en masse* — removing or destroying all provisions — and took refuge in the woods, where they followed the Austro-Prussians like wolves, killing stragglers or small parties. The 'rabble' fought stubbornly, and fell to the cry of 'long live liberty!' When captured, they refused to give information about the French defences or to serve against the Revolution. Meanwhile, behind the front line, at Châlons, Rheims, Soissons and Meaux, volunteers were gathering in their thousands.

The Duke, therefore, was beset by increasing fears and uncertainty. He would have preferred to occupy the frontier fortresses and await collapse of the French from internal unrest and insolvency; but Frederick of Prussia, who despised the French, was convinced that rapid victory was possible, and insisted on an immediate march upon Paris. The Duke, not daring to oppose the King, although convinced that he was mistaken, proceeded to carry out his wishes with infinite precaution, throwing away every advantage that might have been gained either from a rapid blow or from prudent handling of the situation.

On the other hand Dumouriez, active and resolute, always ready to take the initiative without paying heed to the ministers, Assembly, and journalists, who were busy directing the war from Paris, had every quality that the Duke of Brunswick lacked.

At first he had found great difficulty in winning the trust of his men. At Sedan he was received coldly and with suspicion. When he reviewed the troops, they became restive. 'It was he who declared war,' exclaimed a grenadier. 'Do you think you can conquer freedom without fighting?' demanded Dumouriez promptly, with unruffled calm. 'Down with the General!' shouted another. Dumouriez drew his sword, and faced the group from which the voice had issued. 'Let that fellow fall out and cross swords with me!' No one moved. 'My friends, the man is a coward, unworthy to remain among you.' To the volunteers who complained that they had no arms, he replied, 'On the first battlefield you shall collect arms from the dead.' In this way he won the affection of his men, raised their morale and re-established discipline. He realized the danger of exposing an army that consisted of such diverse elements in the open, and wisely kept them on high ground or in wooded country until he was sure of victory. Thus the enemy was harassed at every turn by small, fast-moving detachments of *tirailleurs*, who covered the infantry's movements and retired at an opportune moment.

Up to the beginning of September Dumouriez had intended to invade Belgium and force the Austro-Prussians to follow him beyond the frontiers of France. He clung to this idea, notwithstanding opposition from some of his generals and continual letters from the Executive Council urging him to defend the capital. When Longwy fell and the siege of Verdun began he decided to carry out the Council's wishes. He left Sedan, Montmédy and Mezières to defend themselves, hoping to 'save the trunk by sacrificing the branches', and boldly threw his army into the wooded heights of the Argonne, which divide the basin of the Meuse from the Aisne valley. Here he occupied five outlets from the forest defiles through which the Austro-Prussian forces would have to pass on their advance from Verdun to Paris. Meanwhile, 16,000 men from the Belgian frontier under the command of Beurnonville, and 22,000 from Metz under Kellermann, were coming to his assistance by forced marches.

The Duke of Brunswick, by remaining inactive at Verdun until September 11th, allowed Dumouriez to occupy the Argonne without opposition.

On September 12th the Austrians under Clerfayt seized Croix-sous-Bois in the northern zone of the forest. From this important position, which Dumouriez had unwisely left almost undefended, the invaders were able to penetrate into the valley of the Aisne and swing to the rear of the Argonne, thus threatening to cut off Beurnonville from Dumouriez and Dumouriez from his base. Brunswick, however, dared not exploit this success to the full.

Taking rapid advantage of the Duke's inertia, Dumouriez abandoned by night the now untenable outlets from the forest and concentrated his forces round Sainte-Ménehould on September 15-17th, occupying the southern pass of the Islettes in strength, to secure his rear. On September 19th Beurnonville succeeded in joining him and took up positions on Mont Yvron. The next day Kellermann came up, and occupied the heights from Gizaucourt to Valmy.

The Prussians, who had issued from the Argonne and entered Champagne, deceived by the rumour of a French retirement towards Châlons, swung round Mont Yvron. On the morning of September 20th, turning their backs on Paris and advancing in mist and rain, they came face to face with Kellermann's forces, who were occupying the heights of Valmy.

Twenty-four thousand Prussians with fifty-eight guns confronted thirty-six thousand French with forty guns. The two armies began to bombard one another at about seven in the morning. Kellermann rode up and down the ranks, waving his hat with its tricolour cockade upon the point of his sword, and shouting *Vive la nation!* to encourage his men, who were nervous and unaccustomed to fire. From the heights of the Lune, opposite Valmy, the Duke of Brunswick observed the compact mass of French infantry, noted the enemy's excellent gunnery, and, mindful of the privations and disease that had weakened his troops, dared not order his men to attack. Towards midday, when the weather had somewhat cleared, the King of Prussia insisted on his giving battle, and he ordered an assault. His men had scarcely advanced two hundred yards when, again overtaken by doubts and fears, he sent the order to retire. The cannonade lasted till about six that evening.

Such was the famous battle of Valmy, in which the infantry and cavalry merely remained spectators of an artillery duel; the French losing about 300 men and the Prussians 184. A trivial engagement, from the material point of view. But morally it was a signal defeat for the Prussians and a triumph for the French. The revolutionary armies, instead of being put to ignominious flight, had for a whole day stood their ground and blocked the enemy's way: while the Prussian infantry, which had entered France deriding the leaderless, undisciplined *bourgeois* troops mustered in defence of their country, had not even dared attack them. The victory they missed was a real and true defeat for the Allies. Goethe, who, as adviser to the Grand Duke of Weimar, was present at the Austro-Prussian headquarters, recorded, many years later, in an account of the campaign, that he said to his companions that evening: 'Here and now, a new era begins in the history of the world.' Although it may be that these words are an instance of 'wisdom after the event', they contain a great historic truth, whether they were spoken or not on the day of the battle of Valmy.

During the night of September 20th-21st, the rain poured down in torrents upon the two armies. The Prussians, without shelter, greatcoats, food or drinking-water, plunged in the mud of this hostile and desolate land and discouraged by their failure on the previous day, wholly lost heart. Uncertain what to do, the King of Prussia and the Duke of Brunswick remained before Valmy for another week, their condition worsening from day to day. The Austrian General Staff, instead of sending all the forces at their disposal to support the Duke, kept 25,000 men besieging Lille, in a hope of holding this important fortress when the war was over. The Allied diplomatists were still not agreed upon distributing the conquests which, as yet, they had not made. The Prussian officers were on bad terms with the Austrians, and accused their allies of having failed to fulfil their pledges. Their respect for France was revived, now that she appeared strong, and they regretted the abandonment of Prussia's traditional pro-French and anti-Austrian policy.

Finally, having lost 6000 men through disease, the invaders began to withdraw on the night of October 1st. It was a melancholy retreat, under 'cruel' rain (as Goethe described it). The men were up to their knees in mud; cavalry, infantry, ambulance carts and gun-carriages struggled along in disorder, leaving behind them along the road their dead and dying, their famished horses, with arms and equipment of every kind. By the time the rear-guard had re-crossed the frontier on October 23rd, abandoning Verdun and Longwy, the Prussian army of 42,000 men was reduced to 20,000; and of these, more than half were without muskets or boots. Torn, bleeding, verminous, and weak from dysentery, they were walking skeletons.

The *emigrés*, turned away from every door and accused by the Prussians and Austrians of responsibility for the disaster, were reduced to a pitiful state. Some returned to France and were shot or guillotined. Others went in disguise to the Vendée and Brittany, where a peasant insurrection on a large scale was being prepared. A few, in despair, took their own lives; while a number joined the Republican armies under false names, as volunteers.

While the Duke of Brunswick was forced to evacuate Champagne and Lorraine, the Duke of Saxony-Teschen, too, met with humiliating failure in the north. The city of Lille, having withstood a savage bombardment from September 29th until October 5th, refused to surrender; and on October 8th the Austrian army was forced to withdraw across the frontier.

It was the end of the feudal monarchy in France.

EPILOGUE

I. The negative work of the revolutionaries. — II. Their positive achievements.
— III. *Bourgeoisie* and lower classes in the revolutionary movement.

I

WHEN Louis XVI, by summoning the States-General in
August 1788, openly acknowledged that he and his
ministers were unable to solve the problems confronting
the French State, mediaeval feudalism— both lay and ecclesiastical
— was already in its last throes. The revolutionaries did not destroy,
in the course of a few months, a society that had been the work of
many centuries, as is too often maintained; instead, they brought to
completion in a few months a process of dissolution that had been
going on for many centuries. Their negative work consisted in
finally destroying the prestige of those juridical principles and
political institutions that had outlived the decay of the old social
and economic order, but which, originally, had held it together.
For greater accuracy it must be noted that this had to a great
extent already been achieved by the pre-revolutionary *philosophes*.

This is not to belittle what the revolutionaries accomplished.
Most men tend to accept the legitimacy of everything consecrated
by the past, not only through intellectual laziness but also because
it seems that what is old must be the outcome of very great labour
and experience; or because every change is achieved at some cost
which is only worth while if it leads to a new situation better than
the old, and it is always open to doubt whether an innovation
produces in the end more gain than loss. Moreover, it is not only
those who enjoy the advantages or privileges of any given social
order but also very many excluded from them who are pre-
disposed to this dislike of what is new. In eighteenth-century
France the propaganda of the *philosophes* was confined — owing
to the people's illiteracy and the lack of regular newspapers— to
a limited circle. Traditional standards still exercised a great
influence over the people's minds. It was as though they were
torn between veneration for their ancient legal and political
customs and resentment at the evils which these customs tended

to perpetuate. In the revolutionary period, on the contrary, as de Tocqueville has shown so well, men cleared their minds of those conceptions upon which until then they had based their feelings of respect and obedience; they assailed all the old powers, overthrew authorities which for centuries had been revered, and wiped out traditions which until that moment had seemed imperishable. The ancient institutions were bound up with the whole social body. The revolutionaries tore them out and destroyed them at the cost of a fearful crisis in the life of the community.

Their temerity would seem inconceivable were it not for the fact that so profound a change did not take place all at once in men's minds, but through many partial modifications. The first breach was made by the privileged classes themselves. 'Who had accustomed the people to clamorous meetings and resistance to the Government?' Alexandre de Lameth had acutely inquired in his time, 'The *parlements*. Who had shown most hostility in the provinces towards the Royal officials? The nobility. Who had obstinately refused to contribute towards the State finances? The clergy. *Parlements*, nobility, and clergy — it was they who declared war upon the Government and gave the signal for insurrection.'

When the revolutionaries began to rise against the established order, they appeared uncertain, wavering, and wholly ignorant of what the final results of their work must be. In the early days of 1789 many of the old ideas still dominated not only the minds of the unlettered and ignorant peasants, but also those of the more learned and unprejudiced among would-be innovators. The men who took the oath of the Jeu de Paume, stormed the Bastille, joined in the October rising, confiscated Church property, decreed the Civil Constitution of the Clergy and abolition of titles of nobility, and who hastened in pursuit of the King on his way to Varennes, aghast at the flight of their sovereign and protector, seem to us remote and timid, when we look back at them after September 21st, 1792. As one by one the old ideas were discarded, these men swore with complete sincerity that they would remain faithful to the remaining ones; often they considered the sacrifice of some time-honoured institution as a necessity imposed by the respect owing to other more sacred parts of the old régime. The aristocracy and *parlements*, under Calonne and

Brienne, assailed monarchical absolutism in the name of the legitimacy of feudal privilege. In 1789 the peasants destroyed the *châteaux* in the belief that they were carrying out the King's wishes; and the crowd hastening to Versailles to take the King prisoner deluded themselves with the excuse that they went to make him safe from the plots of the nobles and priests. As each new struggle began, some who had been revolutionaries hitherto refused to go beyond the positions already won and became the conservatives of the day; while others went on to swell the ranks of rebels and newcomers, only to become the conservatives of the morrow. Through this constant process of attack and defence, of enthusiasm and reluctance, the French people, in the end, found that, almost unawares, they had brought about a real republic and a genuine democracy.

The greater part of this radical destruction was the work — not, as is commonly thought — of the two Assemblies, but of the mob, which was swayed by the deputies' will only in so far as the latter accorded with its own destructive fury. Without doubt the deputies, psychologically prepared, as they were, by philosophic criticism of the old order, for the practical destruction of its institutions, often looked on with indulgence at revolutionary violence: justifying it with that optimism which they had absorbed from eighteenth-century philosophy, and willingly awarding the seal of legality to the crowd's actions by translating into juridical *formulae* what took place before their eyes. But it would be a mistake to attribute the fact that various revolutionary events were in harmony with the pre-conceived ideas of the deputies, to active influence by the Assemblies over events; for they were due rather to a spontaneous concordance between events and theories.

If, for example, there had been no reason, other than the physiocrats' dislike of indirect taxation, for abolishing the *octrois* on foodstuffs, the Constituent Assembly would have found great difficulty in suppressing the city customs barriers, as it did on February 17th, 1791. Even Dupont de Nemours, the most influential representative of the physiocratic school in the Assembly, although condemning them in theory, proposed that these tariffs should be retained as a valuable source of income, and wanted the Assembly merely to reduce the revenue from 70 to 24 millions a year by refunding it in the form of a food-subsidy; whilst

Camus — a typical doctrinaire — used to say, despite his theories, that 'in principle there should be nothing but direct taxation; necessity enforces the retention of indirect taxation'. Necessity, however, of a different sort, ended by giving the victory to principle. Throughout the eighteenth century the toll-barriers had been an object of bitter hatred on the part of the townspeople. Rioting in the summer of 1789 had unloosed popular fury against them and their restitution at Lyons had given rise to grave disorders in July 1790.

'Do you want to consolidate the Revolution?' demanded the deputy Boislandry, in opposing the motion of Dupont de Nemours. 'Do you want the Constitution to be secure? Conciliate the city-dwellers. These tariffs will always be a sure weapon in the hands of reactionaries for arousing the people's anger against the Constitution. They will say to them, you pay an enormous tax on wine and on the most necessary of foodstuffs; you are searched and abused at the city gates: what is the good of liberty to you? Be faithful to us, and we will suppress the *octrois* on agricultural produce; only then will you be able to enjoy real freedom.'

These practical considerations ended by producing a decree that seems a logical consequence of physiocratic theories on taxation, although it is not so in reality.

Nor must it be forgotten, in attempting to estimate the work of the Constituent and Legislative Assemblies in its due proportions, that if these two bodies willingly approved and legalized a great deal of destruction, there was much that they tried without success to prevent; giving their consent only when they saw that it could no longer be withheld. A typical example was the abolition of feudal dues, which was achieved by the peasants against the Constituent Assembly's will. Another was destruction of the centralized administrative system, which had once been the chief means of keeping feudal power in check, and was to be the pattern of the future administration. No physiocrat had ever proposed that the State officials, who acted as intermediaries between the central government and the local bodies, should be entirely suppressed. The deputies of the Constituent Assembly themselves would certainly never have come to such a decision on their own account; indeed, they attempted, by passing the municipal law, to impose some control from above into the chaos produced by disintegration of the administrative system in the summer of 1789. But in this field too, as in that of the feudal dues, they came up against the resistance of those groups who had seized power over the new local bodies.

Nevertheless, it would be equally mistaken to deny any direct and independent share on the part of the Assemblies in the destruction of the old France, and to reduce the deputies' work merely to that of registering, more or less voluntarily, what was forced on them by extra-parliamentary pressure. The war, which was a fact of fundamental importance in the history of the Revolution, was without doubt chiefly due to the initiative of the Gironde.

The deputies were not — indeed, how could they be? — superior to their time. They shared the illusions, hopes and prejudices of the nation and social class to which they belonged. They joined with the rest in hewing their share from the stricken oak; and, being in an advantageous position, were able to contribute more effectively to the general break-up than would have been possible had they acted as private citizens.

But this is not to say that the work of the National Assemblies was a predominant factor in the downfall of the old régime. It is impossible to ascribe the whole complicated development of the revolutionary movement to the more or less doctrinaire discussions and decisions of a few hundred men; unless we regard them as endowed, like the magicians in oriental tales, with power to make the old world vanish and a new one appear simply by a wave of the wand.

II

In carrying out their work of destruction, the revolutionaries did not neglect that of reconstruction.

During the preceding centuries, while feudal society was decaying, the first signs of a modern economic system and of its political and juridical framework had begun to appear. Long before the Revolution the commercial, intellectual and rural *bourgeoisie* had already brought property in the capitalist sense into being — in other words, property that was marketable, divisible, accessible to women as well as to men, and subject to confiscation by the

State— as distinct from the old form of feudal and ecclesiastical property, which was almost exclusively in land, could not be transferred or divided up, and, belonging in common either to the family or to a collective religious body, was subject to entail or to the bond of mortmain. In so doing, they had seized on half the landed property in the kingdom, making inroads even upon feudal territory through capitalistic investment, and had undermined it by gradually doing away with the feudal rights. To control and regulate this new form of property they had recourse to the principles of Roman law, which had been formulated at a time when property possessed the mobility that had disappeared in the Middle Ages and was tending to reappear in modern society. It was they who afforded the kings both the support and personnel required in setting up the centralized administration to which the lay and ecclesiastical feudal lords were forced to submit themselves.

But these first attempts, before the Revolution, to create a modern system of property-ownership were everywhere blocked by feudalism. The juridical protection which capitalist property needed for its development was not generally available, and always came into conflict with feudal law. Uniformity of administration by the central government was everywhere obstructed by the remains of primitive feudal administration. In the eyes of the kings and their officials— once contact between *bourgeoisie* and monarchy had been ended in the time of Louis XIV— property *par excellence,* the only property that should be preserved and developed, was still feudal property.

By annulling all the laws of the old régime, the revolutionaries freed the modern world from its mediaeval fetters. They transferred ecclesiastical and corporative landed property to the middle-classes, confiscated most of the nobles' estates on the score of emigration, and made Roman law applicable to the property of all classes by abolishing the rights of primogeniture and mortmain. Moreover, they divided France into uniform administrative districts and sought to make the Government representative in form, so that it might be the administrative council of the new ruling class.

In other words, just as they did not themselves destroy the feudal economic order but abolished its juridical and political basis, so, in the same way, the revolutionaries did not create the modern economic world which, fundamentally, was in existence before their time, but legalized it and endeavoured to set up the political institutions required for its preservation.

But if the jurists who filled the Constituent and Legislative Assemblies found themselves well placed to achieve lasting work in the field of common law, their situation was very different when it became a question of constitutional law.

In the former case, with Roman law as their guide, they had nothing to invent, but a great deal to select, organize and clarify out of the old legislative chaos; and they were well prepared for such an undertaking by their professional experience. For this reason they handled the question of property rights with admirable sureness of touch. And although through lack of time and the multiplicity of material to be dealt with they were not able to complete their work to the last detail, nevertheless, when the Convention opened, the basic principles of a new system of common law were already established, corresponding so well with the needs of the new régime that all nineteenth-century civil legislation was founded upon them.

Among such problems, however, as concerned the Government's future political and administrative form, only reform of penal legislation was facilitated by the deputies' juridical practice and theory: and both the penal code and penal procedure laid down were an undisputed glory of the first revolutionary Assembly. But all other innovations in administrative and constitutional law were hedged about with formidable difficulties. Here the deputies had at their service none of that practical preparation which experience alone can give. They had to fall back upon suggestions contained in writings by the physiocrats and *philosophes*, which were merely a synthesis of pre-revolutionary hopes and criticism. In some cases, these proved useful, but often they came between the deputies and reality, clouding and distorting their vision. If all the deputies had had the practical genius of Mirabeau, or, at least, Danton's unprejudiced good sense, they would have been better equipped to resist these theoretic illusions: and they might perhaps from the first have constructed an administrative and political framework more closely adapted to the real needs of society. But they were men of no more than average ability, and

331

their conduct was influenced, according to circumstances, either by the pressure of events or by philosophic theories. In the latter case, they sometimes took the right way but more often they blundered badly.

Eighteenth-century thinkers had always wavered between belief in popular sovereignty and the hope of an enlightened despotism, dividing their sympathies between the largely imaginary ideal of republican rule in ancient times, and an equally unrealistic conception of the reign of Charlemagne or of Henri IV. A characteristic of their teaching, as we have already seen, was the contradiction inherent in physiocratic theory, which affirmed the necessity for re-establishing local government, and yet preferred French absolutism to English constitutionalism as an instrument of reform. This was inevitable, given, on the one hand, a centuries-old absence of civic life, together with the administrative habits engendered by the centralized system, which created an exaggerated idea of the Government's power; and, on the other, the evil effects of governmental inefficiency, which led many people to seek a remedy for their ills in self-government and political freedom.

The folly of Louis XVI, and the inability of his bureaucracy to break with the past, finally discredited any possible programme of enlightened despotism. The deputies had to construct a new political régime upon the basis of popular sovereignty. They therefore did not defend the old centralized administrative machine from attack by the populace, although it had been in its time the strongest bulwark against feudalism, and was later to become the pattern of the new administration. They set themselves to demolish the State's authority. Transforming public administration into a federation of independent communal republics, they grouped them in uniform *départements*— a uniformity which is still intact— but denied the departmental administrators any effective power. They made the electorate— at first with wide, and later, with universal suffrage— the fount of all authority. They even fashioned the constitution of the Church in accordance with the principle of popular sovereignty.

They thought that in this way they would create a revolutionary clergy, but they only succeeded in turning even the most liberal-minded clerics into a strongly reactionary body. Intending to organize independent local government, they merely codified administrative anarchy. They persuaded themselves that they were founding a republic of free men, but they brought about the despotic rule of the Terror. Their designs, which looked so well on paper, were not made to hold together in real life. As Carlyle wrote, they were simply 'cutting asunder ancient intolerable bonds, and for new ones, assiduously spinning ropes of sand'. It is impossible for a people to pass abruptly from centuries of minority-rule to full self-government. Practical experience in the conduct of affairs cannot be improvised. It is one thing to know Montesquieu and Rousseau by heart and another to govern a democratic republic; one thing to destroy a *château* or kill a non-juring priest, and another to administer a small rural community.

And so seven long years of grievous trials were to pass by, during which the new ruling class blindly groped its way from revolutionary excess to reactionary oppression; until the genius of Napoleon — greater in peace than in war — grasped the necessity of reconstructing the old centralized monarchical administration within the new *départements*, but in a more flexible and manageable form; and of returning, with the Concordat, to the former monarchical method of choosing the bishops by agreement between the Pope and the French Government: enforcing Papal acceptance, in return, of all other revolutionary reforms. In this way, through a fusion of old and new, a solid basis for relations with the Church was obtained which remained unchallenged for more than a century, until the denunciation of the Concordat in 1906 and the separation between Church and State.

III

In their positive work the Assemblies inevitably felt the pressure of a social element which had never, in the eighteenth century, been taken into consideration as an important political factor, and which was brought into the forefront by the course of the Revolution.

In eighteenth-century France the kings, the great lay and ecclesiastical lords, and the higher, ennobled bureaucracy, closely bound together as they were by ties of rank and common interest, and held in check by no effective legal restraint, found it easy

enough— with the aid of a large army— to subdue sporadic outbreaks on the part of their subjects. Having at their service the
whole weight of the administrative machine, they clung tenaciously to their privileges at a time when the country's social life
was undergoing rapid change; and although they allowed the
middle-classes to control administration, they excluded them even
from such honours as had been open to them until the time of
Louis XIV. Not only *bourgeois* interests but those of the lower
clergy and nobility were injured by such irresponsible government; while the common people were treated no better than
beasts, without rights or human dignity.

Thus problems of every sort accumulated. Resentment became
acute. In the end the parasitical minority found itself assailed by
all the other social groups together. And when the forces of
destruction had gathered way, the old régime was overwhelmed
by the onslaught of a great army in which the *bourgeoisie* found
itself fighting side by side with the peasants and the workers.

The first impulse of the jurists in the Constituent Assembly,
after the monarchy had been subdued and the political and civil
privileges of the nobility destroyed, was to hasten to defend rural
feudalism and to exclude 'passive' citizens from the franchise.
But the threats of the privileged classes and the King's anti-
revolutionary policy brought about new conflicts in which alliance
with the lower classes became indispensable to the *bourgeoisie*.
External war, which greatly increased the danger of counter-
revolution, made the rural and city populations protagonists of
the revolutionary drama, inasmuch as it was they who were most
numerous in filling the ranks for defence of the nation, and who
provided the bolder spirits in the campaign against the King and
the aristocrats. The fact that the Assemblies sat in Paris made
them particularly sensitive to pressure by the democratic element.

In the nation's hour of greatest peril, when the peasants were
hastening in their thousands towards the frontiers and the Paris
sansculottes were dealing the monarchy its death-blow, the jurists
of the Legislative Assembly abolished almost all feudal rights and
proclaimed universal suffrage. Thus, not only were the remains
of ancient servitude obliterated from the peasants' lives as they
had been from those of the city-dwellers, but the principle of
equality, which the Constituent Assembly had applied only in

civil and penal law, was extended by the Legislative Assembly to the political field.

Equality, therefore; civil and political equality together. In the three thousand years of European history— which had seen, even under the most democratic republics of classical and mediaeval times, either the working-class majority, or the inhabitants of the provinces and countryside, always excluded from political life — the French Convention of 1792 was the first political Assembly to be, at least in theory, a mandatory body of the whole population through universal suffrage.

It was more than enough for the peasants, who only wanted to sow, reap and sell their grain in freedom. It was too little for the city proletariat, or— to be more precise— for those workers and artisans who, particularly in Paris, crowded the political clubs, shoulder to shoulder with the lesser intellectual *bourgeoisie*. To them, civil and political equality were inseparable from total equality; from the right of every citizen to have a share in all property. And here the problem of a just distribution of wealth, regarded by the eighteenth-century *philosophes* merely as an object of theoretic discussion, began under these new political conditions to arouse interest as something of practical and immediate importance.

Thus the new régime was born carrying within it the seeds of another conflict greater far than that just brought to a close. At the very moment when private property was throwing off its last feudal encumbrances and establishing a juridical system that was suited to the needs of capitalist expansion, a part of that same revolutionary army which until then had devoted all its energies to the destruction of feudal society turned its attention to a new objective, and adopted as its programme the abolition of private ownership.

They were confused, uncertain ideas, and those who spread them were not endowed with outstanding moral or intellectual qualities, nor with any special technical, administrative or political ability. Gracchus Babeuf, who was the first to organize a revolutionary movement against the principle of private ownership, was to leave his head upon the scaffold. Napoleon resorted to military despotism, restored central administration and renewed the alliance between Church and State, in order to preserve private property, proclaimed inviolable under the Civil Code, from being assailed by the Jacobins, as by the feudal serfs. But whereas the feudal classes had already been in their last throes before the Revolution, and the revolutionaries had only to register their death, the working-classes found in the new economic, social and political order that succeeded the old régime, the requisite conditions for their own rise and organization, and for their growing power. Babeuf's ideas were not to perish with him.

BIBLIOGRAPHICAL NOTE

Amid the mass of existing literature on the French Revolution, many conflicting statements and interpretations of historical fact are to be found, and the student is often in a quandary as to which writer's version he should accept and which reject.

It would be convenient if we could assume the more recent works to be the more trustworthy. But the newest book is not always the best, and to have the last word is no proof of being in the right. A single example, applicable to our present case, is that of Tocqueville's brilliant study *L'ancien régime et la Révolution* — famous now for nearly a century — which contains more solid and incontrovertible historical criticism than hundreds of volumes of later date.

The only way of knowing whether the statements of one writer are more reliable than those of another is to refer to the sources, and in every instance to go over the whole ground again on one's own account: an enterprise that would be beyond the strength of any man. For a work of synthesis such as the present book it is impossible not to avail oneself of the knowledge gained by others. One must, therefore, concentrate upon a sufficiently wide, but not unmanageable, body of authoritative works; accepting as true such statements as are not contested, and using one's own judgment where controversy exists.

How, then, are we to discriminate between reliable and untrustworthy works? Here too the only logical way would be to read them all and compare them carefully with the sources. Again it would be madness to attempt such a task. The solution once more is to rely, with due exercise of common sense, on the judgment of others. The bibliographical and critical notices appearing from time to time in the more important reviews will not only keep the student informed of what is being published but enable him to distinguish those worth reading from the rest. A work that receives poor notices or none at all from the principal reviews, or to which no serious writer on the subject ever refers, can be ignored with an easy conscience. Thus the great majority of books that would have been better unborn can be eliminated.

In the same way a check can be kept on such studies as deal with comparatively unimportant issues, not essential to a work with aims like the present. Unless the particulars they cite are of general interest they too may safely be left aside.

Readers who wish to continue their studies on this subject would do well to refer to the excellent bibliographies which the French university presses have issued under the general title of *Clio: introduction aux études historiques*. They consist of two volumes by Joseph Calmette entitled *Le monde féodal* and *L'élaboration du monde moderne;* that of Sée, Rébillon and Préclin on *Le XVI siècle: Renaissance, Réforme, Guerres de religion*; and two volumes by Préclin and Tapié entitled *Le XVIIe siècle* and *Le XVIIIe siècle.* The best and most recent bibliography on the French Revolution is given by Villat, in *La Révolution et l'Empire: 1789-1799* (Paris, Presses Universitaires de France).

INDEX

INDEX

341

INDEX

343